£57.50 Am3 5/11

D1326947

ENGINEERING OF DISTRIBUTED CONTROL SYSTEMS

ENGINEERING OF DISTRIBUTED CONTROL SYSTEMS

LONNI R. WELCH
DIETER K. HAMMER
EDITORS

Nova Science Publishers, Inc.
Huntington, New York

Senior Editors: Susan Boriotti and Donna Dennis
Coordinating Editor: Tatiana Shohov
Office Manager: Annette Hellinger
Graphics: Wanda Serrano
Book Production: Matthew Kozlowski, Jonathan Rose and Jennifer Vogt
Circulation: Cathy DeGregory, Ave Maria Gonzalez

Library of Congress Cataloging-in-Publication Data
               p.   cm.
        Includes bibliographical references and index.
        ISBN 1-59033-102-8

Copyright ©2001 by Nova Science Publishers, Inc.
               227 Main Street, Suite 100
               Huntington, New York 11743
               Tele. 631-424-6682   Fax 631-424-4666
               e-mail: Novascience@earthlink.net
               Web Site: http://www.nexusworld.com/nova

Printed in the United States of America

Contents

Contents

Engineering of Distributed Control Systems

Lonnie R. Welch[1,*]
Dieter K. Hammer[2,*]

The Joint Workshop on Parallel and Distributed Real-Time Systems was held in Santa Barbara, April 1 – 3, 1997 as part of the 9th IEEE International Parallel Processing Symposium (IPPS). The workshop combined the 5th International Workshop on Parallel and Distributed Real-Time Systems (WPDRTS) and the 3rd Workshop on Object-Oriented Real-Time Systems (OORTS). The meeting brought together researchers from different "communities" to address issues of mutual interest since it has become evident that the existing methods employed by these different communities have been unable to solve all the problems associated with the construction of distributed and dependable real-time systems. An example is the domain of object-oriented real-time systems, that has been explicitly addressed at the workshop by members of several different "communities." The event clearly showed that various problems can only be solved if the many relevant disciplines join their forces in an systems engineering approach towards system construction.

To disperse the findings reported at the workshop, several papers from the workshop's proceedings were selected for enhancement and subsequent inclusion in this book. These papers give a good overview about the various issues a system engineer of a complex distributed real-time system is confronted with: Requirements engineering and architecting (H. Gomaa), formal specification and validation of real-time systems (J. Hooman and O. van Roosmalen as well as S. Yamane), formal specification and verification of hybrid systems (R. Huuck, Y. Lakhnech, L. Urbina, S. Engell, S. Kowalewski and J. Preussig), program analysis (J. Gustafsson and A. Ermedahl), distributed real-time scheduling (G. Manimaran, M. Shashidhar, Anand Manikutty and C. Siva Ram Murthy), single-processor real-time scheduling (E.A. de Kock, E.H.L. Aarts and G. Essink) and real-time operating systems (A. Miyoshi and H. Tokuda).

---

[1] University of Texas at Arlington (welch@ohio.uta.edu)
[*] General Co-Chairs of WPDRTS'97
[2] Eindhoven University of Technology (hammer@win.tue.nl)

L. WELCH AND D. HAMMER

The editors would like to express their gratitude to the authors and the reviewers. We would also like to thank Eui-nam Huh whose help in the editorial process was invaluable.

USE CASES FOR DISTRIBUTED REAL-TIME SOFTWARE ARCHITECTURES

Abstract. This paper describes how use cases can be applied to the architectural design of distributed real-time applications. In order to benefit from use cases in distributed real-time design, it is necessary to extend use cases, particularly in the design phase, when important design decisions need to be made. To achieve this, use cases are integrated with CODARTS (Concurrent Design Approach for Real-Time Systems) distributed design concepts. Three different types of architectural use cases are described, client/server use cases, subscription use cases and real-time control use cases. Different forms of message communication are associated with the different use case types. The software architecture of the distributed real-time system is achieved by composing it from the use cases.

1. Introduction. Many software system analysis and design methods, regardless of whether they are functional or object-oriented, take a structural perspective on the system being analyzed, that is they view the system from a static perspective. For many applications, the behavioral or dynamic perspective is very important, and is often more informative than the static perspective. The behavioral aspects of a system are very important in concurrent and real-time applications, as these systems are reactive and often state-dependent. Understanding how the system behaves and reacts to the arrival of external events is essential.

The architecture of a software system defines a system in terms of components and the interconnections among these components [16]. In sequential systems, the interconnections are usually procedure calls between sequential components, e.g., procedures or objects. In distributed systems, the interconnections between concurrent and distributed components are in the form of messages.

CODARTS (Concurrent Design Approach for Real-Time Systems) is a design method for concurrent and real-time applications that emphasizes the structuring of a system into concurrent tasks that can potentially execute on distributed nodes [4,5]. The CODARTS/DA method is an extension of CODARTS that addresses the design of distributed real-time applications.

In the past few years, several object-oriented analysis and design methods have emerged. Initially they emphasized the static aspects of the application with their emphasis on information modeling. Later object-oriented analysis methods emerged that also emphasized the dynamic aspects of the problem, in particular the dynamic modeling view in the Object Modeling Technique (OMT) [15] and use of cases in Object-Oriented Software Engineering (OOSE) [11].

This paper describes how use cases can be applied to the architectural design of distributed real-time applications. Section 2 describes the CODARTS method for distributed real-time applications, Section 3 describes the use case approach to software engineering, Section 4 describes how use cases can be extended and

---

*Department of Information & Software Engineering. George Mason University, Fairfax, VA, E-mail: hgomaa@gmu.edu.

integrated with CODARTS for the design of real-time applications. Section 5 gives an example of applying use cases for the design of a distributed real-time application, namely a distributed factory automation system.

2. Distributed Real-Time Design using CODARTS.

2.1. Design of Distributed Real-Time Applications. The CODARTS/DA (CODARTS for Distributed Applications) design method is used for designing applications such as distributed real-time control systems, distributed real-time data collection systems, distributed client/server systems, and systems that have aspects of all three. With CODARTS/DA, a large-scale distributed real-time system is structured into subsystems. A subsystem is defined as a collection of concurrent tasks executing on one physical node. However, more than one subsystem may execute on the same physical node. Each physical node consists of one or more interconnected processors with shared memory.

The goal of a CODARTS/DA software architecture is to provide a concurrent message based design that is highly configurable. The concept is that the software architecture can be mapped to many different system configurations. Thus, for example, the same application could be configured to have each subsystem allocated to its own separate physical node, or have all or some of its subsystems allocated to the same physical node. To achieve this flexibility, it is necessary to design the application in such a way that the decision about mapping subsystems to physical nodes does not need to be made at design time, but is made later at system configuration time. Consequently, it is necessary to restrict communication between tasks in separate subsystems to message communication.

Subsystem structuring criteria can help guide a designer. For example client subsystems could be real-time control subsystems, data collection subsystems or user interface subsystems. Server subsystems could be database servers, application servers, file servers, printer servers, processing servers, scheduling servers. In addition, a server subsystem may be sequential (designed as one task) or concurrent (designed as several tasks), depending on the processing load the server is expected to handle.

Other issues in distributed application design relate to whether data and/or control should be centralized or distributed. Two approaches to data distribution are the distributed server and data replication. With the distributed server, data that is collected at several locations is stored at those locations. Each location has a local server, which responds to client requests for that location's data. With data replication, the same data is duplicated in more than one location in order to speed up access to the data. With distributed control, a subsystem usually performs a specific site related service controlling a given aspect of the system. For many applications, it is desirable to give distributed control subsystems considerable local autonomy, so that they can operate relatively independently of other nodes and be operational even if other nodes are temporarily unavailable. A real-time subsystem can perform time critical services at a given node, while other non-real-time or less time-critical services are performed elsewhere.

2.2. Steps in Using CODARTS/DA. There are three main steps in designing a large-scale distributed real-time system using CODARTS/DA consisting of subsystems that can be configured to execute on distributed physical nodes:

a) *Distributed Real-Time System Decomposition.* Structure the distributed real-time system into subsystems that potentially could execute on separate nodes in a distributed environment. The message communication interfaces between subsystems are defined. A set of subsystem structuring criteria is used for determining the subsystems.

b) *Subsystem Decomposition.* Structure subsystems into concurrent tasks and information hiding modules. Since by definition, a subsystem can only execute on one physical node, each subsystem can be designed using a design method for non-distributed concurrent systems, such as DARTS, ADARTS or CODARTS [4,5]. Thus, tasks within the same subsystem, which by definition always reside on the same physical node, may use inter-task communication and synchronization mechanisms that rely on shared memory.

c) *Distributed Real-Time System Configuration.* Once a distributed real-time system has been designed, instances of it may be defined and configured. During this stage, the subsystem instances of the real-time system are defined, interconnected, and mapped onto a hardware configuration [12].

2.3. Message Communication Services in CODARTS/DA. In several object-oriented methods, objects conceptually communicate by means of messages. However, this form of message passing is often very restrictive, consisting of a sequential system where an operation in one object calls an operation provided by another object.

A designer of a distributed application, where distributed subsystems potentially reside on different nodes, needs to consider a wide variety of alternatives for message communication. This section describes the message communication services provided by CODARTS/DA for the design of distributed real-time applications. As distributed subsystems potentially reside on different nodes, all communication between subsystems is restricted to message communication. Tasks in different subsystems communicate with each other as follows:

a) Tightly coupled (synchronous) message communication, also referred to as a Remote Procedure call, either in the form of single client/server communication or multiple client/server communication. In both cases a client sends a message to the server and waits for a response; in the latter case a queue may build up at the server. In a client/server architecture, it is also possible for a server to delegate the processing of a client's request to another server, which then responds directly to the original client.

b) Loosely coupled (asynchronous) message communication, either by means of FIFO message queues or priority message queues. In distributed environments, loosely coupled message communication is used wherever possible for greater flexibility. This approach can be used if the sender does not need a response from the receiver. Alternatively, if it does not need an immediate response, the sender can receive it later.

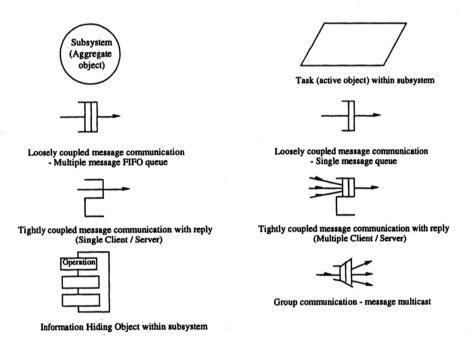

Figure 1: Notation for Distributed Real-Time Applications

c) Connections. If the client and server are to have a dialog that involves several messages and responses, a connection may be established between the client and the server. Messages are then sent and received over the connection.

d) Group communication. With group communication, one message is sent to several recipients, e.g., from the server to its clients. Group communication may be broadcast or multicast communication. With broadcast communication, an unsolicited message may be broadcast to several clients, e.g., informing them of a pending shutdown. The client then decides whether to act on the event or not.

With multicast communication, clients may subscribe to events they wish to be notified of. When an event of interest arises, a message is sent to all clients on the subscription list notifying them of the event.

e) Transaction support. For transactions that need to be atomic, services are needed to begin the transaction, commit the transaction, or abort the transaction. This is typically used for updates to a distributed database that need to be atomic, e.g., transferring funds from one account to another. Using this approach, updates to the database are coordinated, such that they are either all performed (commit) or all rolled back (abort).

f) Brokered communication. An object request broker mediates interactions between clients and servers. It frees the client from having to maintain information about where a particular service is provided and how to obtain the service. Servers register their location and services they provide with the broker. Clients can query the broker for available services. One option is for the broker to forward a client request to a server, receive the server's reply, and then forward the reply to the client. A more efficient approach for a prolonged dialog, is for the broker to return a service handle to the client, who then uses the handle to request the service from the server. The server replies directly to the client.

3. The Use Case Approach to Software Engineering. As pointed out in the introduction, the behavioral aspects of a system are a very important consideration in the design of concurrent and real-time applications. In the analysis phase of CODARTS, scenarios are developed to show how the system reacts to external events. Event sequence scenarios are depicted on data flow diagrams and state transition diagrams. OMT uses statecharts [10] and scenarios to describe how the system reacts to external events. OOSE use cases [11] are similar to scenarios. However, they are applied to the analysis and design of a system in a more systematic way. Thus the use case approach is applied throughout the software life cycle from requirements definition through system testing.

A use case defines a sequence of interactions between one or more users (referred to as actors) and the system. An actor initiates the use case. Actors model external entities that need to interact with the system. Actors can model human users and external I/O devices, as well as external systems that communicate with this system. Simple use cases may involve only one interaction with one actor, while more complicated use cases may involve several interactions with more than one actor. Dependencies between use cases can also be defined.

A use case can be viewed at different levels of detail. In a Requirements Model, the functional requirements of the system are defined in terms of actors and black box use cases, which describe the system's response to the actor's inputs. In an Analysis Model, the use case is refined to show the objects that participate in the use case. In the Design Model, implementation considerations are added and object interaction diagrams are developed that define the detailed communication among the objects in the use case.

Benefits of a behavioral approach in general, and the use case approach in particular, are that it provides a good way of ensuring that all the requirements of the system have been satisfied in the subsequent design and implementation through traceability by use case, as well as a means of testing that the design satisfies the requirements, by design walkthroughs on a use case basis. It also has potential for reuse, as use cases, and the objects that are needed to support them, can be reused. This is a larger grained form of reuse than the traditional single component.

4. Use Cases in Distributed Real-Time Design.

4.1. Architectural Use Cases. The use case approach is a general approach for software design. In order to benefit from use cases in distributed real-time design, it is necessary to extend use cases, particularly in the design phase, when important design decisions need to be made. To achieve this, use cases are integrated in this paper with CODARTS distributed design concepts.

In this paper, architectural use cases are introduced, which are an architectural realization of black box and analysis use cases. Architectural use cases are defined in terms of distributed real-time components, namely subsystems, tasks and information hiding modules. Using the terminology given in [1], a subsystem is an aggregate object composed of active and passive objects, a task is an active object, which has its own thread of control, and an information hiding module is a passive object, which does not have its own thread of control.

OOSE uses object interaction diagrams to show the sequence of communication among objects to satisfy a use case. In a sequential system, inter-object communication is simple, consisting of one object invoking an operation provided by another object. However, in a distributed real-time design, there is a great choice in the type of message communication (see 2.2) between distributed objects. To emphasize the semantics of the message communication between distributed subsystems and between tasks within a subsystem, the architectural use cases are therefore depicted on event sequence diagrams, based on the distributed architecture diagrams used by CODARTS, which show the sequence and type of message communication.

In addition, OOSE does not address state dependent use cases in much detail, where it is necessary to consider how the behavior pattern varies by state. State dependent use cases are an important aspect of architectural use cases.

4.2. Categorization of Use Cases in Distributed Real-Time Design. In distributed real-time applications, different kinds of use cases can be identified. Three different categories of use cases are described here, client/server use cases, subscription use cases and real-time control use cases. It is possible for one application to have all three kinds of use cases. Different forms of message communication are associated with the different use case types.

Each use case is supported by an event sequence diagram, which shows the event sequence numbers superimposed on a distributed subsystem architecture diagram. An overall distributed system architecture diagram represents the integration of the subsystem architecture event sequence diagrams for each of the use cases.

It should be noted that an object may participate in more than one use case. Thus a server object may participate in a client/server use case where it responds to messages from several clients, including subscription requests, and also participate in a subscriber notification use case, where it distributes newly received messages to subscribers.

5. Case Study for Use Cases in Distributed Real-Time Designs. As an example of applying use case technology in the design of a distributed real-time application, a factory automation problem is considered [4]. In a high volume low flexibility assembly plant, manufacturing workstations are physically laid out in an assembly line. Parts are moved between workstations on a conveyor belt. A part is processed at each workstation in sequence. Since workstations are programmable, different variations on a given product may be handled. Typically, a number of parts of the same type are produced, followed by a number of parts of a different type.

Each manufacturing workstation has an assembly robot for assembling the product, and a pick-and-place robot for picking parts off and placing parts on the conveyor. Each robot is equipped with sensors and actuators. Sensors are used for monitoring operating conditions, e.g. detecting part arrival, while actuators are used to switch automation equipment on and off, e.g. switching the conveyor on and off.

The manufacturing steps required to manufacture a given part in the factory, from raw material to finished product, are defined in a process plan. The process plan defines the part type and the sequence of manufacturing operations. Each operation is carried out at a workstation.

The processing of new parts in the factory is initiated by the creation of a work order by a human production manager. The work order defines the quantity of parts required for a given part type. Factory operators monitor the processing of parts in the factory by viewing workstation status and factory alarms.

6. Architectural Use Cases in Distributed Real-Time Design.

6.1. Client/server Use Cases. With client/server use cases, a client object interacts with a server object to store or retrieve information. Both the client and server objects may be aggregate objects. The client object may be a user interface object, a data collection object, or a real-time control object [6]. In the design model, these objects are mapped to distributed subsystems. The simplest client/server use cases are designed using the multiple client/server message communication service, described in Section 3. With this communication, the client waits for the server to respond. Other use cases can use loosely coupled communication, where the client continues processing after sending the message and receives the server response later.

An example of a client/server use case from the distributed factory automation case study is the *View Alarms* use case, which is developed as part of the Requirements Analysis stage. First a summary of the black box description (Section 3) is given, which is an entirely external view of the system.

The factory operator views outstanding alarms and acknowledges that the cause of an alarm is being attended. The operator may also subscribe to receive notification of alarms of a given type.

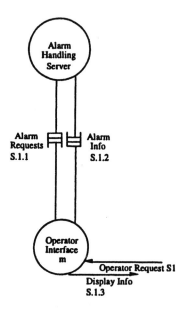

Figure 2: View Alarms Architectural Use Case

An event sequence diagram is given in Figure 2 to show the architectural use case for the *View Alarms* use case. The distributed objects participating in this use case are multiple user interface client objects, one of which (Operator Interface m) is shown in Figure 2, and the server object, Alarm Handling Server (AHS). The AHS provides several services and responds to alarm requests made by client Operator Interface objects. As one of these services, an operator may subscribe to receive alarms of a specific type (event S1 in Figure 2). The Operator Interface object sends an alarm subscription message (S1.1) to the Alarm Handler Server, which acknowledges receipt (S1.2, S1.3). The message communication is loosely coupled to allow the Operator Interface object to continue with other activities.

Other client/server use cases are View Workstation Status, where an operator may view the status of the factory workstations, and View Process Plans, where the production manager can view available process plans before creating a work order to manufacture parts according to a specific process plan.

6.2. Subscriber Notification Use Cases. A subscriber notification use case deals with a server receiving messages for information that some clients wish to be notified of. The server multicasts the newly received message to those clients who have subscribed to receive messages of this type.

An example of a subscriber notification use case in the Factory Automation case study is the *Alarm Generation and Notification* use case; a brief black box description of this use case is given next. If an alarm condition is detected during part processing, an alarm is sent to the Alarm Handling Server. Operators are notified of alarms they have subscribed to.

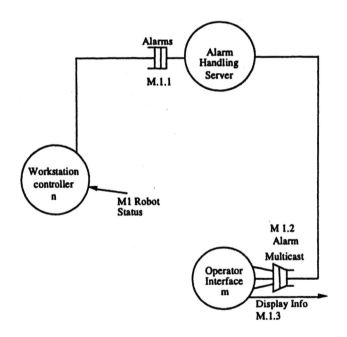

Figure 3: Alarm Generation and Notification Architectural Use Case

The event sequence diagram for the architectural use case is shown on Figure 3. In addition to the Alarm Handling Server and Operator Interface objects, Workstation Controller objects, which are real-time control objects, also participate in this use case.

A Workstation Controller object receives robot status indicating a problem condition (M1), so it sends an alarm to the Alarm Handling Server (M1.1), which then sends a multicast message (M1.2) containing the alarm to all subscribers registered to receive messages of this type.

Another subscriber notification use case in the Factory Automation case study is the *Workstation Status Generation and Notification* use case, in which operators can subscribe to be notified of workstation status events, such as part y completed at workstation z.

6.3. Architecture of Alarm Handling Server. Both the *Alarm Generation and Notification* and *View Alarms* architectural use cases may be depicted at a greater level of detail by considering the architecture of the Alarm Handling Server. Servers may be sequential or concurrent. The Alarm Handling Server is designed as a concurrent server for improved throughput, as shown in Figure 4. In a concurrent server, which resides on one node, objects may be active (referred to as task or thread) or passive (referred to as information hiding object [13,14]).

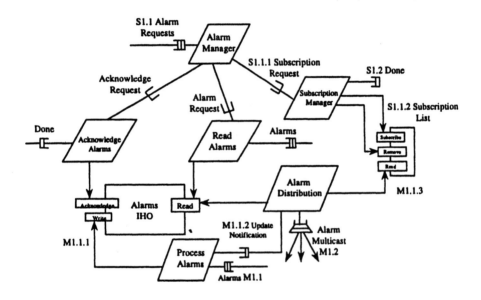

Figure 4: Architecture of Alarm Handling Server -
Alarm Handling Architectural Use Cases

The Alarm Handling Server subsystem provides several services for clients including Read Alarms, Acknowledge Alarms and Subscription Management. Each of the services provided by the concurrent server subsystem is implemented as a concurrent task type, which is instantiated to provide the service. The Read Alarms service is a reader only service while the others are writer services. Alarm status is maintained in the Alarms information hiding object (IHO). The Alarm Manager is the server supervisor task, which receives client requests. It delegates processing an alarm message request to one of the service tasks, which processes the request and then responds directly to the client. Thus the Alarm Manager instantiates a server task to handle a client request, e.g., a Read Alarms task to handle an alarm request. The Read Alarms task invokes the Read operation of the Alarms information hiding object and sends the requested information directly to the requesting client Operator Interface object. A client may also subscribe to receive alarms in which case the subscription request is forwarded to the Subscription Manager Task, which updates the subscription list. The request is for the client to be either subscribed or removed from the subscription list. The event sequence scenario for alarm subscription is shown on Figure 4 and described next:

S1.1 The Operator Interface client sends a Subscription Request message for alarms of a specific type, e.g., high priority alarms.

S1.1.1 The Alarm Manager task forwards the client request message to the Subscription Manager task.

S1.1.2 The Subscription Manager adds the subscription request to the subscription list it maintains by calling the Subscribe operation of the Subscription List object.

S1.2 The Subscription Manager sends an acknowledgement of the client subscription to the client.

Alarm updates from the Workstation Controller are received by the Process Alarms task. The Process Alarms task updates the Alarms repository, which is maintained by the Alarms information hiding object, and then sends an update notification message to the Alarm Distribution task. The Alarm Distribution task then reads the subscription list and sends a copy of the new data to each registered client, as indicated in their subscription specification. This is handled by means of multicast message communication.

The *Alarm Generation and Notification* event sequence scenario is also shown in Figure 4.

M1.1 An alarm update message, e.g., Workstation X robot malfunctioning, arrives at the Process Alarms task.

M1.1.1 The Process Alarms task updates the Alarm IHO with the new alarm by calling the Write operation of the Alarms object.

M1.1.2 The Process Alarms task sends an Update Notification message to the Alarm Distribution task.

M1.2 The Alarm Distribution task calls the Read operation of the Subscription List object, which reads the subscription list in order to determine which client tasks are registered for this event. The names of the client tasks are passed back to the Alarm Distribution task.

M1.2 The new alarm is multicast to all client tasks that have registered for this event.

Since there are multiple readers and writers accessing the Alarm IHO, an appropriate synchronization algorithm must be used, such as the mutual exclusion algorithm or the multiple readers/ multiple writers algorithm. In the latter case, multiple readers are allowed to access the product archive concurrently; however a writer must have mutually exclusive access to the archive. The synchronization is done entirely in the bodies of the Read, Write, and Acknowledge operations of the Alarms IHO, and is thus a "secret" of this object [13] and not a concern of the tasks that use the object.

6.4. Distributed Real-Time Control Use Cases. In distributed real-time systems, distributed real-time control use cases are the most complex. They involve multiple distributed real-time objects cooperating to provide a real-time service and are frequently state dependent. Distributed real-time control use cases involving peer-to-peer communication between real-time objects provided by loosely coupled (asynchronous) message communication. Sometimes, client/server tightly coupled communication is also required.

A distributed real-time control use case for the factory automation system consists of manufacturing a part through the factory. The objects participating in this use case (Figure 5) are the Production Manager Interface, the Process Planning Server, and three real-time control objects, the Receiving Workstation Controller, the Line Workstation Controller and the Shipping Workstation Controller, which interface to pick-and-place and assembly robot controllers, and control the processing of each part. There is one instance of the Line Workstation Controller subsystem for each manufacturing workstation (only one is shown in Figure 5), and the instances are connected in series. Real-time control objects are defined by means of state diagrams, as depicted for the Line Workstation Controller in Figure 6.

A just-in-time algorithm is used in the factory. This means that a workstation only requests a part when it is ready to process it, so that parts do not pile up at a workstation. The use case is initiated by the Production Manager Interface object sending a Start Part message to the Receiving Workstation Controller (RWC), which initiates the manufacture of the part by commanding a robot to place the raw material on a conveyor. The RWC sends a part coming message to the first Line Workstation Controller (LWC). The part is processed at each Line Workstation Controller in sequence until it arrives at the Shipping Workstation Controller (SWC), which sends a Part Complete message to the Production Manager Interface object. Figure 5 shows an event sequence diagram for the Part Manufacturing use case. Each independent event sequence starts with a letter. Since each Line and Shipping Workstation Controller sends a Part request message to its predecessor workstation at initialization (actor is the system), this is shown by the B1.1 and C1.1 messages (also shown on the state diagram in Figure 6). The main event sequence is initiated by the production manager actor creating a work order (A1). The event sequence is as follows:

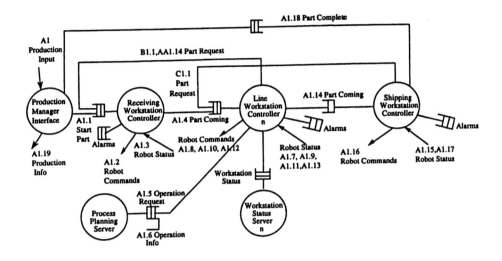

Figure 5: Part Manufacturing Architectural Use Case

B1.1, C1.1) Workstation Controller object sends Part Request message to predecessor Workstation Controller object.

A1) Actor (human production manager) creates work order.

A1.1) Production Manager Interface sends Start Part message to Receiving Workstation Controller.

A1.2, 1.3) RWC informs Robot to place part on conveyor.

A1.4) RWC sends Part Coming message to LWC.

A1.5, A1.6) On receiving Part Coming message, LWC requests and receives operation information for manufacturing the part from Process Planning Server.

A1.7) Robot detects part arrival and sends a Part Arrived message to LWC.

A1.8, A1.9) LWC sends a Pick command to the Pick Place robot, which picks the part off the conveyor and sends an acknowledgement to the LWC.

A1.10, A1.11) LWC sends an Assembly command to the Assembly robot, which assembles the part and then sends an Operation End status message to the LWC.

A1.12, A1.13) LWC sends a Place command to the Pick Place robot, which places the part on conveyor and sends an acknowledgement to the LWC.

A1.14) LWC sends Part Coming message to the successor workstation.

AA1.14) LWC sends Part Request message to the predecessor workstation.

A1.15 - A 1.17) Eventually, the part arrives at the Shipping Workstation Controller where it is stored in the parts completed inventory.

A1.18) The SWC sends a Part Complete message to the Production Manager Interface.

All message communication is loosely coupled apart from the interaction between the LWC and the Process Planning Server, which is tightly coupled.

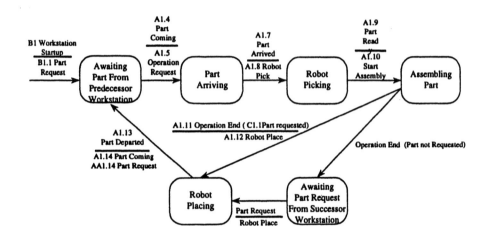

Figure 6: Line Workstation Controller State Diagram

The state diagram (Figure 6) for the LWC shows the influence of different event sequences. Each incoming message to the LWC corresponds to an event on the state diagram. Each action on the state diagram corresponds to an outgoing message from the LWC. The event sequence numbers on Figure 6 correspond to those on Figure 5. Thus at workstation startup, the startup event (B1) causes the LWC to enter Awaiting part from Predecessor Workstation state and send the Part Request message (B1.1) to its predecessor Workstation Controller object. LWC then waits for the Part Coming event (A1.4) from the main part processing event sequence to transition to the Part Arriving state. It sends an output event Operation Request (A1.5). The LWC progresses in a similar way to Assembling Part state. From Assembling Part state, there are two possible transitions, depending on whether the part has been requested by the successor workstation. The condition Part requested is set to True when the Part Request message (C1.1) arrives. Thus, when the assembly operation ends (A1.11), the LWC transitions directly to Robot Placing state.

7. Composing a Software Architecture from Use Cases. The overall design of the distributed real-time system is achieved by composing it from the use cases. Each black box use case describes a functional requirement, while each architectural use case describes the realization of the black box use case in terms of the objects that cooperate to execute the use case. In the same way as the requirements of the system are defined as the sum of the black box use cases, the software architecture of the system is composed from the architectural use cases. Although each object may contribute to several use cases in the architectural use cases, it only appears once in the composed software architecture. Objects that only participate in one use case are depicted on the composed software architecture as they appear in the architectural use case. Contributions by an object to different use cases are synthesized in the composed software architecture.

The caveat is that the black box use cases must cover all the requirements, and that each architectural use case covers the black box use case it is based on. The former needs active user involvement and review, as well as prototyping the requirements [8] where necessary. A practical way to achieve the latter is to review the composed software architecture against the original requirements, analyzing the contribution of each architectural use case. A use case traceability matrix can also be developed to relate use cases to objects. This concisely shows the objects that participate in each use case as well as the use cases that a specific object participates in.

For the factory automation system, the composition of the software architecture involves the three architectural use cases described above, namely *View Alarms*, *Alarm Generation and Notification*, and *Part Manufacturing*, together with the three other use cases previously mentioned, *View Workstation Status*, *View Process Plans* and *Workstation Status Generation and Notification*. The software architecture composed from these use cases is depicted in Figure 7. It shows the aggregate objects in the form of distributed subsystems and their message communication interfaces. The Part Processing subsystem shown in Figure 7 corresponds to an aggregate subsystem composed of four subsystems shown on Figure 5: one instance of a Receiving Workstation Controller, one instance of a Shipping Workstation Controller, n instances of a Line Workstation Controller, and n instances of a Workstation Status Server. The architecture for the Part Processing aggregate subsystem is shown on Figure 8.

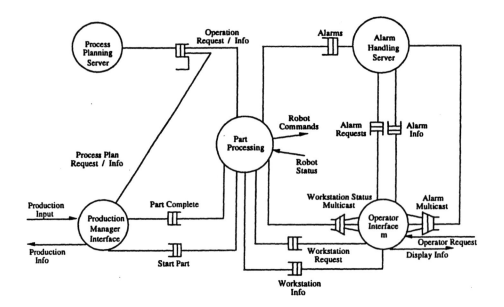

Figure 7: Software Architecture of Factory Automation System System

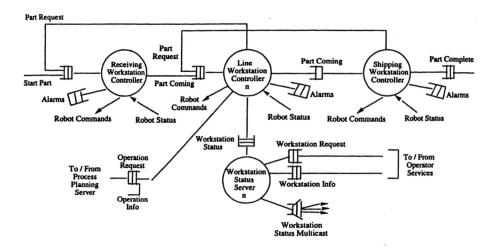

Fig. 8: Architecture of Part Processing Aggregate Subsystem

Consider the Alarm Handling Server object (Figure 7): its contribution to the *Alarm Generation and Notification* use case (Figure 3) is shown by its communication with the Workstation Controller objects of the Part Processing subsystem and the Operator Interface object. Its participation in the *View Alarms* use case (Figure 2) is shown by its communication with the Operator Interface object, which is different from its communication with the same object in the *Alarm Generation and Notification* use case.

8. Conclusions. This paper has described how use cases can be applied in the design of distributed real-time applications. The architectural use cases, based on distributed real-time software architectures, depict the objects participating in the use case and the type of message communication used. These architectural use cases can be considered domain-specific design patterns [2] with the potential of being reused in other applications for the same application domain. Current research is also investigating how use cases can be applied to the design of families of distributed applications [7,9].

REFERENCES

[1] G. Booch. Object-Oriented Analysis and Design. Second Edition, Prentice Hall, 1994.
[2] Gamma, R. Helm, R. Johnson and J. Vlissides. Design Patterns: Elements of Reusable Object-Oriented Software. Addison Wesley, 1995.
[3] H. Gomaa. A Reuse-Oriented Approach to Structuring and Configuring Distributed Applications. The Software Engineering Journal, March 1993.
[4] H. Gomaa. Software Design Methods for Concurrent and Real-Time Systems. Addison-Wesley, 1993.
[5] H. Gomaa. Software Design Methods for Large Scale Real-Time Systems. Journal of Systems and Software, Vol. 25, No. 2, May 1994.
[6] H. Gomaa, D. Menasce, L. Kerschberg. A Software Architectural Design Method for Large-Scale Distributed Information Systems. Journal of Distributed Systems Engineering, September 1996.
[7] H. Gomaa and G.A. Farrukh. An Approach for Configuring Distributed Applications from Reusable Architectures. Proceedings of IEEE International Conference on Engineering of Complex Computer Systems, Montreal, Canada, October 1996.
[8] H. Gomaa. The Impact of Prototyping on Software Systems Engineering in System and Software Requirements Engineering. edited by R. Thayer and M. Dorfman, IEEE Computer Society Press, Second Edition,1997.
[9] H. Gomaa and G. Farrukh. Automated Configuration of Distributed Applications from Reusable Software Architectures. Proceedings IEEE International Conference on Automated Software Engineering, Lake Tahoe, November 1997.
[10] D. Harel. On Visual Formalisms. CACM 31, 5 (May 1988), 514-530.
[11] I. Jacobson et al. Object-Oriented Software Engineering. Addison-Wesley, 1992
[12] Magee J, N. Dulay and J. Kramer. A Constructive Development Environment for Parallel and Distributed Programs. Second International Workshop on Configurable Distributed Systems, Pittsburgh, PA, March 1994.
[13] Parnas D. On the Criteria for Decomposing a System into Modules. Communications ACM, December 1972.
[14] Parnas D., P. Clements and D. Weiss. The Modular Structure of Complex Systems. Proc. Seventh IEEE International Conference on Software Engineering , Orlando, Florida, March 1984.
[15] Rumbaugh, J., et al. Object-Oriented Modeling and Design Prentice Hall, 1991.

[16] M. Shaw and D. Garlan. Software Architecture: Perspectives on an Emerging Discipline. Prentice Hall, 1996.

FORMAL DESIGN OF REAL-TIME SYSTEMS IN A PLATFORM-INDEPENDENT WAY

JOZEF HOOMAN* AND ONNO VAN ROOSMALEN†

Abstract. To design distributed real-time systems, we distinguish two activities: (1) a platform-independent programming activity and (2) the realization of the resulting program on a particular execution platform. This paper concentrates on the first activity, proposing an extension of conventional (non-real-time) programming languages with so called timing annotations that specify the required timing constraints on an abstract level. A formal, axiomatic, semantics of a simple programming language with timing annotations is formulated, using specifications that are based on pre- and postconditions. Program correctness is independent of any underlying execution platform and can be proved by means of compositional proof rules. This is illustrated by a small example of a control system.

1. Introduction. It is generally recognized that problem decomposition and stepwise refinement [1, 11] are important programming strategies. When only functional aspects of programs are considered, there are no major problems in applying these strategies. The functional behavior of a component, specified in terms of its interface, can be implemented independently of other components. Thus, based on the interface properties, functionality can be combined to form more complex behavior. This composability property is essential to enable software reuse and the efficient construction of complex systems.

In contrast, if one considers timing behavior of a program component, implementation details of other, concurrently executing components may become important. E.g., in a multitasking system the time required to complete a certain computation is sensitive to claims on the processor(s) made by other program parts that solve completely independent concerns. We will refer to these other program parts as the *context*. The hidden coupling, i.e. dependences that are not explicitly mentioned in the interface description of components, is called *context dependence* here. Thus, timing aspects of a program or program part, in particular execution durations, may be context dependent. In addition, timing behavior usually depends on the execution platform.

Non-real-time programming approaches provide a context and platform-independent way of describing algorithms. The design decisions and the resulting program are not influenced by details of context and execution platform but solely depend on the specification of the system or subsystem that is to be constructed. This abstraction from platform and context, which is so typical in non-real-time, is also desired for real-time problems. It is a prerequisite for composability and reusability.

1.1. Platform-independent real-time programming. As a solution to the previously mentioned composability problems, we distinguish two activities

---

*Dept. of Computing Science. Eindhoven University of Technology, P.O. Box 513, 5600 MB Eindhoven, The Netherlands (hooman@win.tue.nl).

†Dept. of Computing Science. Eindhoven University of Technology, P.O. Box 513, 5600 MB Eindhoven, The Netherlands (wsinonno@win.tue.nl).

in real-time software development:

1. a completely platform-independent programming activity, and
2. a system generation activity where all platform and context dependencies are addressed.

During the first activity, we achieve platform independence by extending the programming language with *timing annotations* that enable the expression of timing constraints without describing the implementation. Using our timing annotations it is possible to limit the programmed timing constraints to the ones that are implied by the problem specification. No additional constraints need to be programmed to realize or "implement" the timing requirements specified in the problem. Timing annotations thus allow a minimally constrained solution to a real-time problem.

In the system generation activity it must be established that the program can be realized on the selected platform, i.e. that the platform is powerful enough to satisfy the timing constraints that are expressed in the program. This usually comes down to scheduling the application appropriately. The main difference between such a system generation activity and the compilation step in non-real-time system development is the possibility for the system generator to conclude that no implementation can be found for the selected platform (i.e. a feasible schedule cannot be found). Then the platform can be changed or the program can be adapted.

Example 1 Consider, as a simple example, a heating system. If the temperature drops below a critical level, a heating unit should be started within δ time units. Suppose the temperature can be read from a certain device register.

Often such a specification is directly implemented by choosing a period P in which an execution block is scheduled. This block contains a read of the register and, if needed, activation of the heating unit. Let D be the worst-case execution time of this block.

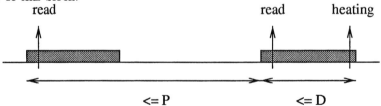

Observe that the temperature might drop below the critical level just after the device register has been read. Then it takes P time units before the register is read again and then at most D time units before the heating is switched on. Hence $P + D \leq \delta$ is required. Note that a large reading period gives a low load of the system, but leads to a strong constraint on the worst-case execution time D. Clearly the choice of the values of P and D depends on the execution platform. Moreover, frequently hard-coded priorities are used to schedule the execution blocks of several processes appropriately, thus introducing a strong context dependency.

During the first activity of our approach we design untimed programs for the processes. For instance, for the heating system this programs is a simple loop in which the register is read and, if needed, the heating unit is activated. Timing is only specified by means of timing annotations, expressing that the heating action should occur within δ after the previous read.

In the second activity, we derive scheduling blocks and timed precedence relations from the annotated program. Given a particular execution platform, the worst-case execution times can be computed and a feasible schedule has to be found. *End Example*

1.2. Compositional Verification. It is important to note that in our approach software components can be programmed independently. Their behavior, including the timing behavior, is constrained only by the specification of the problem or sub-problem they address. This makes it possible to apply compositional verification techniques to our programs with timing annotations. A formal method is called *compositional* if it allows reasoning with the specifications of components, without knowing their implementation.

In this paper we formulate a compositional proof method, that is, a set of axioms and compositional rules that can be used to establish program correctness against the functional as well as the timing specification, independent of the context and the platform. It can also be considered an axiomatic semantics of the programming language, including a formalization of timing annotations. Our specifications are based on Hoare triples [3] (precondition, program, postcondition) that have been extended to deal with real-time.

Not treated here is the verification involved in the second activity; establishing the existence of a feasible and correct schedule (i.e. one that satisfies the constraints expressed in the program) to execute the system on a specified platform.

1.3. Overview. Summarizing, we propose a real-time programming approach with the following properties:

- timing annotations and a programming notation for the functional behaviour are integrated in a single language;
- program semantics is context and platform independent;
- it yields composability and enables abstraction and stepwise refinement of timing behavior;
- correctness of a program or a program part can be formally established in a compositional way (i.e. program component can be proved correct taking into account relevant interfaces of other components only, not their implementation).

The remainder of this paper is structured as follows. Section 2 contains a simple programming language and we explain how timing aspects of systems can be expressed in a platform-independent way. In section 3 we give an axiomatic semantics of this language. This also provides a method to prove correctness, as illustrated by an example of a small control program of a water level monitoring system. Concluding remarks can be found in section 4.

2. A simple parallel programming language. In previous work, our approach has been introduced informally in the object-oriented programming language *Deal*, as part of the Dependable Distributed Operating System (Dedos) project [2]. Here we concentrate on the formal semantics and verification of platform-independent real-time programs. For this purpose we introduce a simple programming language and show how it can be augmented with timing annotations. This also indicates that the basic ideas are more generally applicable to any programming notation describing functional behaviour.

Here our starting point is a normal imperative programming language. Timing constraints are expressed by adding annotations to statements. To illustrate the basic idea, consider the simple example

$$in(d_1, x)[\, m? \,]; \quad \ldots \quad y := f(x) \quad \ldots; \quad out(d_2, y)[\, < m + U \,]$$

The functional part of the program,

$$in(d_1, x); \quad \ldots \quad y := f(x) \quad \ldots; \quad out(d_2, y)$$

expresses that the value of device register d_1 is stored in x, next some computations are done, and then device register d_2 gets the value of y. The timing annotations between the brackets [$\cdots$] express that first the execution moment of $in(d_1, x)$ is assigned to timing variable m. (Typically the execution moment of $in(d_1, x)$ is the moment the value x is taken from the register.) Then the timing annotation of the $out(d_2, y)$ statement expresses that the execution moment of this statement falls before $m + U$.

To give a formal description of the syntax, let *VAR* be a nonempty set of program variables, with typical elements $x, x_1, \ldots, x_n, y, \ldots$ and *RTVAR* be a nonempty set of timing variables, such as $m, m_0, m_1, \ldots, m_n, \ldots$. We also introduce a nonempty set of device variables *DEV*, with typical elements $d, d_1, \ldots, d_n, \ldots$, which enable communication with devices. It is split into devices that are read, *RDEV*, and devices that are written *WDEV*. Let *CONST* be a domain of constants such as $0, 1, \ldots$, using μ for an element of this set. These sets are disjunct, e.g., $VAR \cap RTVAR = \emptyset$. The syntax of our programming language is given in the next table.

Value Expression	$e ::=$	$\mu \mid x \mid e_1 + e_2 \mid e_1 - e_2 \mid e_1 \times e_2$
Boolean Expression	$b ::=$	$true \mid e_1 = e_2 \mid e_1 < e_2 \mid \text{not } b \mid b_1 \text{ or } b_2 \mid b_1 \text{ and } b_2$
Moment Expression	$me ::=$	$\mu \mid m \mid me_1 + me_2 \mid me_1 - me_2 \mid me_1 \times me_2$
Timing Annotation	$TA ::=$	$m := me \mid ?m \mid R\, me \mid TA_1 ; TA_2$
Primitive Statement	$PS ::=$	$\text{skip} \mid x := e \mid in(d, x) \mid out(d, e)$
Statement	$S ::=$	$PS \mid PS[TA] \mid S_1 ; S_2 \mid \text{if } b \text{ then } S_1 \text{ else } S_2 \text{ fi}$ $\mid \text{while } b \text{ do } S \text{ od}$
Program	$P ::=$	$S \mid P_1 \parallel P_2$

We first describe the informal meaning of the normal programming constructs and then explain the added timing annotations.

Informal meaning conventional programming language

Most of the programming constructs are well-known and are assumed to have the conventional untimed semantics in which no assumptions are made about the speed of actions. Statement $in(d, x)$ denotes reading a device variable (register) d and assigning the obtained value to the variable x. Statement $out(d, e)$ denotes writing the value of expression e into the device register d. For the parallel composition $P_1 \parallel P_2$ we require that the variables of P_1 and P_2 are disjoint (i.e., there are no global variables). For simplicity, inter-process communication has not been included in the syntax here. The basic primitives for communication via channels are discussed in section 4.

We use **if** b **then** S **fi** as an abbreviation of **if** b **then** S **else skip fi**.

Informal meaning timing annotations

New is the addition of a time-annotated primitive statement, $PS[TA]$. Timing annotations are used to restrict the set of possible behaviors and they can be seen as constraints on the implementation/scheduler. Since there is no notion of platform in the programming activity, the definition of time units is provided by the problem domain. Therefore, we describe the timing behavior of a program from the viewpoint of an external observer with his own clock. We use the non-negative reals as our (dense) time domain: $TIME = \{\tau \in \mathbb{R} \mid \tau \geq 0\}$. All times are taken relative to the start of the program, taken at time 0.

To describe the meaning of $PS[TA]$ we first define the *execution moment* of a primitive statement PS, denoted by $em(PS)$. The execution moment of PS is a point in time between (or possibly at) the start and the termination time of PS. It usually corresponds to the moment at which the state change that is the result of the statement is effectuated. $PS[TA]$ has the following meaning, using $\equiv$ to denote syntactic equality.

- If $TA \equiv m := me$ then the value of the moment expression me is assigned to m. This is called a *timing assignment*.
- If $TA \equiv ?m$ then the execution moment of statement PS, $em(PS)$, is assigned to m. This is called a *time measurement*.
- Henceforth we identify relation symbol R and its interpretation.
  If $TA \equiv R\,me$ then we have $em(PS)\,R\,me$. This is called a *timing requirement*.
- if $TA \equiv TA_1 \, ; \, TA_2$ then we have the sequentially combined effect of TA_1 and TA_2.
  (If this leads to $false$ the timing constraint can never be satisfied and an implementation of the program cannot be constructed. E.g., **skip**[$<$ $5\,;\,>5$] has an unsatisfiable constraint.)

Thus, we have three types of statements in the annotation:

1. timing assignments, that enable the manipulation of timing variables;
2. time measurements which can be used to record the execution moment

of the annotated program statement;

3. timing requirements, which expresses a timing constraint on the execution moment of the annotated statement.

Henceforth $[TA]$ is used as an abbreviation of **skip**$[TA]$.

Example 2 Consider the following annotated program.

$[m := 0]$;

while *true* **do**

$\quad\quad in(d_1, x)[\ > m + L \ ; \ < m + U \ ; \ ?m \ ]$;

$\quad\quad \dots$

$\quad\quad out(d_2, y)[\ < m + \delta \ ]$

od

This expresses that a read of d_1 occurs between L and U after the previous one (or 0 if there is no such one). Further, it is specified that a write of d_2 occurs in less than δ time units after the preceding read.   *End Example*

Given a particular program, all execution traces are allowed that satisfy the specified timing constraints and additionally guarantee progress (any enabled programming statement will eventually be executed) and finite variability (only a finite amount of progress will happen within a finite amount of time). Additionally, reading and writing of device variables takes a positive amount of time. Apart from this nothing is known about the speed of statement execution.

To solve a real-time programming problem, it is usually not necessary for the programmer to put constraints on the execution moment of every statement in the program. Almost always, requirements only exist for the execution moment of statements that are related to some (observable) external event. Hence, the timing annotations usually only refer to execution moments of a few relevant statements. There is no need to explicitly consider the execution duration of every statement in between: this can be deferred to the system generation activity.

Observe that expressions in the annotations are syntactically isolated from the rest of the program by using square brackets. We distinguish time domain variables (variables of $RTVAR$ used in between square brackets) and program variables (of VAR). Since $RTVAR$ and VAR are disjoint, the scope of variables is restricted to one domain only. This way separability of real-time constraints and functional aspects is achieved. In principle this syntactic restriction is not necessary, but it has been introduced for the following reasons.

1. By not introducing timing variables in the program domain, it is possible to first construct a functionally correct program, and then consider timing requirements.

2. By forbidding the use of program variables in the time domain, it becomes syntactically impossible to introduce data dependencies in the timing requirements. Such data-dependencies usually complicate correctness proofs considerably.

3. Formal verification of programs with timing annotations. A formal, axiomatic, semantics of the language is presented by formulating rules and axioms which express when a program satisfies a certain specification. First the specifications are introduced, using an extended and modified version of Hoare triples (program, precondition, postcondition), similar to [5]. Next the axiomatic semantics is given by formulating a set of compositional rules and axioms. This is also called a proof system, since it can be used to prove program correctness. Compositionality implies that one can reason with the specifications of components without knowing their program text. Program verification is illustrated by a small example of a water level control program.

3.1. Specifications. Specifications have the form $\langle\!\langle A \rangle\!\rangle \ S \ \langle\!\langle C \rangle\!\rangle$ where A is an assertion called *assumption*, S a program, and C an assertion called *commitment*. In the assertions we use program variables, such as x, y, etc., and two special variables *em* and *term*. These terms are only used for local reasoning of a sequential program and are not part of the external interface of a component. They have the following meaning.

- In A, x represents the value of program variable x in the state before the execution of S. If S terminates, then in C it represents the value of x in the final state of S.
- *em* denotes the last *execution moment*; in A the execution moment of the statement preceding S (0 if there is no such statement) and in C the execution moment of the last executed primitive statement of S.
- *term* is a boolean variable denoting termination; in A termination of the statement preceding S (*true* if there is no such statement) and in C it denotes whether S terminates.

Example 3 We present a few simple examples of specifications. The first example is similar to classical Hoare triples, except that we additionally express that the execution moment of a statement (as denoted in the commitment) is not smaller than that of the preceding statement.

$$\langle\!\langle x = 3 \wedge em = 5 \wedge term \rangle\!\rangle \ x := x + 1 \ \langle\!\langle x = 4 \wedge em \geq 5 \wedge term \rangle\!\rangle.$$

We can generalize specifications by using logical (rigid) variables, such as v and t below.

$$\langle\!\langle x = v \wedge em = t \wedge term \rangle\!\rangle \ x := x + 1 \ \langle\!\langle x = v + 1 \wedge em \geq t \wedge term \rangle\!\rangle.$$

The next two examples show some consequences of timing annotations.

$$\langle\!\langle x = 3 \wedge em = 5 \wedge term \rangle\!\rangle \ x := x + 1[\,?m\,] \ \langle\!\langle x = 4 \wedge m \geq 5 \wedge em \geq 5 \wedge term \rangle\!\rangle.$$
$$\langle\!\langle x = 3 \wedge term \rangle\!\rangle \ x := x+1[\, > 6; < 9\,] \ \langle\!\langle x = 4 \wedge 6 < m < 9 \wedge term \rangle\!\rangle. \quad \text{End Example}$$

For a predicate P **at** t, expressing that P occurs at time t, and a set (usually an interval) $I \subseteq TIME$, we use the abbreviations

$$P \textbf{ during } I \equiv \forall t \in I : P \textbf{ at } t$$
$$P \textbf{ in } I \equiv \exists t \in I : P \textbf{ at } t$$

3.1.1. Specification of device registers. The programming language offers device registers for the program to communicate with its environment. A device register can either be set by the environment and read by one process in the program or it can be set by one of the processes and read by the environment. In the former case the state of the environment will be reflected in the value obtained by the read action, in the latter the program will determine the state of the device and influence the environment that way. The following primitives are added to the assertion language.

- $read(d, v)$ **at** t to express that value v is read from d at time t, and
- $set(d, v)$ **at** t to express that d is set to v at time t.

To abstract from read or written values, two abbreviations are introduced.

- $read(d)$ **at** $t \equiv \exists v : read(d, v)$ **at** t
- $set(d)$ **at** $t \equiv \exists v : set(d, v)$ **at** t

Further we introduce the notation $d(t)$ to represent the value of register d at time t. Henceforth, frequently $(d = v)$ **at** t is used as another notation for $d(t) = v$, and similarly for $(d > v)$ **at** t, etc.

The next property expresses that the value read corresponds to the actual value of the device register.

PROPERTY 1 (ReadVal). *For $d \in RDEV$,*

$$read(d, v) \text{ at } t \rightarrow d(t) = v$$

Further, if a process writes a device register d, the value of d equals the last written value (or the initial value at 0).

PROPERTY 2 (WriteVal). *For $d \in WDEV$,*

$$d(t) = v \leftrightarrow (\exists t_0 \leq t : set(d, v) \text{ at } t_0 \wedge \forall v_0 \neq v : \neg set(d, v_0) \text{ during } [t_0, t]) \vee$$
$$(v = d(0) \wedge \neg set(d) \text{ during } [0, t])$$

At most one value is written at any point in time.

PROPERTY 3 (Uniqueness). *For $d \in WDEV$,*

$$set(d, v_1) \text{ at } t \wedge set(d, v_2) \text{ at } t \rightarrow v_1 = v_2$$

Finally, only a finite number of write actions can be performed in a finite amount of time. Hence there exists a last write in any finite period I which contains at least one write.

PROPERTY 4 (Finiteness). *For $d \in WDEV$,*

$$set(d) \text{ in } I \rightarrow \exists t \in I : set(d) \text{ at } t \wedge (\neg set(d)) \text{ during } \{t_0 \in I \mid t_0 > t\}$$

Example 4 We present a few simple specifications, to give an indication of what can be expressed. First consider a statement $in(d, y)$ which reads a device (taking a positive amount of time).

$$\langle\!\langle x = 7 \wedge em = 3 \wedge term \rangle\!\rangle$$

$in(d, y)$

$\langle\!\langle x = 7 \wedge em > 3 \wedge read(d, y) \textbf{ at } em \wedge term \rangle\!\rangle.$

The next example shows an *out* statement and the use of logical variables (v and t).

$\langle\!\langle x = v \wedge em = t \wedge read(d_1, 6) \textbf{ at } 5 \wedge term \rangle\!\rangle$

$\qquad out(d_2, x + 3)$

$\langle\!\langle x = v \wedge em > t \wedge read(d_1, 6) \textbf{ at } 5 \wedge set(d_2, v + 3) \textbf{ at } em \wedge term \rangle\!\rangle.$

The following example contains timing annotations.

$\langle\!\langle x = 1 \wedge \delta = 10 \wedge m = 15 \wedge term \rangle\!\rangle$

$\qquad out(d, x + 3)[\ < m + \delta \ ]$

$\langle\!\langle x = 1 \wedge set(d, 4) \textbf{ at } em \wedge em < 25 \wedge term \rangle\!\rangle.$

The next, non-terminating, program sets d infinitely often with a distance of at most δ time units.

$\langle\!\langle em = 0 \wedge term \rangle\!\rangle$

$\qquad [\, m := 0 \,] \, ;$

$\qquad \textbf{while } true \textbf{ do } out(d, 0)[\ < m + \delta \, ; \, m? \,] \textbf{ od}$

$\langle\!\langle \neg term \wedge \forall t : set(d, 0) \textbf{ in } [t, t + \delta] \rangle\!\rangle.$ $\hfill$ *End Example*

3.2. Proof system. We briefly present the rules and axioms for our programming language and refer to [5] for more explanation on the rules for the conventional programming constructs. We assume that all new (logical) variables which are introduced in the rules are fresh.

3.2.1. Axiomatization of Programming Constructs. Let $A[exp/x]$ denote the assertion obtained by substituting expression exp for all free occurrences of variable x in A. In the rule for a **skip** statement, the last execution moment before this statement is represented by t_0 (replacing em in A by t_0).

RULE 1 (Skip).

$$\frac{A[t_0/em] \wedge term \wedge em \geq t_0 \rightarrow C}{\langle\!\langle A \wedge term \rangle\!\rangle \textbf{ skip } \langle\!\langle C \rangle\!\rangle}$$

As mentioned above we assume that t_0 does not occur free in C. Note that execution of the **skip** statement may take 0 time (it is possible that $em = t_0$). In the rule for assignment $x := e$, similarly the execution moment of the preceding statement is represented by t_0 and the initial value of x is represented by v (by means of the substitution $A[t_0/em, v/x]$).

RULE 2 (Assignment).

$$\frac{A[t_0/em, v/x] \wedge term \wedge x = e[v/x] \wedge em \geq t_0 \rightarrow C}{\langle\!\langle A \wedge term \rangle\!\rangle \ x := e \ \langle\!\langle C \rangle\!\rangle}$$

Example 5 The formula

$$\langle\langle x = 4 \wedge 5 < em \wedge em < 7 \wedge term \rangle\rangle \quad x := x + 2 \quad \langle\langle x = 6 \wedge em > 5 \wedge term \rangle\rangle$$

can be derived by the assignment rule, since

$(x = 4 \wedge 5 < em \wedge em < 7)[t_0/em, v/x] \wedge term \wedge x = (x + 2)[v/x] \wedge em \geq t_0$

equals

$v = 4 \wedge 5 < t_0 \wedge t_0 < 7 \wedge term \wedge x = v + 2 \wedge em \geq t_0$ which implies

$x = 6 \wedge em > 5 \wedge term.$ *End Example*

Similarly, rules for access to device registers are formulated.

RULE 3 (Read).

$$\frac{A[t_0/em, v/x] \wedge term \wedge read(d, x) \text{ at } em \wedge}{(\neg read(d)) \textbf{ during } (t_0, em) \wedge em > t_0 \rightarrow C}{\langle\langle A \wedge term \rangle\rangle \; in(d, x) \; \langle\langle C \rangle\rangle}$$

Note that in the rule above and the one below, $em > t_0$ has been used instead of $em \geq t_0$ to express that these statements take some positive amount of time.

RULE 4 (Set).

$$\frac{A[t_0/em] \wedge term \wedge set(d, e) \text{ at } em \wedge}{(\neg set(d)) \textbf{ during } (t_0, em) \wedge em > t_0 \rightarrow C}{\langle\langle A \wedge term \rangle\rangle \; out(d, e) \; \langle\langle C \rangle\rangle}$$

The rules for sequential composition and choice are identical to the classical rules of Hoare logic [3].

RULE 5 (Sequential Composition).

$$\frac{\langle\langle A \rangle\rangle \; S_1 \; \langle\langle B \rangle\rangle, \quad \langle\langle B \rangle\rangle \; S_2 \; \langle\langle C \rangle\rangle}{\langle\langle A \rangle\rangle \; S_1; S_2 \; \langle\langle C \rangle\rangle}$$

RULE 6 (If-then-else).

$$\frac{\langle\langle A \wedge b \rangle\rangle \; S_1 \; \langle\langle C \rangle\rangle, \quad \langle\langle A \wedge \neg b \rangle\rangle \; S_2 \; \langle\langle C \rangle\rangle}{\langle\langle A \rangle\rangle \textbf{ if } b \textbf{ then } S_1 \textbf{ else } S_2 \textbf{ fi } \langle\langle C \rangle\rangle}$$

The rule for the while construct is more complicated, since our framework considers both terminating and non-terminating computations. For simplicity, we only present the rule for a while construct with a true boolean guard. Clearly **while** *true* **do** S **od** does not terminate and there are two classes of computations: either S always terminates and we have an invariant I which holds after each execution of S for increasing execution moments (represented by I_1 below) or eventually S does not terminate (represented by its invariant I).

RULE 7 (While true).

$$\frac{\langle\langle I \wedge term \rangle\rangle \; S \; \langle\langle I \rangle\rangle,}{\forall t_1 \; \exists t_2 > t_1 : I[t_2/em] \rightarrow I_1, \quad loc(I_1) = \emptyset,}{term \text{ does not occur in } I_1}{\langle\langle I \wedge term \rangle\rangle \textbf{ while } true \textbf{ do } S \textbf{ od } \langle\langle\langle (I \vee I_1) \wedge \neg term \rangle\rangle}$$

See [5] for a general rule, and similarly for more details on sequential and parallel composition.

RULE 8 (Parallel Composition).

$$\frac{\langle\!\langle A_1\rangle\!\rangle \ P_1 \ \langle\!\langle C_1\rangle\!\rangle, \quad \langle\!\langle A_2\rangle\!\rangle \ P_2 \ \langle\!\langle C_2\rangle\!\rangle}{\langle\!\langle A_1 \wedge A_2\rangle\!\rangle \ P_1\|P_2 \ \langle\!\langle C_1 \wedge C_2\rangle\!\rangle}$$

provided

- the commitment of one process should not refer to local objects of the other process;
- assertions in the specification of a process refer only to the interface of the process itself;
- *em* and *term* do not occur in the commitments C_1 and C_2.

3.2.2. Axiomatization of Timing Annotations. Next we introduce a few new rules to reason about timing annotations. Since a timing annotations is not a statement (recall that the statement $[TA]$ is an abbreviation of **skip**$[TA]$), we introduce some auxiliary notation. For a timing annotation we use $\langle\!\langle\!\langle A\rangle\!\rangle\!\rangle \ [TA] \ \langle\!\langle\!\langle C\rangle\!\rangle\!\rangle$.

As a simple example, to show the main idea, consider the formula

$\langle\!\langle x = 3 \wedge m_0 = 5 \wedge term\rangle\!\rangle$

$\quad out(d, x + 3)[\ > m_0 + 2 \ ; \ < m + 4 \ ; \ ?m_0 \ ; \ m_0 := m_0 + 10 \,]$

$\langle\!\langle x = 3 \wedge set(d, 6) \ \textbf{at} \ em \wedge em > 7 \wedge \ em < m + 4 \wedge m_0 = em + 10 \wedge term\rangle\!\rangle.$

This is proved by first deriving

$\langle\!\langle x = 3 \wedge m_0 = 5 \wedge term\rangle\!\rangle$

$\quad out(d, x + 3)$

$\langle\!\langle x = 3 \wedge m_0 = 5 \wedge set(d, 6) \ \textbf{at} \ em \wedge term\rangle\!\rangle$

with the Set Rule above. Next we will present rules to derive

$\langle\!\langle\!\langle x = 3 \wedge m_0 = 5 \wedge set(d, 6) \ \textbf{at} \ em \wedge term\rangle\!\rangle\!\rangle$

$\quad [\ > m_0 + 2 \ ; \ < m + 4 \ ; \ ?m_0 \ ; \ m_0 := m_0 + 10 \,]$

$\langle\!\langle\!\langle x = 3 \wedge set(d, 6) \ \textbf{at} \ em \wedge em > 7 \wedge \ em < m + 4 \wedge m_0 = em + 10 \wedge term\rangle\!\rangle\!\rangle.$

Then the following rule leads to the desired formula.

RULE 9 (Timing Annotation Introduction).

$$\frac{\langle\!\langle A\rangle\!\rangle \ S \ \langle\!\langle B\rangle\!\rangle, \quad \langle\!\langle\!\langle B\rangle\!\rangle\!\rangle \ [TA] \ \langle\!\langle\!\langle C\rangle\!\rangle\!\rangle}{\langle\!\langle A\rangle\!\rangle \ S[TA] \ \langle\!\langle C\rangle\!\rangle}$$

To derive formulas of the form $\langle\!\langle\!\langle A\rangle\!\rangle\!\rangle \ [TA] \ \langle\!\langle\!\langle C\rangle\!\rangle\!\rangle$ we introduce three axioms and a rule.

AXIOM 1 (Timing Assignment).

$$\langle\!\langle\!\langle C[me/m]\rangle\!\rangle\!\rangle \ [\ m := me \,] \ \langle\!\langle\!\langle C\rangle\!\rangle\!\rangle$$

AXIOM 2 (Time Measurement).

$$\langle\!\langle\!\langle C[em/m]\rangle\!\rangle\!\rangle \; [\,?m\,] \; \langle\!\langle\!\langle C\rangle\!\rangle\!\rangle$$

Example 6 As a simple example, observe that we can derive $\langle\!\langle\!\langle em = 5\rangle\!\rangle\!\rangle \; [\,?m\,] \; \langle\!\langle\!\langle m = 5\rangle\!\rangle\!\rangle$. *End Example*

AXIOM 3 (Timing Requirement).

$$\langle\!\langle\!\langle A\rangle\!\rangle\!\rangle \; [\,R\,me\,] \; \langle\!\langle\!\langle A \wedge em \, R \, me\rangle\!\rangle\!\rangle$$

RULE 10 (Timing Annotation Sequential Composition).

$$\frac{\langle\!\langle\!\langle A\rangle\!\rangle\!\rangle \; [\,TA_1\,] \; \langle\!\langle\!\langle B\rangle\!\rangle\!\rangle, \langle\!\langle\!\langle B\rangle\!\rangle\!\rangle \; [\,TA_2\,] \; \langle\!\langle\!\langle C\rangle\!\rangle\!\rangle}{\langle\!\langle\!\langle A\rangle\!\rangle\!\rangle \; [\,TA_1; TA_2\,]\langle\!\langle\!\langle C\rangle\!\rangle\!\rangle}$$

Example 7 With these rules we can derive, e.g., formulae of the form
$\langle\!\langle term\rangle\!\rangle$
$$S_1[\,?m_2\,]; \; S_2[\,?m_1\,]; \; \textbf{if } b \textbf{ then } S_3[\, \le m_2 + \delta_1\,] \textbf{ else } S_4[\, \le m_2 + \delta_2\,] \textbf{ fi}$$
$\langle\!\langle m_2 \le m_1 \le m_2 + max(\delta_1, \delta_2)\rangle\!\rangle$. *End Example*

3.2.3. General Rules and Axioms. The proof system contains several general rules such as the consequence rule which allows strengthening of assumptions and weakening of commitments.

RULE 11 (Consequence).

$$\frac{\langle\!\langle A_0\rangle\!\rangle \; P \; \langle\!\langle C_0\rangle\!\rangle, A \rightarrow A_0, C_0 \rightarrow C}{\langle\!\langle A\rangle\!\rangle \; P \; \langle\!\langle C\rangle\!\rangle}$$

Here we only list the rules pertaining to the particulars of our real-time language, and refer to [5] for other rules. The first axiom expresses that a terminating program takes only a finite amount of time.

AXIOM 4 (Finite Time).

$$\langle\!\langle em = t_0 \wedge term\rangle\!\rangle \; S \; \langle\!\langle term \rightarrow \exists \delta \ge 0 : em \le t_0 + \delta\rangle\!\rangle$$

For a statement S, let $write(S)$ be the set of device variables that might be set by S, i.e. the set of variables d such that $out(d, e)$ occurs in S. Similarly, $read(S)$ is the set of device variables that might be read by S, i.e. the set of variables d such that $in(d, x)$ occurs in S. We assume that at most one process can access a device variable.

AXIOM 5 (Read Invariance).　　If $d \notin read(S)$,

$$\langle\!\langle em = t_0 \rangle\!\rangle \; S \; \langle\!\langle\!\langle (\neg read(d)) \; \textbf{during} \; (t_0, em] \rangle\!\rangle\!\rangle$$

AXIOM 6 (Write Invariance).　　If $d \notin write(S)$,

$$\langle\!\langle em = t_0 \rangle\!\rangle \; S \; \langle\!\langle\!\langle (\neg set(d)) \; \textbf{during} \; (t_0, em] \rangle\!\rangle\!\rangle$$

3.3. Verification of a simple control system. We specify, implement and verify the control program of a water level monitoring system. A water vessel has limited but unknown influx of water. A pump, with a larger capacity than this influx, is installed to be able to remove water from it. Activation or deactivation of a pump must prevent that the vessel overflows or runs dry. A device measuring the water level is installed. Critically low and high water levels are selected. Using the maximal flow in and out of the vessel and the critical levels, the response time D for the control system to switch the pump on or off is calculated. This leads to the control requirement

$\forall t_1, t_2$: (water critically high) **during** $[t_1, t_2] \rightarrow$ (pump is on) **during** $[t_1 + D, t_2]$

and similarly for the critically low value. Because of symmetry we only show the high value case here. For simplicity we assume that two device variables, water and pump, represent the water level and the pump state instantaneously. Assume pump ranges over $\{on, off\}$. The aim is to design a control system satisfying:

$\forall t_1, t_2$: (water > high) **during** $[t_1, t_2] \rightarrow$ (pump = on) **during** $[t_1 + D, t_2]$

Since the right-hand side is trivially true if $t_1 + D > t_2$, it is equivalent to

$CTL_1 \equiv \forall t_1, t_2$: $t_1 + D \leq t_2 \wedge$ (water > high) **during** $[t_1, t_2] \rightarrow$ (pump = on) **during** $[t_1 + D, t_2]$

Similarly we have CTL_2 for water < low and pump = off. The aim is to design a control system Contr such that

$$\langle\!\langle em = 0 \rangle\!\rangle \; \text{Contr} \; \langle\!\langle CTL_1 \wedge CTL_2 \rangle\!\rangle.$$

The program must keep the pump in the correct state. It can do so by setting the variable pump at selected moments. Hence we refine the specification to

$CP_1 \equiv \forall t_1, t_2$: $t_1 + D \leq t_2 \wedge$ (water > high) **during** $[t_1, t_2] \rightarrow$
$\qquad\qquad \exists t_3 \leq t_1 + D : set(\text{pump}, on) \; \textbf{at} \; t_3 \wedge (\neg set(\text{pump}, off)) \; \textbf{during} \; [t_3, t_2]$

Similarly, CP_2 is defined for water < low. Then we can prove the following lemma.

LEMMA 3.1.　$CP_1 \wedge CP_2$ implies $CTL_1 \wedge CTL_2$

Proof. To prove CTL_1, assume for t_1, t_2 that $t_1 + D \leq t_2$ and (water > high) **during** $[t_1, t_2]$.
By CP_1, there exists a t_3 with $t_3 \leq t_1 + D$, $set(\text{pump}, on)$ **at** t_3, and $(\neg set(\text{pump}, off))$

during $[t_3, t_2]$. By Property 2 (WriteVal) this implies (pump $= on$) during $[t_3, t_2]$, and hence
(pump $= on$) during $[t_1 + D, t_2]$.
The proof of CTL_2 proceeds similarly. $\square$

Hence it remains to implement Contr such that
$$\langle\!\langle em = 0 \rangle\!\rangle \ \text{Contr} \ \langle\!\langle CP_1 \wedge CP_2 \rangle\!\rangle.$$

Next we use device variable water to read the value of the water level. A possible step in the design is now to choose a certain reading period R and to specify that the pump should be switched on in less than $D - R$ time units when reading a value greater than high. Here we avoid the choice of periods and corresponding internal reaction times, by specifying that a response is needed in less than D time units after the previous read, since this represents the worst-case assumption about the water level. See the figure below.

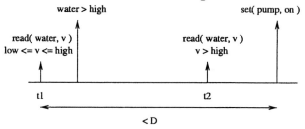

To specify this design idea, we do not explicitly refer to the previous read, but only to the preceding interval without read actions. Abbreviation $ReadPeriod(t_1, t_2, v)$ expresses that after t_1 the first read action of water is at t_2 and value v is read.
$$ReadPeriod(t_1, t_2, v) \equiv (t_1 < t_2) \wedge read(\text{water}, v) \ \text{at} \ t_2 \wedge (\neg read(\text{water})) \ \textbf{during} \ (t_1, t_2)$$
Next a few additional abbreviations.
$$ReadPeriod(t_1, t_2) \equiv \exists v : ReadPeriod(t_1, t_2, v)$$
$$ReadPeriodHigh(t_1, t_2) \equiv \exists v : v > \text{high} \wedge ReadPeriod(t_1, t_2, v)$$
$$ReadPeriodLow(t_1, t_2) \equiv \exists v : v < \text{low} \wedge ReadPeriod(t_1, t_2, v)$$
To specify the control program, commitment CC_1 expresses that a value is read at least once every period of D time units.
$$CC_1 \equiv \forall t \ \exists t_1, t_2 : t_1 < t \le t_2 < t + D \wedge ReadPeriod(t_1, t_2)$$

If the first read after t_1 takes place at t_2 and yields a high value then the pump should be switched on. Since it is possible that the water was already high immediately after t_1, the deadline on the set action is $t_1 + D$.
$$CC_2 \equiv \forall t_1, t_2 : ReadPeriodHigh(t_1, t_2) \rightarrow set(\text{pump}, on) \ \text{in} \ [t_2, t_1 + D]$$

Finally we specify that the pump is only switched off at time t if a low value has been read at t_2 before t and no value has been read between t_2 and t.
$$CC_3 \equiv \forall t : set(\text{pump}, off) \ \text{at} \ t \rightarrow \exists t_1, t_2 : t \in [t_2, t_1 + D] \wedge ReadPeriodLow(t_1, t_2) \wedge$$

$$(\neg read(\text{water})) \text{ during } (t_2, t]$$

In addition, the symmetric case is described by CC_4 and CC_5, interchanging high and low, and also *on* and *off*. Let $CC \equiv CC_1 \wedge CC_2 \wedge CC_3 \wedge CC_4 \wedge CC_5$. Then we have the following lemma.

LEMMA 3.2. If low $\leq$ high then CC implies $CP_1 \wedge CP_2$.

Proof. By symmetry, it is sufficient to show CP_1. Suppose the premise of the implication in CP_1 is satisfied and there exists a t_1 and t_2 with

(3.1) $$t_1 + d \leq t_2 \wedge (\text{water} > \text{high}) \text{ during } [t_1, t_2]$$

By CC_1, the water level was read in $[t_1, t_1 + D]$ and unfolding the abbreviations, we obtain t_{11}, t_{21} and v with

(3.2) $$t_{11} < t_1 \leq t_{21} \leq t_1 + D \wedge read(\text{water}, v) \text{ at } t_{21} \wedge$$
$$(\neg read(\text{water})) \text{ during } (t_{11}, t_{21})$$

Observe that $t_{21} \in [t_1, t_2]$, thus assumption (3.1) leads to $\text{water}(t_{21}) > \text{high}$. By Property 1 (ReadVal) we have $\forall t : read(\text{water}, v) \text{ at } t \to \text{water}(t) = v$. Hence $v > \text{high}$, and thus

(3.3) $$ReadPeriodHigh(t_{11}, t_{21})$$

By CC_2 we obtain $set(\text{pump}, on)$ in $[t_{21}, t_{11} + D]$. That is, there exists a t_3 with

(3.4) $$t_{21} \leq t_3 \leq t_{11} + D \wedge set(\text{pump}, on) \text{ at } t_3$$

Since, using (3.2), $t_3 \leq t_{11} + D < t_1 + D$, it remains to show $(\neg set(\text{pump}, off))$ **during** $[t_3, t_2]$.

Suppose $set(\text{pump}, off)$ in $[t_3, t_2]$, i.e., assume there exists a $t_4 \in [t_3, t_2]$ with $set(\text{pump}, off)$ at t_4. Then by CC_3 there exist t_{12} and t_{22} such that $t_4 \in [t_{22}, t_{12}+D]$, $ReadPeriodLow(t_{12}, t_{22})$, and $(\neg read(\text{water}))$ **during** $(t_{22}, t_4]$. Given the last formula, observing that $t_4 \geq t_3 \geq t_{21}$ and using $read(\text{water})$ at t_{21} from (3.2), we obtain that $t_{21} \leq t_{22}$. By (3.2) we have $t_1 \leq t_{21}$ thus $t_1 \leq t_{22}$. Since $t_{22} \leq t_4 \leq t_2$ this leads to $t_{22} \in [t_1, t_2]$. Then (3.1) implies that $\text{water}(t_{22}) > \text{high}$, and thus low $<$ high leads to $\neg(\text{water}(t_{22}) < \text{low})$. By Property 1 (ReadVal) this yields a contradiction with $ReadPeriodLow(t_{12}, t_{22})$.

Hence $(\neg set(\text{pump}, off))$ **during** $[t_3, t_2]$ and CP_1 has been proved. $\square$

Consequently, control program Contr is specified by

$$\langle\!\langle em = 0 \rangle\!\rangle \text{ Contr } \langle\!\langle CC \rangle\!\rangle.$$

Note that CC_3 is stronger than strictly necessary for the proof. It incorporates the design decision that no additional read action will take place between reading a low water level and setting the pump. Similarly for CC_5. This excludes programs in which such read and set actions are performed by different processes and they need not alternate.

To satisfy the commitment CC we propose the following program.

Contr $\equiv$

$[\, m_1 := 0 \,]$;

while *true* **do**

      $[\, m_2 := m_1 \,]$;

      $in(\text{water}, x)[\ < m_2 + D \,;\ ?m_1 \,]$;

      if high $< x$ **then** $out(\text{pump}, on)[\ < m_2 + D \,]$

        else **if** $x <$ low **then** $out(\text{pump}, off)[\ < m_2 + D \,]$

      fi fi

od

The program should be read as follows. Initially timing variable m_1 is set to 0. On the first sweep of the repetition, m_2 obtains this value in the first annotated statement. The first execution of the *in* statement takes place before time D, and m_1 records the actual execution moment. If subsequently a pump action is required, the state change corresponding to the relevant *out* statement is realized before the deadline D. In the next sweep m_2 gets the old value of m_1 and m_1 records the execution moment of the next *in* statement that inspects the environment. A possible response to the value obtained must now take place before $m_2 + D$, i.e. within time D from the one but last inspection. Since the *out* statements need not be executed, the maximal distance D between successive reads is specified separately. This pattern is repeated forever.

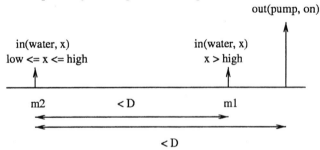

Considering the specification, this program can be motivated as follows. CC_1 is satisfied by allowing at most D time units to pass between two consecutive sensor readings. This is expressed in the annotation of the *in* statement. The maximum *ReadPeriod* that ends at a particular read action extends backwards to the moment of the previous read action. Thus, CC_2 is realized by imposing a deadline D on the *out*(pump, *on*) statement counted from the execution moment of the one but last inspection of the water level. Similarly, it is easy to see that CC_3 holds, since the pump is only switched off within D time units after a low value has been read.

LEMMA 3.3. $\langle\!\langle em = 0 \rangle\!\rangle$ Contr $\langle\!\langle CC \rangle\!\rangle$

Proof. To prove CC_1, define

$$CC_1(t) \equiv \exists t_1, t_2 : t_1 \leq t \leq t_2 \leq t + D \wedge\ ReadPeriod(t_1, t_2)$$

The proof is based on a loop invariant I_1 which expresses essentially that $CC_1(t)$ holds for all $t < m_1$, where m_1 is a timing variable. Since additionally $m_1 \geq em - D$, the property that the while loop yields unbounded values of em leads to $CC_1(t)$, for all t.

$I_1 \equiv term \wedge m_1 \leq em \leq m_1 + D \wedge \neg read(\text{water})$ **during** $(m_1, em) \wedge \forall t < m_1 :$ $CC_1(t)$

The proof is represented by a so called proof outline; a program where assertions have been inserted at the location where they should hold. Motivated by the timing annotation introduction rule, the proof of $\langle\!\langle A \rangle\!\rangle S[TA] \langle\!\langle C \rangle\!\rangle$ is represented by the proof outline $\langle\!\langle A \rangle\!\rangle S \langle\!\langle B \rangle\!\rangle TA \langle\!\langle C \rangle\!\rangle$. In the proof outline below we use the auxiliary assertion A_1.

$A_1 \equiv term \wedge m_2 < m_1 < em \wedge \neg read(\text{water})$ **during** $(m_2, em) \wedge read(\text{water})$ **at** $m_1 \wedge$

$\qquad \forall t < m_2 : CC_1(t)$

We assume that initially $em = 0$, representing the assumption that nothing is executed before this program.

$\langle\!\langle term \wedge em = 0 \rangle\!\rangle$

$[\, m_1 := 0 \,] ; \ \langle\!\langle term \wedge m_1 = em = 0 \rangle\!\rangle$

while $true$ **do** $\langle\!\langle I_1 \rangle\!\rangle$

$\qquad [\, m_2 := m_1 \,] ; \ \langle\!\langle B_1 \equiv I_1[m_2/m_1] \rangle\!\rangle$

$\qquad in(\text{water}, x) \ \langle\!\langle C_1 \equiv B_1 \wedge read(\text{water}) \ \textbf{at} \ em \rangle\!\rangle \ [\ < m_2 + D \ ; \ ?m_1 \,] ;$

$\qquad \langle\!\langle D_1 \equiv C_1 \wedge em < m_2 + D \wedge m_1 = em \rangle\!\rangle$

$\qquad \textbf{if high} < x \ \textbf{then} \ \ \langle\!\langle D_1 \rangle\!\rangle \ out(\text{pump}, on) \ \langle\!\langle A_1 \rangle\!\rangle \ [\ < m_2 + D\,] \ \langle\!\langle I_1 \rangle\!\rangle$

$\qquad \textbf{else if } x < \textbf{low then} \ \ \langle\!\langle D_1 \rangle\!\rangle \ out(\text{pump}, off) \ \langle\!\langle A_1 \rangle\!\rangle \ [\ < m_2 + D\,] \ \langle\!\langle I_1 \rangle\!\rangle$

$\qquad \textbf{fi fi} \langle\!\langle I_1 \rangle\!\rangle$

od

$\langle\!\langle CC_1 \rangle\!\rangle$

The last step, the proof of CC_1, follows from Rule 7 (While true), since $I_1 \wedge \neg term$ is equivalent to $false$ and $\forall t_1 \exists t_2 > t_1 : I_1[t_2/em]$ implies $\forall t_1 \exists t_2 > t_1 : t_2 \leq m_1 + D \wedge \forall t < m_1 : CC_1(t)$. We show that this leads to $\forall t_0 : CC_1(t_0)$. Consider a point of time t_0. Let $t_1 = t_0 + D$. Then there exists a $t_2 > t_1$ such that $t_2 \leq m_1 + D$, and thus $m_1 \geq t_2 - D > t_1 - D = t_0$. I.e., $t_0 < m_1$ which leads to $CC_1(t_0)$. Finally note that $\forall t_0 : CC_1(t_0)$ implies CC_1.

To prove CC_2 define

$CC_2(t_2) \equiv \forall t_1 : ReadPeriodHigh(t_1, t_2) \rightarrow set(\text{pump}, on) \ \textbf{in} \ [t_2, t_1 + D]$

Then proof proceeds similarly to the one above, using the invariant

$I_2 \equiv term \wedge \neg read(\text{water})$ **during** $(m_1, em) \wedge (m_1 = 0 \vee read(\text{water})$ **at** $m_1) \wedge$ $\forall t < em : CC_2(t)$

Similarly, CC_3 is proved by means of

$CC_3(t) \equiv set(\text{pump}, off) \ \textbf{at} \ t \rightarrow \exists t_1, t_2 : t \in [t_2, t_1 + D] \wedge ReadPeriodLow(t_1, t_2) \wedge$
$\qquad\qquad\qquad\qquad\qquad (\neg read(\text{water}))$ **during** $(t_2, t]$

and the invariant

$I_3 \equiv term\wedge \neg read(\text{water}) \textbf{ during } (m_1, em)\wedge \forall t < em : CC_3(t)$ □

4. Concluding remarks. We have described how a programming language can be extended with timing annotations to describe real-time constraints. The syntax of the programming language used here was just a vehicle to illustrate the approach and details of the syntax and semantics are not essential. We believe, however, that the following properties *are* essential for any successful approach to real-time programming.

1. Formal techniques are essential, at least to define a real-time programming paradigm. Many current proposals are hard to understand and difficult to apply because a formal semantics of new constructs is not provided.
2. A strict separation of concerns in the programming and system generation activities should be used. All platform and context dependencies should be addressed during system generation. In this respect, the only difference with non-real-time programming is that the system generator may decide not to implement the program on the specified platform.
3. Real-time programs *can* and *should* be designed *and verified* independently of an execution platform.
4. Over-specification of timing behavior should be avoided. Usually over-specifications are made on the basis of platform considerations.

An important aspect of our work is the possibility to formally establish program correctness without making any assumptions about the platform that will execute the program.

Concerning the second point, observe that in contrast with other formal methods for real-time systems (see, e.g., [8]), in our approach program correctness does not require any assumption about the underlying platform. No assumptions are made about the duration of statements, the number of processors, the mapping of processes to processors, the scheduling policy, etcetera. We are not aware of any other programming framework that provides a similar rigorous abstraction from the execution platform.

4.1. Communication between parallel processes. In a technical report [6] we have given a more detailed description of our approach, illustrated by a larger example of a mine pump system. In that example the design leads to a program with several parallel processes and we show that this program can be scheduled on various platforms.

To denote synchronization and communication between parallel processes in an abstract way, two new statements are introduced:

- $send[\ !me\ ](c, e)$ denotes an asynchronous send action, that is, the value e is transmitted along channel c. Further, moment expression me is communicated to the receiver (conceptually, i.e., this need not be physically sent). We assume that messages are stored in an infinite FIFO buffer.

- $receive[\,?m\,](c, x)$ denotes a receive action which receives a value from channel c, namely the first available message in the FIFO buffer of this channel, and assigns this value to x. Further a timing value is received (conceptually) and assigned to m. This statements waits until a message is available.

With this notation, there is no need to split global deadlines into local deadlines for the processes, thus avoiding over-specification (see point 4. above). The basic idea is that constraints on actions can be passed from one process to another (conceptually).

Example 8 Assume given two functions f_1 and f_2 on the data domain. It is specified that after reading a value v from register d_1, a computed value $f_2(f_1(v))$ should be written into register d_2 in less than δ time units. Thus

$$\forall t, v : read(d_1, v) \text{ at } t \to set(d_2, f_2(f_1(v))) \text{ in } [t, t + \delta)$$

Additional constraints, such as a certain frequency of reading input, are omitted here. Suppose we decide to implement this by means of two processes, where the first one computes f_1 and sends the result to the second process which then computes f_2. Then we can avoid the decision to split up δ into deadlines for each of the processes, which would depend on the execution time of the computations needed for f_1 and f_2. The next parallel program specifies only the constraints on the external input-output behaviour.

```
while true do                    ||   while true do
    in(d₁,x)[ ?m₁ ] ;                    receive[ ?m₂ ](c, w) ;
    y := f₁(x) ;                         z := f₂(w) ;
    send[ !m₁ + δ ](c, y)                out(d₂, z)[ < m₂ ])
od                                   od
```

Note that the annotation of the send statement does not represent a constraint, but merely propagates a constraint to the receiver. *End Example*

4.2. Comparison. Technical report [6] also contains a comparison with other real-time languages, notably Ada95 and a couple of recent object-oriented real-time languages (e.g. those published in [7, 9, 10]). We summarize here the major differences with other approaches.

Usually timing requirements pertain to the control of observable events. In our approach the related timing constraints can be formulated without constraining unnecessarily the sub-actions carried out between the statements relevant to these events. Consider for example the water level control program. In other languages strictly periodic release-times for processes that inspect sensors must be specified. This requires additional design choices. Consider in our example, e.g., the constraint on the time between a measurement of the water level and the related response of the pump. In other approaches this interval must be divided into a fixed release-period for the process making the measurement and a deadline of the pump-response within such a period. When the period is made smaller, the system load is increased; when it is made larger, the available time to the deadline is smaller and the number of platforms that can execute the process is reduced. Thus, the programmer is enticed to take platform properties into consideration. In our approach such decisions are moved to the system generation activity and the program is kept more general.

Most languages that support timing constraints use timing constraints that are attached to program blocks. In our opinion this choice is inspired by implementation considerations (the relative ease of scheduling blocks) and not by considerations of what the proper abstraction for the programmer should be. Many languages offer process priorities in addition to constructs for timing constraints. Priorities are heuristics concerned with the realization of constraints. They introduce platform and context dependencies in a program component; the choice of the priority for a particular process depends on the scheduling mechanisms offered by the platform and also depends on priorities of other processes with which no explicit interface exists.

4.3. Future work. Concerning the formal verification of programs, we are currently working with the verification system PVS to be able to check proofs mechanically. Earlier work on the compositional verification of real-time programs in PVS [4] has to be extended to be able to reason with timing annotations.

The main ideas of our approach have been devised in the context of the object-oriented language Deal. Future work will address the extension of our formal framework towards object-orientation. More research is also needed on the development of a design methodology, that is, a method to design programs with timing annotations in a systematic way.

In addition to establishing program correctness, it must be shown that a program is correctly implemented on a particular platform. Therefore, applicability of our approach requires suitable tool support for the compilation activity in which a program is mapped onto a particular platform. Some experience has been obtained by building prototypes for a timing analyzer and tool support for the generation of a static off-line schedule.

REFERENCES

[1] E.W. Dijkstra. Notes on structured programming. *A.P.I.C. Studies in Data Processing*, 8:1–81, 1972.
[2] D. Hammer, E. Luit, O. van Roosmalen, P. van der Stok, and J. Verhoosel. Dedos: A distributed real-time environment. *IEEE Parallel & Distributed Technology, Systems & Applications*, 2(4):32–47, 1994.
[3] C.A.R. Hoare. An axiomatic basis for computer programming. *Communications of the ACM*, 12(10):576–580,583, 1969.
[4] J. Hooman. Correctness of real time systems by construction. In *Formal Techniques in Real-Time and Fault-Tolerant Systems*, pages 19–40. LNCS 863, Springer-Verlag, 1994.
[5] J. Hooman. Extending Hoare logic to real-time. *Formal Aspects of Computing*, 6(6A):801–825, 1994.
[6] J. Hooman and O. van Roosmalen. A programming-language extension for distributed real-time systems. Computing Science Report 97/02, Department of Mathemat-

ics and Computing Science, Eindhoven University of Technology, The Netherlands, 1997.

[7] Y. Ishikawa. Object-oriented real-time language design. *ACM SIGPLAN Notices*, 25(10):289–298, 1990.

[8] H. Langmaack, W.-P. de Roever, and J. Vytopil, editors. *Formal Techniques in Real-Time and Fault-Tolerant Systems*. LNCS 863. Springer-Verlag, 1994.

[9] K. Lin, J. Liu, K. Kenny, and S. Natarajan. FLEX: A language for programming flexible real-time systems. In M. van Tilborg and G. Koob, editors, *Foundations of Real-Time Computing (Formal Specifications and Methods)*, pages 251–289. North Holland, 1991.

[10] K. Takashio and M. Tokoro. DROL: An object-oriented programming language for distributed real-time systems. *ACM SIGPLAN Notices*, 27(10):276–294, 1992.

[11] N. Wirth. Programming development by stepwise refinement. *Communications of the ACM*, 14(4):221–227, 1971.

AUTOMATIC EFFECTIVE VERIFICATION METHOD FOR DISTRIBUTED AND CONCURRENT SYSTEMS USING TIMED LANGUAGE INCLUSION

SATOSHI YAMANE *

Abstract. In distributed and concurrent systems, the notions of fairness and time are important as follows: (1)Fairness is a mathematical abstraction in distributed and concurrent systems. Fairness abstracts the details of fair schedulers and the speeds of independent processors. (2)The distributed and concurrent systems have to meet certain hard real-time constraints, and the correctness of them depends on the actual values of the delays.

In this paper, we propose the specification and verification method of fairness and time in distributed and concurrent systems as follows: (1)In order to specify fairness, an enable condition and a performed condition are attached to a finite set of states in our proposed specification method. (2)In order to effectively verify distributed and concurrent systems, we restrict timing constraints of timed automaton such that in cycles we must specify timing constraints about the clock variables after they are reset to zero.

1. Introduction. As many processes concurrently behave and timing conditions are strict in distributed and concurrent systems, it is important to formally specify and verify systems. In distributed and concurrent systems, the notions of fairness [1] and time [2] are important as follows:

1. The systems would be reasonable to assume that each sequential process is assigned to its own physical processor. Depending on the relative rates of speed at which the physical processors ran, we would expect that the corresponding choices would favor the faster procceses more often. On the other hand, under the assumption that each processor is always running at some positive, we would expect to see fair sequences where each process is executed infinitely often. In general, fairness is a mathematical abstraction in distributed and concurrent systems. Fairness abstracts the details of fair schedulers and the speeds of independent processors. By fairness, we can distinguish the issue of correctness from its performance.

2. The systems have to meet certain hard real-time constraints, and the correctness of them depends on the actual values of the delays. For the specification and verification of such systems we need to develop effective methods for quantitative temporal reasoning.

As time is an interesting notion, many researchers have studied timed automaton [3] and timed process algebra [4], timed Petri-Net [5]. On the other hand, fairness has well been discussed in untimed distributed and concurrent systems [6]. But by existing methods, it is not easy to specify fairness conditions, and many discussions have not done in timed distributed and concurrent systems. In this paper, we propose the formal methods of specification and automatic verification about time and fairness in timed distributed and concurrent systems as follows:

---

*Dept. of Computer Science, Shimane University, 1060 Nishikawatu, Matue City, Japan, TEX : +81.852.32.6481, FAX : +81.852.32.6489, (EMAIL : yamane@cis.shimane-u.ac.jp)

1. First, we propose the specification method about timing constraints and fairness by extending timed automaton with attributes.
2. Second, our verification method is based on timed language inclusion method, that is the automata-theoretic approach [7], by representing timing constraints as Difference Bounds Matrices(DBMs) [8].

Moreover, formal verification methods of both untimed and timed systems are almost classified into language inclusion [3] [7] and model-checking [9] [10], bisimulation [11] [12]. In this paper, we use language inclusion method by the following reasons :

1. The language inclusion method decouples the logical and algorithmic components of finite-state-system verification, and yields clear and general verification algorithms.
2. If we verify systems by language inclusion method, we can specify both system specification and verification property specification by timed automaton.

The remainder of the paper is organized as follows. In the section 2, we propose the specification method of distributed and concurrent systems. Section 3 presents the effective verification method. In section 4, we introduce the verification system and example based on our proposed method. In section 5, we conclude the paper by the future works.

2. Specification method.

2.1. Specification automaton. We usually extend existing timed automata [3] in order to realize fairness specification and effective verification as follows.

(1)Extension for fairness specification We specify acceptance conditions of timed automata by accepting states or acceptance families, which are infinitely often repeated [3]. On the other hand, we define fairness by "infinitely often enable → infinitely often performed" based on both enable states and performed states [13] [14]. As we can not express both enable states and performed states, we must specify fairness by defining complex acceptance conditions. We extend timed automata by "enable attributes" and "performed attributes" in order to easily specify fairness.

(2)Restriction for effective verification We must generate region graphs in order to verify timed automata. But the verification costs are very large as the size of region graph is exponential in the length of timing constraints of the given timed automaton [3]. In order to avoid the exponential blow-up, we restrict timed automata such that in cycles we must specify timing constraints about the clock variables after they are reset to zero. We believe this restriction is acceptable and practical.

(3)Extension for mutual communications We can not specify input events and output events by timed automata. In order to specify mutual communications, we introduce output events and synchronous behaviors, asynchronous behaviors into timed automata based on process algebra [11]. From this extensions, we can explicitly and simply specify mutual communications between timed automata. Since the inputs originate from an external, uncontrolled environment, the timed automata receive any combination of input values.

First, we define the notions of fairness and events, and propose specification automaton.

DEFINITION 1 (Fairness).
We define a finite set of accepting states SF(L, U) which satisfies fairness, as follows.

$$SF(L, U) = \{X | X \subseteq S, X \cap L = \phi \vee X \cap U \neq \phi\}$$

where

S : a finite set of states in specification automaton
$L \subseteq S$: a finite set of states with enable conditions
$U \subseteq S$: a finite set of states with performed conditions
If L and U are given, we can compute a finite set of states SF(L, U) satisfying fairness. ∎

For example, if we verify protocols, we express the set of states (at which we send messages) as a set of states with enable conditions and the set of states (at which we receive messages) as a set of states with performed conditions. If we can specify them, we can verify whether the protocol will eventually deliver every message using SF(L,U). SF(L,U) is equal to the acceptance families of ω-automata.

Next, we define events of specification automaton. Events consist of communication events and internal events such as input and output events.

DEFINITION 2 (Events). *We define events as follows.*
(1) a set A of input event names and use a,b,... to range over A
(2) a set $\overline{A}$ of output event names and use $\overline{a}, \overline{b}, \ldots$ to range over $\overline{A}$
(3) τ (tau) is an internal event
(4) a set $N(= A \cup \overline{A})$ of communication event names and use n,n',... to range over N
(5) a set $\Sigma(= N \cup \{\tau\})$ of communication and internal events and use $\alpha, \beta, \ldots$ to range over Σ ∎

DEFINITION 3 (Specification automaton). *Specification automaton P is a tuple $(\Sigma, S, s_0, C, E, L, U)$, where*
Σ : a finite set of events
S : a finite set of states
$s_0 \in S$: an initial state
C : a finite set of clocks
$E \subseteq S \times S \times \Sigma \times 2^C \times \Phi(C)$ gives the set of transitions.
$L \subseteq S$: a finite set of states with enable conditions
$U \subseteq S$: a finite set of states with performed conditions
We can compute an acceptance family SF(L, U) satisfying fairness by [Definition 1]. For a set $C(\ni x)$ of clocks, the set of $\Phi(C)$ of clock constraints δ is defined inductively

$$\delta ::= x \leq d | d \leq x | \neg \delta | \delta_1 \wedge \delta_2$$

where x is a clock in C and d is a constant in integer. We assign a real value to each clock. P changes state from s to s' using some transition of the form

$(s, s', \alpha, \lambda, \delta)$ *reading the input* α *if the current values of clocks satisfy* δ. *With this transition the clocks in* λ *are reset to 0, and thus counting time with respect to the time of occurrence of this transition. In the following, we denote this transition as*

$$s \xrightarrow{\alpha, \lambda, \delta} s'$$

In order to avoid the exponential blow-up, we restrict specification automata such that in cycles we must specify timing constraints about the clock variables after they are reset to zero.

We call $r \in (\Sigma \times 2^C \times \Phi(C))^*$ *"run* r*". For such a run, the set* $inf(r)$ *consists of the states* $s \in S$ *such that* s *is infinitely often visited. We define* $E \subseteq S \times S \times (\Sigma \times 2^C \times \Phi(C))^*$ *as follows. For a given* $\forall q \in S$,

(1)$(q, q, \varepsilon) \in E$

(2)$\forall w \in (\Sigma \times 2^C \times \Phi(C))^*$, $a = (\alpha, \lambda, \delta) \in \Sigma \times 2^C \times \Phi(C)$, *for a given* $\exists q', q'' \in S$,$(q, q', w) \in E \wedge (q', q'', \alpha, \lambda, \delta) \in E \rightarrow (q, q'', wa) \in E$

For a given specification automaton $P = (\Sigma, S, s_0, C, E, L, U)$ *and run* $r \in (\Sigma \times 2^C \times \Phi(C))^*$, r *is accepting when* $\{s | (s_0, s, r) \in E, s \in inf(r)\} \in SF(L, U)$. *The set* $\{r | \{s | (s_0, s, r) \in E, s \in inf(r)\} \in SF(L, U)\}$ *is defined as the language accepted by* P *and it is denoted by* $L(P)$.   ∎

The specification automaton is equal to deterministic timed Muller automaton [3], which is restricted such that in cycles we must specify timing constraints about the clock variables after they are reset to zero.

EXAMPLE 1 (Example of specification automaton). *The example of specification automaton is shown in Fig.1. When* $(s, s', \alpha, \lambda, \delta) \in E$, *we specify as follows.*

$$s \xrightarrow{\alpha, \lambda, \delta} s'$$

Event α *and a set of reset formulas* λ, *timing constraints formula* δ *are attached to edges in a directed graph. When* $s_0 \rightarrow s_1$ *occurs by event* a, *a clock variable* x *is reset to zero. For a given* $L = \{s_1\}$ *and* $U = \{s_2\}$, *we can calculate an acceptance family* $SF(L, U)$ *as follows.*

$\{X | X \subseteq S, X \cap L = \phi\} = \{\phi, \{s_0\}, \{s_2\}, \{s_0, s_2\}\}$

$\{X | X \subseteq S, X \cap U \neq \phi\} = \{\{s_2\}, \{s_0, s_2\}, \{s_1, s_2\}, \{s_0, s_1, s_2\}\}$

From (1), (2) and [Definition 1], $SF(L, U) = \{\phi, \{s_0\}, \{s_2\}, \{s_0, s_2\}, \{s_1, s_2\}, \{s_0, s_1, s_2\}\}$ *is calculated.*   ∎

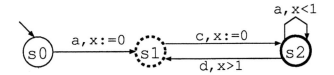

where

⦙⁑⦙ :a state with an enable condition

◯ :a state with a performed condition

Fig.1 Example specification automaton

It is convenient to automatically calculate an acceptance family from L and U. Without L and U, it is difficult to define fairness. From this convenience, it is important to specify a finite set of states with enable conditions and a finite set of states with performed conditions.

2.2. System specification. We generate system specification by choice and parallel composition like usual process algebra [11] as follows.

DEFINITION 4 (Generation rule). *For given specification automata* $P_1 = (\Sigma_1, S_1, s_{01}, C_1, E_1, L_1, U_1)$ *and* $P_2 = (\Sigma_2, S_2, s_{02}, C_2, E_2, L_2, U_2)$, *we define* s_1 *and* $s_2, s_1{\prime}, s_2{\prime}$ *as follows:*

(1)Case : $\alpha_1 \in \Sigma_1$

$$s_1 \overset{\alpha_1, \lambda_1, \delta_1}{\longrightarrow} s_1{\prime}$$

(2)Case : $\alpha_2 \in \Sigma_2$

$$s_2 \overset{\alpha_2, \lambda_2, \delta_2}{\longrightarrow} s_2{\prime}$$

where $s_1, s_1{\prime} \in S_1$, $s_2, s_2{\prime} \in S_2$

In this case, we define choice and parallel composition as follows:

(1)choice composition$(P = P_1 + P_2)$ *We generate specification automaton* $P=(\Sigma, S, s_0, C, E, L, U)$ *by choice composition of* P_1 *and* P_2, *where,* $\Sigma = \Sigma_1 \cup \Sigma_2$, $S = S_1 \cup S_2$, $s_0 = s_{01} \cup s_{02}$, $E = E_1 \cup E_2$, $L = L_1 \cup L_2$, $U = U_1 \cup U_2$, $C = C_1 \cup C_2$. *We define E according to whether an event is included in* Σ_1 *or* Σ_2 *in detail as follows:*

(a)Case : $n \in \Sigma_1$

$$s_1 \cup s_2 \overset{n, \lambda_1, \delta_1}{\longrightarrow} s_1{\prime}$$

,where the clocks in λ_1 *are reset to zero and* δ_1 *is a timing constraint over* C_1.

(b)Case : $n \in \Sigma_2$

$$s_1 \cup s_2 \overset{n, \lambda_2, \delta_2}{\longrightarrow} s_2{\prime}$$

,where the clocks in λ_2 *are reset to zero and* δ_2 *is a timing constraint over* C_2.

(2)parallel composition $(P = P1 \parallel P2)$ *We generate specification automaton*

P by parallel composition of P_1 and P_2, where, $\Sigma = \Sigma_1 \cup \Sigma_2$, $S = S_1 \times S_2$, $s_0 = s_{01} \times s_{02}$, $E = E_1 \times E_2$, $C = C_1 \cup C_2$, $L = L_1 \cup L_2$, $U = U_1 \cup U_2$.
We can specify asynchronous systems by following (a) and (b), synchronous systems by following (c).

(a)Case : $n \in \Sigma_1$

$$s_1 \times s_2 \xrightarrow{n,\lambda_1,\delta_1} s_1{}' \times s_2$$

(b)Case : $n \in \Sigma_2$

$$s_1 \times s_2 \xrightarrow{n,\lambda_2,\delta_2} s_1 \times s_2{}'$$

(c)Case : $n \in \Sigma_1$ and $n \in \Sigma_2$

$$s_1 \times s_2 \xrightarrow{\tau,\lambda_1\cup\lambda_2,\delta_1\wedge\delta_2} s_1{}' \times s_2{}'$$

The computation of the choice or parallel composition requires $O(card(S) + card(E))$ or $O(card(S) \times card(E))$ in time complexity. ∎

3. Formal verification method.

3.1. Verification method by language inclusion method. In this paper, we reduce verification problems to language inclusion problems. First, we formally define language inclusion method.

DEFINITION 5 (Language inclusion method). *The language inclusion method is defined as follows.*
$$L(M_1) \subseteq L(M_2)$$
This formality is equal to the followings.
$$L(M_1) \cap \overline{L(M_2)} = \phi$$
where

M_1 : *system specification*
$L(M_1)$: *language accepted by M_1*
M_2: *verification property specification*
$L(M_2)$: *language accepted by M_2* ∎

We can show $L(M_1) \subseteq L(M_2)$ if and only if the intersection of $L(M_1)$ with the complement of $L(M_2)$ is empty. Here we need to prove the closure property of the complementation of specification automaton.

THEOREM 3.1 (Closure property of complementation). *The specification automaton is closed under complementation.*
(Guideline of proof)
In general, if we complement deterministic automaton, we calculate the complementation of acceptance families [15]. By the way, our proposed specification automaton is a deterministic timed automaton. Moreover, we can calculate acceptance families of specification automaton from [Definition 1]. As we can calculate the complementation of acceptance families of specification automaton, it is closed under complementation. ∎

From the above theorem, we can reduce verification problem to language inclusion problem. Finally, we explain the problem of deciding whether specification automaton is contained in specification automaton is PSPACE-complete.

THEOREM 3.2 (Decidability of language inclusion). *The problem of deciding whether specification automaton is contained in specification automaton is PSPACE-complete.*

(Guideline of proof)
We can prove the theorem in the same way the problem of deciding whether timed Buchi automaton is contained in deterministic timed Muller automaton is PSPACE-complete [3].
(1)First, we deal with PSPACE-membership. It is possible to check for emptiness of the region graph of product automaton(the intersection of specification automaton with the complement of specification automaton) by guessing a path of the desired form using on polynomial space.
(2)Secondly, we deal with PSPACE-hardness. We construct product automaton such that its language is nonempty if and only if a linear bounded automaton halts on a given input. ∎

3.2. Verification algorithm based on language inclusion method.

3.2.1. Survey of verification algorithm. The verification algorithm based on language inclusion method reduces to checking emptiness of the intersection of system specification with the complement of verification property. We define the verification algorithm as follows.

DEFINITION 6 (Verification algorithm). *The verification algorithm is to find a cycle (satisfying acceptance conditions and reachable from an initial state) by Tarjan's depth-first search algorithm [16].*
(1)When there is no cycle *If there is no cycle, verification property specification is satisfiable in system specification.*
(2)When there is a cycle *If there is a cycle, we must check whether timing constraints are satisfiable from an initial state to the cycle.*
(2-a)When timing constraints are satisfiable *If timing constraints are satisfiable, verification property specification is not satisfiable in system specification.*
(2-b)When timing constraints are not satisfiable *If timing constraints are not satisfiable, verification property specification is satisfiable in system specification.* ∎

We explain finding an accepting cycle by finding a cycle, and the method of checking timing constraints as follows.

3.2.2. Finding an accepting cycle using finding a cycle. In finding a cycle, as we visit a set of states only once, we can not find such an accepting cycle $s_0 \rightarrow s_1 \rightarrow s_3 \rightarrow s_2 \rightarrow s_3 \rightarrow s_1$ as shown in Fig.2. We prove that we can find an accepting cycle using finding a cycle.

THEOREM 3.3 (Validity of finding an accepting cycle). *We can find an accepting cycle by finding a cycle.*
(Proof by example)

The accepting cycle such as $s_0 \to s_1 \to s_3 \to s_2 \to s_3 \to s1$ exists in Fig.2. But we can find only $s_0 \to s_1 \to s_3 \to s_1$ by finding a cycle. We can not find $s_0 \to s_1 \to s_3 \to s_2 \to s_3$ for visiting a set of states only once. We show finding an accepting cycle is realized by finding a cycle by classifying following two cases.
(1)When timing constraints are not satisfiable in $s_0 \to s_1 \to s_3 \to s_1$
In this case, as timing constraints are not satisfiable in $s_0 \to s_1 \to s_3 \to s_2 \to s_3 \to s_1$, there is no accepting cycle.
(2)When timing constraints are satisfiable in $s_0 \to s_1 \to s_3 \to s_1$
In this case, there is an accepting cycle in $s_0 \to s_1 \to s_3 \to s_1$. $s_0 \to s_1 \to s_3 \to s_2 \to s_3 \to s_1$ is classified into the following (a) and (b) by depending on the satisfiability of timing constraints of $s_3 \to s_2 \to s_3$.
(a)When timing constraints are satisfiable in $s_3 \to s_2 \to s_3$ *The accepting cycle in $s_0 \to s_1 \to s_3 \to s_2 \to s_3 \to s_1$ exists, and its result is equal to the result of $s_0 \to s_1 \to s_3 \to s_1$.*
(b)When timing constraints are not satisfiable in $s_3 \to s_2 \to s_3$ *As the accepting cycle in $s_0 \to s_1 \to s_3 \to s_2 \to s_3 \to s_1$ does not exist, we must find the accepting cycle of $s_0 \to s_1 \to s_3 \to s_1$.*
From the above (1) and (2), we can find an accepting cycle by finding a cycle. Also, we can explain finding an accepting cycle including more cycles in the same way.
We can find an accepting cycle by finding a cycle.   ■

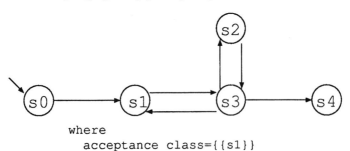

where
acceptance class={{s1}}

Fig.2 Example of search for a cycle

3.2.3. Checking whether timing constraints are satisfiable. We are now explain the method of checking whether timing constraints are satisfiable from an initial state to a cycle. We check it by using the DBMs(Difference Bounds Matrices) [8] by D. Dill.

DEFINITION 7 (Checking timing constraints). *Verification algorithm of checking timing constraints consists of the following steps.*
(1)Constructing the DBMs for each state.
(2)Constructing the canonical DBMs by Floyd-Warshall's algorithm.
(3)Analyzing the forward reachability of state transitions by the intersection of DBMs.   ■

DEFINITION 8 (DBMs(Difference Bounds Matrices)). *The DBMs consist of the matrix of timer valuations. Timer valuations are defined as follows.*

$\forall i, j \in C : t_i - t_j \leq d_{ij}$

where

t_i, t_j are clock variables

d_{ij} is a clock constant

The (i,j)-th element of the DBMs is equal to d_{ij}. A fictitious clock t_0 that is always exactly zero is introduced. We define $d_{ij} \subseteq \{\ldots, -2, -1, 0, 1, 2, \ldots\} \cup \{\ldots, -2^-, -1^-, 0^-, 1^-, 2^-, \ldots\} \cup \{-\infty\} \cup \{\infty\}$. The ordering $<$ over the integers is extended to d_{ij} by the following laws:

for any integer a, $-\infty < a^- < a < (a+1)^- < \infty$ ∎

DEFINITION 9 (Canonical DBMs). We can represent DBMs as a graph consisting of a finite set of nodes(clock variables) and a finite set of edges(clock constants). We show the example consisting of clock variables $(t_1, t_2, \ldots, t_n)$ and clock constants $(d_{1,2}, d_{2,3}, \ldots, d_{n,1})$ in Fig.3, where $t_i - t_j \leq d_{ij}$. From this graph, we can derive the canonical DBMs by Floyd-Warshall's algorithm. ∎

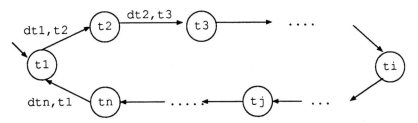

Fig.3 The graph representation of DBMs

Finally, we define the algorithm for checking whether timing constraints are satisfiable as follows.

DEFINITION 10 (Checking timing constraints). Generate the intersection of canonical DBMs, check reachability between two states. Here we check whether state $D \rightarrow$ state $D\prime$ is possible or not.

(1)Compute canonical DBMs D by Floyd-Warshall's algorithm

(2)Compute the time successors of DBMs D

(3)Canonize the DBMs $D\prime$

(4)Intersect the time successors of DBMs D with canonical DBMs $D\prime$

Intersection DBMs $= min\{d_{ij}, d_{ij}\prime\}$

where

$[d_{ij}]$: the time successors of DBMs D

$[d_{ij}\prime]$: canonical DBMs $D\prime$

(5)Canonize Intersection DBMs

(6)If there is a negative-cost cycle in intersection DBMs, it is impossible to reach $D\prime$ from D. If there is no negative-cost cycle in intersection DBMs, it is possible to reach $D\prime$ from D. ∎

Next, we explain the validity of algorithm of checking whether timing constraints are satisfiable or not as follows.

THEOREM 3.4 (Validity of checking timing constraints). If there is a negative-cost cycle in intersection DBMs of D and $D\prime$, it is impossible to reach

$D\prime$ from D.

(proof)

We call a sequence of clock variables $t_1, t_2, \ldots, t_n$. The cost of the path in intersection DBMs is $d_{1,2} + d_{2,3} + \ldots + d_{n,1}$. We can define $d_{1,2}, d_{2,3}, \ldots, d_{n,1}$ as follows: $t_1 - t_2 \leq d_{1,2},\ t_2 - t_3 \leq d_{2,3},\ \ldots,\ t_n - t_1 \leq d_{n,1}$. *The cost is $(t_1 - t_2) + (t_2 - t_3) + \ldots (t_n - t_1) = t_1 - t_1$. If there is a negative-cost cycle($t_1 - t_1 < 0$), it is impossible to reach $D\prime$ from D.*   ∎

It is difficult to check whether timing constraints are satisfiable in usual timed automaton because accepting conditions are infinitely often run. We show the comparison of the verification of proposed specification automaton with the verification of usual timed automaton as follows.

EXAMPLE 2 (Example of timing verification). *We compare the verification of our proposed timed automaton with the verification of usual timed automaton as follows.*

(1)Verification of usual timed automaton *We show the verification of usual timed automaton in Fig.4(1). In this example, an initial state is s_0 and acceptance family is $\{\{s_2, s_4\}\}$. In this case, we can find a cycle $s_0 \rightarrow s_1 \rightarrow s_2 \rightarrow s_3 \rightarrow s_4 \rightarrow s_1$ satisfying accepting conditions. When first we visit it, its timing constraints are satisfiable. But when twice we visit it, its timing constraints are not satisfiable for $x \leq 2$. In the case of usual timed automaton, in general we must visit a cycle many times.*

(2)Verification of our proposed timed automaton *We show the verification of our proposed timed automaton in Fig.4(2). In the case of our proposed specification automaton, we can check timing constraints only by one visit for reset formula in a cycle in Fig.4(2). From this result, we can reduce verification costs in time complexity, and timing constraints are independent on clock constants.*   ∎

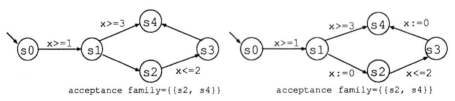

acceptance family={{s2, s4}}   acceptance family={{s2, s4}}

(1)Example of usual timed automaton   (2)Example of specification automaton

Fig.4 The satisfiability of timing constraints

3.3. Verification costs of specification automata. Finally we show the verification costs of our proposed method and timed automata as follows.

THEOREM 3.5 (Verification costs). $0(|S| + |E|) + 0(|AS| \bullet n3)$, *where*

S : *the number of states of product automaton*

E : *the number of transitions of product automaton*

AS : *the number of states reachable from an initial state to a cycle($AS \leq S$)*

n : *the number of clock variables*

(Guideline of proof)
(1) $0(|S| + |E|)$: *It is clear from the cost of depth-first search [16].*
(2) $0(|AS| \bullet n3)$: *It is clear from the cost of Floyd-Warshall's algorithm [16].* ∎

DEFINITION 11 (Verification cost of timed automaton). *[3]*
$0[(|S| + |E|) \times 2^{|\delta(A)|}]$, *where*
    S : *the number of states of product automaton A*
    E : *the number of transitions of product automaton A*
    $|\delta(A)|$: *the length of clock constants of product automaton A*   ∎

Our proposed verification method is more effective than existing verification method of timed automaton, because (1)we visit a cycle only once, and (2)we need not to make region graphs.

3.4. Verification example. EXAMPLE 3 (Example of verification). *System specification and verification property specification are given in Fig.5(1) and (2).*
(1)System specification $L = \{s_0\}$ *and* $U = \{s_1\}$, $S = \{s_0, s_1\}$ *are given in Fig.5(1). The acceptance family is calculated as follows.*
    (a) $\{X | X \subseteq S, X \cap L = \phi\} = \{\phi, \{s_1\}\}$
    (b) $\{X | X \subseteq S, X \cap L \neq \phi\} = \{\{s_1\}, \{s_0, s_1\}\}$
From (a) and (b), $SF(L, U) = \{\phi, \{s_1\}, \{s_0, s_1\}\}$ *is calculated.*
(2)Verification property specification $L = \{p_0\}$ *and* $U = \{p_1\}$ *are given in Fig.5(2). The acceptance family is calculated as follows.* $SF(L, U) = \{\phi, \{p_1\}, \{p_0, p_1\}$
(3)Product automaton *We calculate the intersection of system specification with the complement of verification property specification as shown in Fig.5(3). The acceptance family of product automaton is* $\{\{s_1 \times p_0\}, \{s_0 \times p_0, s_1 \times p_0\}\}$.
(4)Verification
(a)Search for accepting cycles *We can find the following accepting cycles by depth-first search algorithm.*
    (i) $(s_0, p_0) \rightarrow (s_1, p_0) \rightarrow (s_0, p_0) \rightarrow \dots$
    (ii) $(s_0, p_0) \rightarrow (s_1, p_0) \rightarrow (s_1, p_0) \rightarrow \dots$
(b)Checking whether timing constraints are satisfiable *We check whether timing constraints are satisfiable from an initial state to cycles. We show the example of checking the transition from DBMs D1 at* (s_1, p_0) *to DBMs D2 at* (s_0, p_0) *in Fig.5(4). DBMs* D_1 *is defined from* $x \geq 0, y \geq 6, y \geq x$ *as follows.*
    (i)From $x \geq 0$, $t_0 - x \leq 0(d_{01} = 0)$
    (ii)From $y \geq 6$, $t_0 - y \leq -6(d_{02} = -6)$
    (iii)From $y \geq x$, $x - y \leq 0(d_{12} = 0)$
Next, we calculate the canonical form of DBMs D1 and the time-successor of the canonical form. Next, we calculate the canonical form of DBMs D2 from $x \leq 5, y \geq x$. *Finally, we calculate the intersection of the time-successor of DBMs D1 with the canonical DBMs D2, and check whether there is a negative-cost cycle in intersection DBMs. As there is no negative-cost cycle in intersection DBMs, timing constraints of the transition from* $(s_1, p_0) \rightarrow (s_0, p_0)$ *are satisfiable.*
From above results, verification property specification is not satisfiable in system

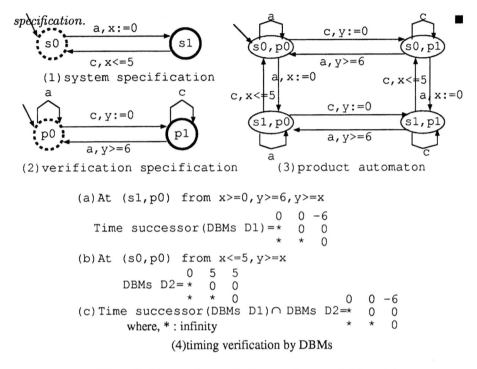

(1) system specification

(2) verification specification

(3) product automaton

(a) At (s1,p0) from x>=0,y>=6,y>=x

$$\text{Time successor(DBMs D1)} = \begin{matrix} 0 & 0 & -6 \\ * & 0 & 0 \\ * & * & 0 \end{matrix}$$

(b) At (s0,p0) from x<=5,y>=x

$$\text{DBMs D2} = \begin{matrix} 0 & 5 & 5 \\ * & 0 & 0 \\ * & * & 0 \end{matrix}$$

(c) Time successor(DBMs D1) ∩ DBMs D2 = $\begin{matrix} 0 & 0 & -6 \\ * & 0 & 0 \\ * & * & 0 \end{matrix}$

where, * : infinity

(4) timing verification by DBMs

Fig.5 Example of formal verification

4. Verification system and verification example.

4.1. Verification system. We have developed the verification system on SUN4/IP(main memory 8MB). The configuration is shown in Fig.6. It consists of compiler and timing verifier, which are implemented in C language(3kstep). We input specifications by programming format, and convert them into intermediate format(adjacency-matrix representation) using compiler. We can check whether system specification is included in property specification or not using language inclusion verifier.

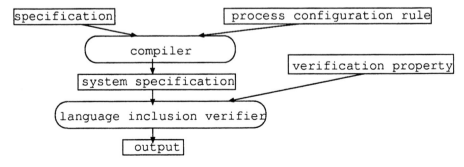

Fig.6 Configuration of verification system

4.2. Verification example. Alternating Bit Protocol [17] is a simple communication protocol that provides error free communication over a medium which may lose messages. Our specification of Alternating Bit Protocol consists of four entities such as a sender and two media(medium, Ack-medium), a receiver. The structure of the communication system, as well as the communication primitives are shown in Fig.7.

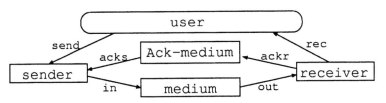

Fig.7 Configuration of Alternating Bits Protocol

We show example of system specification by specification automaton in Fig.8. We can calculate acceptance families by L and U. System behaves as *sender* ‖ *medium* ‖ *Ack − medium* ‖ *receiver* ‖ *user*, where ‖ means parallel composition operator.

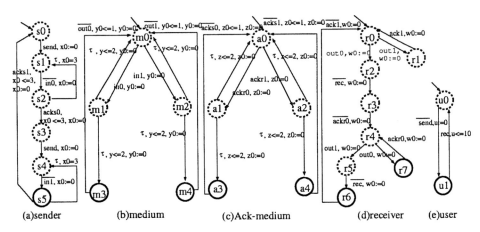

Fig.8 Timed Alternating Bit Protocol

We show example of verification property specification in Fig.9. These properties mean response properties.

(1) response property (false)   (2) response property (true)

Fig.9 Verification property specification

If we input system specification and verification property specification, we can test whether system specification is included in verification property specification or not((1) is false and (2) is true). The number of states of system specification is 2400, and verification costs are about 100 seconds and 4.6MB on SUN4/IP without the costs of choice and parallel composition. These costs reduce to (1/100) compared with region graph method, and they reduce to (9/10) compared with usual timed automata.

```
System specification ;
System configuration ;
  system=sender||medium||Ack-medium||receiver||user ;
Process specification(sender) ;
  State definition part s0,s1,s2,s3,s4,s5 ;
  Event definition part send,in0,in1,acks0,acks1,τ ;
  Initial state definition part s0 ;
  Enable condition part s0,s1,s2,s3,s4 ;
  Performed condition definition part s5 ;
  Clock variable definition part x0 ;
  Transition definition part
    s0->send,x0:=0->s1 ;
    s1->in0,x0:=0->s2 ;
                :
end ;
```

Fig.10 Example of specification by specification automata

5. Conclusion and future works. In this paper, we propose the method, in which we can easily specify fairness and timing constraints by the specification method and can effectively verify distributed and concurrent systems.

1. In order to specify fairness, an enable condition and a performed condition are attached to a finite set of states in our proposed specification method.
2. In order to effectively verify distributed systems, we restrict timing constraints of timed automaton such that in cycles we must specify timing constraints about the clock variables after they are reset to zero.

We have developed the verifier based on our proposed method and shown it effective by timed Alternating Bit Protocol.

In the future, we will develop effective verifier, because the number of regions in a region graph of timed automaton is exponential in the total number of clocks, and is proportional to the magnitudes of constants in the clock constraints. To avoid this blow-up a variety of heuristics have been proposed as follows.

1. Difference Bounds Matrices(DBMs) verification
   In this paper, we have proposed effective verification method based on DBMs. The DBMs verification directly verify timed automata using DBMs without constructing region graphs. KRONOS [18] is the first symbolic model checker based on DBMs verification. But this method causes the state explosion problem by explicit state enumeration.
2. Iterative verification
   Alur et al. [19] and Balarin et al. [20] describe iteration algorithms. These approaches assumes that not many timing constraints in the system are necessary for its correct operation. They initially attempt to verify the system based on only logical constraints. Additional untimed processes are added as need to reintroduce timing information.
3. Compositional verification
   Larsen et al. [21] describe compositional verification and develop UP-PAAL. This approach generate a compositional quotient construction, which allows components of a system to be gradually moved from the system description into the temporal logic formula specification. The intermediate specifications are kept small using minimization heuristics.
4. Symbolic verification
   Symbolic verification is useful in timed systems [22] as well as in timed systems. Balarin [23] and Pnueli et al. [24] [25] have used BDDs to represent matrices. This method can take advantage of the symbolic representation of the untimed state-space. But the analysis of timed automata with many clocks is not yet feasible.
5. Approximations
   Dill et al. [26] describe approximations of reachability analysis of timed automata combining BDDs and DBMs. We have developed the first symbolic model checker based on this method [27].

Now we do not know the best verification method of all the above methods such as compositional verification and symbolic verification, approximations. We believe approximations of combining BDDs and DBMs, and will implement our proposed method based on approximations.

REFERENCES

[1] Dijkstra E.W. Cooperating sequential processes. *Programming Languages*, pp.41-112, 1968.

[2] Aggarwal S., Kurshan R. P. Modeling elapsed time in protocol specification. *PSTV III*, pp.51-62, 1983.

[3] Alur R., Dill D. A Theory of timed automata. *Theoretical Computer Science*, No. 126,pp.183-235, 1994.

[4] Nicollin X., Sifakis J. An overview and synthesis on timed process algebra. *Real-Time : Theory in Practice, LNCS 600*, pp.526-548, 1992.

[5] Berthomieu B., Diaz M. Modeling and verification of time dependent systems using timed Petri Nets. *IEEE TOSE*, Vol.17,No.3,pp.259-273, 1991.

[6] Francez N. Fairness. *Texts and monographs in computer science*, Springer-verlag, P.295, 1986.

[7] Vardi M. Y., Wolper P. An automata-theoretic approach to automatic program verification. *LICS 86*, pp.332-344, 1986.

[8] Dill D. Timing assumptions and verification of finite-state concurrent systems. *CAV 89, LNCS 407*, pp.197-212, 1989.

[9] Clarke E.M., Emerson E.A., Sistla A.P. Automatic verification of finite state concurrent system using temporal logic. *ACM TOPLAS*, Vol.8, No.2, pp. 244-263, 1986.

[10] R. Alur, C. Courcoubetis, D.L. Dill. Model checking for real-time systems. *LICS 90*, pp. 414-425, 1992.

[11] Milner R. Communication and Concurrency. *Prentice Hall*, P.260, 1989.

[12] Cerans K. Decidability of bisimulation equivalences for parallel timer processes. *CAV 92, LNCS 663*, pp.302-315, 1992.

[13] Emerson E.A., Lei C. Modalities for model checking:branching time logic strikes back. *Science of computer programming*, No.8, pp.275-306, 1987.

[14] Kurshan R.P. Computer-aided verification of coordinating processes: The automata-Theoretic Approach. *Princeton University Press*, P.270, 1994.

[15] Hopcroft J.E., Ullman J.D. Introduction to Automata Theory, Language, and Computation. *Addison-Wesley Publishing Company*, P.418, 1979.

[16] Cormen T.H., Leiserson C.E., Rivest R.L. Introduction to algorithms. P.1028,MIT PRESS, 1989.

[17] Bartlett K., Scantlebury R., Wilkinison P. A note on reliable full-duplex transmissions over half duplex lines. *CACM*, Vol.12, No.5, pp.260-261, 1969.

[18] Henzinger T.A., Nicollin X., Sifakis J., Yovine S. Symbolic model checking for real-time systems. *LICS 92*, pp. 394-406, 1992.

[19] Alur R., Itai A., Kurshan R.P., Yannakakis M. The timing verification by successive approximation. *CAV 92, LNCS 663*, pp. 137-150, 1992.

[20] Balarin F., Sangiovanni-Vincentelli A.L. A verification strategy for timing constrained systems. *CAV 92, LNCS 663*, pp. 151-163, 1992.

[21] Kim G. Larsen, Paul Pettersson, and Wang Yi. Compositional and Symbolic Model-Checking of Real-Time Systems. *RTSS 96*, pp. 76-87, 1996.

[22] McMillan K.L. Symbolic Model Checking. Kluwer, P.194, 1993.

[23] Balarin F. Approximate reachability analysis of timed automata. *RTSS 96*, pp. 52-61, 1996.

[24] Asarin E, Bozga M., Kerbrat A., Maler O., Pnueli A., Rasse A. Data structures for the verification of timed automata. *Hybrid and Real-time Systems, LNCS 1201*, pp. 575-586, 1997.

[25] Bozga M., Maler O., Pnueli A., Yovine S. Some progress in the symbolic verification of

timed automata. *CAV 97, LNCS 1254*, pp. 179-190, 1997.

[26] Dill D., Wong-Toi H. Verification of real-time systems by successive over and under approximation. *CAV 95, LNCS 939*, pp.409-422, 1995.

[27] Yamane S. Symbolic Model Checking Method based on Approximations and BDDs for Real-Time Systems. *TACS 97, LNCS 1281*, pp. 562-582, 1997.

INTEGRATING TIMED CONDITION/EVENT SYSTEMS AND TIMED AUTOMATA FOR THE VERIFICATION OF HYBRID SYSTEMS*

R. HUUCK[†], Y. LAKHNECH[†], B. LUKOSCHUS[†], AND L. URBINA[†]

S. ENGELL[‡], S. KOWALEWSKI[‡], AND J. PREUßIG[‡]

Abstract. In this paper we integrate two different approaches for the specification and verification of timed systems being used in control theory and computer science. These are the timed condition/event systems and the timed automata formalisms. Our main result states that timed condition/event systems can be efficiently transformed into timed automata which then can be analyzed automatically.

1. Introduction. Many computer-controlled systems consist of discrete components interacting with continuously evolving sub-systems. Such systems can be found in avionics, robotics, chemical plants, and other fields. Systems involving discrete as well as continuous or sectionally continuous components are called *hybrid systems*. A very important sub-class of hybrid systems consists of *real-time systems* which are systems depending on hard deadlines and on real-time constraints. A typical real-time constraint is that the response time of the controller to some events generated by the controlled components does not exceed a given amount of time; another typical constraint is that the controlled components do not generate such events too fast. Obviously, the analysis of real-time systems is in general not as involved as the verification of hybrid systems, since these may involve complex differential equations which describe the behavior of the continuous components. However, in many cases hybrid systems can be faithfully considered as real-time systems. Indeed, there are techniques which allow to abstract a hybrid system to obtain a real-time system [12] such that if the real-time system satisfies the wanted properties, so does the hybrid system, too.

Hybrid and real-time systems can often be found in applications where faults can lead to the loss of human lives, pollution of the environment, or important financial loss. Therefore, methods based on mathematical logic should be applied to verify the absence of faults in hybrid systems. An essential ingredient in such a method is a formal model $\mathcal{M}$ which allows to model hybrid systems.

In general, one can distinguish between operational models for hybrid and real-time systems, on the one hand, and axiomatic models on the other hand.

---

*This work has been supported by the German Research Council (DFG) within the special program KONDISK (Analysis and Synthesis of Technical Systems with Continuous-discrete Dynamics) under the grants Ro 1122/2 and En 152/19. URL: http://www.informatik.uni-kiel.de/~kondisk/, Email: kondisk@informatik.uni-kiel.de

†Institut für Informatik und Praktische Mathematik der Christian-Albrechts-Universität zu Kiel, Preußerstr. 1–9, D-24105 Kiel, Germany.

‡Lehrstuhl für Anlagensteuerungstechnik, Fachbereich Chemietechnik, Universität Dortmund, Emil-Figge-Straße 70, D-44221 Dortmund, Germany.

While axiomatic models are usually more suitable for a proof rule-based reasoning, operational models are more suitable for algorithmic reasoning.

In this paper we consider two important mathematical operational models for real-time systems, namely *timed automata* [2] and *timed condition/event systems* [8]. Timed automata are by now a standard model for real-time systems and have been intensively studied from different points of view including the automata theoretic view [2], the verification view [1, 11, 5, 19], and the logic view [25, 5, 19]. This led to a variety of tools, for example KRONOS [22], UPPAAL [4], and HyTech [10], that can analyze real-time systems modeled by timed automata.

It has been demonstrated that timed condition/event systems are suitable for modeling hybrid systems such as chemical plants [15, 16, 18]. Timed condition event/systems are particularly suitable for a modular specification of the considered system. There are, however, hardly any tools which support the analysis of timed condition/event systems.

Our main objective in the present paper is to show that timed condition/event systems can be transformed into timed automata which then can be analyzed automatically using for instance one of the tools mentioned above. Indeed, we show that, given a timed condition/event system $\mathcal{S}$, we can construct a timed automaton $\Psi(\mathcal{S})$ which admits the same behaviors as $\mathcal{S}$. Moreover, any reachability problem for $\mathcal{S}$, that is, the question whether a particular state of $\mathcal{S}$ is reachable, can be transformed into a reachability problem for $\Psi(\mathcal{S})$.

Notations. Given a set X, we denote by $2_\emptyset^X$ the set of non-empty subsets of X. Given a Cartesian product $B_1 \times B_2$ of sets and an element $b = (c, d) \in B_1 \times B_2$, we denote by b_1, respectively, b_2, the projection of b on the first, respectively, second component, i.e. $b_1 = c$ and $b_2 = d$. For a finite-variable function $f : \mathbb{R}_{\geq 0} \to D$, and $t > 0$, we denote by $f(t^-)$ the limit $\lim_{\epsilon \to 0} f(t - \epsilon)$, if it exists. As convention, we define $f(t^-)$ for $t = 0$ as $f(0)$.

2. Condition/Event Systems, their Composition and Real-Time Version.

Condition/event systems (CESs for short) are introduced in [24] as a modeling paradigm for discrete event systems (DESs) and have gained increasing interest from the DESs and hybrid systems community (cf. [9], [13], [7]). The main motivation for developing CESs is to provide a framework for modeling DESs based on block diagrams and signal flows as is standard practice in system theory. A CES allows to model a system as a relation between its input and output signals. The particularity of CESs is that they distinguish between two sorts of signals which correspond to two kinds of interactions between interconnected systems, namely *enabling/disabling* of transitions and, on the other hand, *forcing* of transitions. The first kind of interaction is modeled by *conditions* which can be seen as state variables. Enabling of transitions depends on the values of such conditions. Forcing is implemented by *events*. An enabled transition which is labeled by an event e has to be taken as soon as the event e occurs. When more than one transition is enabled, one of them is nondeterministically chosen.

In this section we recall the definition of condition/event systems and their discrete version. Then, we introduce operators which allow to compose condition/event systems. The operators we consider are variants of the composition operators given in [24]. Finally, we define a real-time version of condition/event systems.

2.1. Condition/Event Systems.
Condition/event systems describe the behavior of a system in terms of an input-output relation on *condition*, respectively, *event* signals.

DEFINITION 2.1.

- *Given a nonempty finite set U, called* condition alphabet, *of* condition symbols, *a function $s_u : \mathbb{R}_{\geq 0} \to U$ is called* condition signal *over U, if it is right-continuous and finite-variable. A function f is called* finite-variable, *if f has a finite number of discontinuity points in every bounded subinterval of dom(f). The set of all condition signals over U is denoted by $C(U)$.*

- *Given a finite set V, called* event alphabet, *of* event symbols *containing a special null symbol 0_V, a function $s_v : \mathbb{R}_{\geq 0} \to V$ is called* event signal *over V, if $s_v(0) = 0_V$ and if there are finitely many points $t \in I$ such that $s_v(t) \neq 0_V$, for every bounded interval I in $\mathbb{R}_{\geq 0}$. The set of all event signals over V is denoted by $E(V)$.*

□

Thus, condition signals are piecewise constant functions which associate with each time point a value in U; while event signals take on values indicating events only at single discrete points on the continuous time axis. Henceforth, we write 0 instead of 0_V, if the alphabet V is understood from the context. Moreover, if V is the product of alphabets $V_1, \cdots, V_n$ then we identify 0_V with $(0_{V_1}, \cdots, 0_{V_n})$. We call an event e with $e \neq 0$ *proper* event.

DEFINITION 2.2. *A condition/event system S is given by a tuple (U, V, Y, Z, S), where*

- *U is the* input condition alphabet,
- *Y is the* output condition alphabet,
- *V is the* input event alphabet,
- *Z is the* output event alphabet, *and*
- *$S : C(U) \times E(V) \to 2_{\emptyset}^{C(Y) \times E(Z)}$ is the* system behavior function.

□

We identify the function S with a *behavior relation* $S_R \subseteq \mathcal{B}(U, V, Y, Z) = C(U) \times E(V) \times C(Y) \times E(Z)$. An element of $\mathcal{B}(U, V, Y, Z)$ is called *behavior*. Henceforth, given a behavior $s \in \mathcal{B}(U, V, Y, Z)$, we denote by s_u, s_v, s_y, and s_z the signals such that $s = (s_u, s_v, s_y, s_z)$.

2.2. Discrete Condition/Event Systems.
Condition/event systems with discrete state realizations are condition/event systems that can be described operationally.

DEFINITION 2.3. *A discrete condition/event system (DCES) is given by a tuple $D = (U, V, Q, Y, Z, f, g, h, q_0)$, where*

- U, V, Y and Z are as above, Q is a finite set of states,
- $f : Q{\times}U{\times}V \to 2_\emptyset^Q$ is the state transition function,
- $g : Q{\times}U \to Y$ is the condition output function,
- $h : Q{\times}Q{\times}V \to Z$ is the event output function, and
- $q_0 \in Q$ is the initial state.

□

An event input signal can be used to force state transitions in a CES in the sense that a state transition has to take place simultaneously with a synchronizing event indicated by the event input signal. Whereas, a condition input signal can be used to enable/disable transitions.

DEFINITION 2.4. *A DCES is called* well-behaved, *if it satisfies the following conditions:*

- *Stuttering:* $\forall q \in Q.\ \forall u \in U.\ q \in f(q, u, 0)$, *i.e., the system is allowed to stay in the same state as long as the value of the event input signal does not show a proper event.*
- *Output triggering:* $\forall q \in Q.\ h(q, q, 0) = 0$, *i.e., the system can only output a proper event while remaining in the same state when it receives a proper input event; this is a causality condition.*

□

Henceforth, we only consider well-behaved DCESs and call them simply DCESs. To assign a semantics to DCESs, we introduce the notion of a *run*.

DEFINITION 2.5. *Given a DCES* $D = (U, V, Q, Y, Z, f, g, h, q_0)$, *we call a run of* D *over* $s \in \mathcal{B}(U, V, Y, Z)$ *any right-continuous and finite-variable function* $r : \mathbb{R}_{\geq 0} \to Q$ *which satisfies the following conditions for each* $t \in \mathbb{R}_{\geq 0}$:

- $r(t) \in f(r(t^-), s_u(t^-), s_v(t))$,
- $s_y(t) = g(r(t), s_u(t))$,
- $s_z(t) = h(r(t^-), r(t), s_v(t))$, *and*
- $r(0) = q_0$.

□

We define the behavior relation S_D of a discrete condition/event system D as the set consisting of all behaviors $s \in \mathcal{B}(U, V, Y, Z)$ such that there exists a run of D over s. We also write S_D to denote the condition/event system (U, V, Y, Z, S_D).

2.3. Composition of Condition/Event Systems. When a complex system model is designed, it is often divided into smaller parts, called *modules*, which more or less represent "real world" parts of the system. Interaction of these parts is achieved by connections between them. When using condition/event systems as the underlying model, these connections are condition and event signals.

When dealing with a network of interconnected condition/event systems, one is interested in the semantics of this whole network. There are mainly two ways of defining this. One way is to define a *global* semantics which takes all single systems and a description of their interconnections and computes the network semantics following a given rule. In this case, the network is composed in a single step, and hence, reflects a flat structure. The other way is to define composition operators on condition/event systems which take some of the systems and descriptions of how they are connected and replace these systems by a single one having their "overall" behavior. The result is a network of systems equivalent to the original one, but with a reduced number of single systems. Repeated application of these operators finally results in one condition/event system having the overall semantics of the original network. Thus, a network described using such operators is composed in several steps to a single system and reflects a certain composition structure.

In [24] two composition operators are defined: the *cascade interconnection* and the *feedback connection*. In the following, we introduce and discuss slight variants of these operators.

2.3.1. Cascade Interconnection. Given two condition/event systems, the cascade interconnection describes the connection of the first system's outputs with the second system's inputs. Obviously, the alphabets of the connected signals have to be equal. The result of this connection is a system having the first system's inputs and the second system's outputs, and as semantics we have the composition of the single systems' behaviors. In contrast to Sreenivas and Krogh's definition, according to our definition, the "intermediate" signals between the two systems remain visible in the resulting system (see Fig. 2.1).

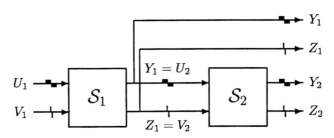

FIG. 2.1. *Condition/Event System Cascade Interconnection of S_1 and S_2*

First, we define the cascade interconnection for condition/event systems. Given condition/event systems $S_i = (U_i, V_i, Y_i, Z_i, S_i)$, for $i = 1, 2$, we say that S_1 and S_2 are *compatible*, if $Y_1 = U_2$ and $Z_1 = V_2$.

DEFINITION 2.6. *Let $S_i = (U_i, V_i, Y_i, Z_i, S_i)$, $i \in \{1, 2\}$, be two compatible C/E systems. A condition/event system $S = (U, V, Y, Z, S)$ is called cascade interconnection of S_1 and S_2, if and only if the following conditions hold:*

- *$U = U_1$, $V = V_1$, $Y = Y_1 \times Y_2$, $Z = Z_1 \times Z_2$,*
- *for any $s \in B(U, V, Y, Z)$, we have $s \in S$ iff $(s_{y_1}, s_{z_1}) \in S_1(s_u, s_v)$ and $(s_{y_2}, s_{z_2}) \in S_2(s_{y_1}, s_{z1})$.*

□

Having defined the cascade interconnection for condition/event systems, we are interested in the following question: If we have two compatible *discrete* condition/event systems, can we always construct a *discrete* condition/event system that is cascade interconnection of them? The answer is positively answered in [24]. For the sake of self-containedness we restate the theorem and recall its proof.

THEOREM 2.7. *[24] Given two compatible DCESs $D_i = (U_i, V_i, Q_i, Y_i, Z_i, f_i, g_i, h_i, q_{0,i})$, for $i \in \{1, 2\}$, a DCES D can be effectively constructed such that S_D is a cascade interconnection of S_{D_1} and S_{D_2}.* □

Proof. Let D_1 and D_2 be given as above. We construct a DCES D such that S_D is cascade interconnection of S_{D_1} and S_{D_2}. Let $D = (U, V, Q, Y, Z, f, g, h, q_0)$ be the DCES with $U = U_1$, $V = V_1$, $Y = Y_1 \times Y_2$, $Z = Z_1 \times Z_2$, $Q = Q_1 \times Q_2$, $q_0 = (q_{0,1}, q_{0,2})$, and for all $q = (q_1, q_2) \in Q$, $q' = (q_1', q_2') \in Q$, $u \in U$, $v \in V$,

- $q' \in f(q, u, v)$ iff $q_1' \in f_1(q_1, u, v)$ and $q_2' \in f_2(q_2, g_1(q_1, u), h_1(q_1, q_1', v))$,

- $g(q, u) = \big(g_1(q_1, u), g_2(q_2, g_1(q_1, u))\big)$,

- $h(q, q', v) = \big(h_1(q_1, q_1', v), h_2(q_2, q_2', h_1(q_1, q_1', v))\big)$.

It is easy to check that S_D is cascade interconnection of S_{D_1} and S_{D_2}. □

Finally, we define the cascade interconnection operator for discrete condition/event systems.

DEFINITION 2.8. *Let D_1 and D_2 be two compatible DCESs as in Theorem 2.7. The DCES D gained from the construction above is called* discrete cascade interconnection *of D_1 and D_2, denoted by $D_1 \to D_2$.* □

2.3.2. Feedback Connection. In [24], for a given condition/event system where the input and output alphabets are equal, for both condition and event signals, the feedback connection describes the connection of the system's outputs with the system's inputs ("feedback loop"). The signals in this loop remain visible. In contrast to Sreenivas and Krogh's definition, we have additional inputs and outputs in the system (see Fig. 2.2). As we discuss later this makes the condition under which the feedback connection of a condition/event system is well-defined slightly more complicated.

DEFINITION 2.9. *Let $S = (U_1 \times U_2, V_1 \times V_2, Y_1 \times Y_2, Z_1 \times Z_2, S)$ be a condition/event system with $Y_2 = U_2$ and $Z_2 = V_2$. A condition/event system $S' = (U, V, Y, Z, S')$ is called* feedback connection *of S, if and only if the following conditions hold:*

- $U = U_1$, $V = V_1$, $Y = Y_1 \times Y_2$, $Z = Z_1 \times Z_2$,
- *for any $s \in \mathcal{B}(U, V, Y, Z)$, we have $s \in S'$ iff $\big((s_u, s_{y_2}), (s_v, s_{z2}), s_y, s_z\big) \in S$.*

□

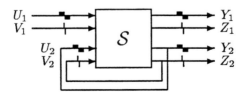

FIG. 2.2. *Condition/event System Feedback Connection of S*

In contrast to cascade interconnection not every *discrete* condition/event system (with adequate alphabets) can be transformed to a *discrete* condition/event system that is a feedback connection of the original one. This is the case because there is not always a solution to the equations $g(x, u)_2 = u_2$ and $h(x, x', v)_2 = v_2$. Therefore, we have to require that there exists a *unique* solution to each of the equations. However, it would be sufficient to require that there is *at least one* solution to each of the equations. This weaker requirement is used in Sreenivas and Krogh's definition, leading to a larger state space $\mathcal{Q}$ in the new system. For our construction, we use the *unique solution property*.

THEOREM 2.10. *Given a DCES* $D = (U_1 \times U_2, V_1 \times V_2, \mathcal{Q}, Y_1 \times Y_2, Z_1 \times Z_2, f, g, h, q_0)$, *with* $Y_2 = U_2$ *and* $Z_2 = V_2$, *a DCES* D' *can be effectively constructed such that* $\mathcal{S}_{D'}$ *is feedback connection of* $\mathcal{S}_D$, *if the following* unique *solution property* holds for D:

- *For all* $q \in \mathcal{Q}$ *and* $u_1 \in U_1$ *there exists a unique* $y_2 \in Y_2$ *such that* $g\big(q, (u_1, y_2)\big)_2 = y_2$.
- *For all* $q, q' \in \mathcal{Q}$ *and* $v_1 \in V_1$ *there exists a unique* $z_2 \in Z_2$ *such that* $h\big(q, q', (v_1, z_2)\big)_2 = z_2$.

□

Proof. Let D be given as above and let the unique solution property hold. Let $G(q, u_1)$ and $H(q, q', v_1)$ be the unique solutions y_2 and z_2, respectively. We construct a DCES D' such that $\mathcal{S}_{D'}$ is a feedback connection of $\mathcal{S}_D$. Let $D' = (U_1, V_1, \mathcal{Q}, Y_1 \times Y_2, Z_1 \times Z_2, f', g', h', q_0)$ be the DCES with

- $q' \in f'(q, u_1, v_1)$ if and only if $q' \in f\Big(q, \big(u_1, G(q, u_1)\big), \big(v_1, H(q, q', v_1)\big)\Big)$,
- $g'(q, u_1) = g\Big(q, \big(u_1, G(q, u_1)\big)\Big)$,
- $h'(q, q', v_1) = h\Big(q, q', \big(v_1, H(q, q', v_1)\big)\Big)$,

for all $q, q' \in \mathcal{Q}$, $u_1 \in U_1$, $v_1 \in V_1$.

It is easy to check that $\mathcal{S}_{D'}$ is feedback connection of $\mathcal{S}_D$. □

Finally, we define the feedback connection operator for discrete condition/event systems.

DEFINITION 2.11. *Let* D *be given as in Theorem 2.10. The DCES* D' *gained from the construction above is called the* discrete feedback connection of D, *denoted by* $D \hookleftarrow$. □

2.4. Timed Condition/Event Systems.

Since the behavior of condition/event systems is defined over continuous time, it is straightforward to incorporate quantitative timing or continuous dynamics. Because the communication between condition/event systems is already defined in terms of continuous time signals, it is a natural way to add so-called *c/e timers* to the model as a special class of c/e systems communicating with the original untimed ones. A c/e timer behaves like an alarm clock, that is, it counts the elapsed time since the last time the timer has been reset. Moreover, time can be compared to certain thresholds and the timer sends an alarm if some specified threshold is reached. To formally define the behavior of a timer we use a function τ_θ, which models for a given event signal s the time elapsed since the last reset point.

DEFINITION 2.12. *Let s be an event signal. Let $\alpha = t_0 t_1 \cdots$ be the maximal ordered finite or infinite sequence of time points such that $s(t_i) \neq \mathbf{0}$. Let $t_{-1} = 0$ and let k be the length of α (thus $k \in \omega \cup \{\omega\}$). A timer function $\tau_\theta(s) : \mathbb{R}_{\geq 0} \to \mathbb{R}_{\geq 0}$ associated to s is determined by*

$$\tau_\theta(s)(t) = \begin{cases} t - t_{j-1} & \text{if } \exists j \geq 0.\ t_{j-1} < t \leq t_j \wedge j < k \\ t - t_j & \text{if } k \in \omega \wedge j = k - 1 \wedge t > t_j \end{cases}.$$

□

Intuitively, we interpret $\tau_\theta(s)(t)$ as the value of the timer at time point t. Indeed, since the occurrence of a proper event resets the timer to zero, between two resets time increases by the distance between the times at which these resets occur.

DEFINITION 2.13. *A condition/event timer (c/e timer) θ is a pair consisting of a condition/event system[1] $(Res_\theta, Int_\theta, Ala_\theta, S_\theta)$ and a vector $T_\theta = (T_\theta^1, \cdots, T_\theta^m)$ of constants $T_\theta^i \in \mathbb{N}_{>0}$ such that $T_\theta^1 < \cdots < T_\theta^m$ and*

- *$Res_\theta = \{\text{``}\theta := 0\text{''}, \mathbf{0}\}$ is the input event alphabet,*
- *$Int_\theta = \{\text{``}\theta < T_\theta^{1}\text{''}, \text{``}T_\theta^1 \leq \theta < T_\theta^{2}\text{''}, \cdots, \text{``}T_\theta^{m-1} \leq \theta < T_\theta^{m}\text{''}, \text{``}\theta \geq T_\theta^{m}\text{''}\}$ is the output condition alphabet,*
- *$Ala_\theta = \{\text{``}\theta = T_\theta^{i}\text{''} \mid i = 1, \cdots, m\} \cup \{\mathbf{0}\}$ is the output event alphabet, and*
- *for every $(s_v, s_y, s_z) \in \mathcal{B}(Res_\theta, Int_\theta, Ala_\theta)$, $(s_y, s_z) \in S_\theta(s_v)$ iff for every $t \in \mathbb{R}_{\geq 0}$ the signal s_y satisfies*

$$s_y(t) = \begin{cases} \text{``}\theta < T_\theta^{1}\text{''} & \text{if } \tau_\theta(s_v)(t) < T_\theta^1 \\ \text{``}T_\theta^i \leq \theta < T_\theta^{i+1}\text{''} & \text{if } i \in \{1, \cdots, m-1\} \wedge \tau_\theta(s_v)(t) \in [T_\theta^i, T_\theta^{i+1}) \\ \text{``}\theta \geq T_\theta^{m}\text{''} & \text{if } \tau_\theta(s_v)(t) \geq T_\theta^m \end{cases}$$

and the signal s_z satisfies

$$s_z(t) = \begin{cases} \text{``}\theta = T_\theta^{i}\text{''} & \text{if } i \in \{1, \cdots, m\} \wedge \tau_\theta(s_v)(t) = T_\theta^i \\ \mathbf{0} & \text{otherwise} \end{cases}.$$

□

In words, a c/e timer θ is a condition/event system with specific input and output signals and an additional set of thresholds $T_\theta = (T_\theta^1, \cdots, T_\theta^m)$. The behavior of the c/e timer is completely determined by its input event signal. A c/e timer behaves as follows: The internal time given by the timer function is always compared to the thresholds and the result is passed to the environment. The output condition signal always states the interval the timer function is in at the moment, i.e. it produces the conditions "$\theta < T_\theta^{1}$", "$T_\theta^i \leq \theta < T_\theta^{i+1}$", and "$\theta \geq T_\theta^{m}$". The output event signal alarms the environment by generating the output event "$\theta = T_\theta^{i}$" when a specific threshold T_θ^i is reached. The value of the timer function is set to 0 when the c/e timer receives "$\theta := 0$" as input event.

Since a timer is completely determined by its threshold vector we identify a timer with this vector. Moreover, when we consider a set $\{\theta_i \mid 1 \leq i \leq n\}$ of

---

[1]The input condition alphabet of this system is a singleton and therefore omitted.

timers, we denote by $T_{\theta_i} = (T_i^1, \cdots, T_i^{m_i})$ the threshold vector of timer θ_i, and by $\text{Res}_i, \text{Int}_i, \text{Ala}_i$ its signal alphabets. For the sake of presentation we use the following abbreviations: U^+ for $U \times \Pi_{i=1}^n \text{Int}_i$, V^+ for $V \times \Pi_{i=1}^n \text{Ala}_i$, and Z^+ for $Z \times \Pi_{i=1}^n \text{Res}_i$. Then, we define timed condition/event systems as condition/event systems which are determined by a set of timers and a discrete condition/event system D. The behavior of the discrete condition/event system D depends on the output signals of the timers and is able to reset these timers by sending a reset signal.

DEFINITION 2.14. *A timed condition/event system (TCES) is a tuple* $T = (U, V, Y, Z, D, \Theta)$, *where*

- $\Theta = \{\theta_i \mid 1 \le i \le n\}$ *is a set of c/e timers and*
- $D = (U^+, V^+, \mathcal{Q}, Y, Z^+, f, g, h, q_0)$ *is a discrete condition/event system.*

□

In order to assign a semantics to a timed condition/event system, we associate to each timed condition/event system T a condition/event system $\mathcal{S}_T$ with behavior function S_T.

DEFINITION 2.15. *Given a timed condition/event system* $T = (U, V, Y, Z, D, \Theta)$. *Its behavior function* $S_T : C(U) \times E(V) \to 2_\emptyset^{C(Y) \times E(Z)}$ *is defined as follows:*

For any $s \in \mathcal{B}(U, V, Y, Z)$, *we have* $(s_y, s_z) \in S_T(s_u, s_v)$ *iff there exist* $s'_u \in \Pi_{i=1}^n C(\text{Int}_i)$, $s'_v \in \Pi_{i=1}^n E(\text{Ala}_i)$, *and* $s'_z \in \Pi_{i=1}^n E(\text{Res}_i)$, *such that the following conditions are satisfied:*

- $(s'_{u_i}, s'_{v_i}) \in S_{\theta_i}(s'_{z_i})$, *for each* $i = 1, \cdots, n$, *and*
- $(s_y, (s_z, s'_z)) \in S_D((s_u, s'_u), (s_v, s'_v))$.

□

In the above definition the first condition ensures that the timer signals associated to the timers are legal and the second condition ensures the same for the DCES. Thus, a timed condition/event system is a connection between a finite set of timers, each one behaving like a condition/event system and a DCES also behaving like a condition/event system. The connection is established as follows: The output signals of the timers are part of input signals of the TCES and the input event signals of the timers are part of the output event signals of the TCES. Since the signals from timer are not observable for an environment, we call them *internal signals*. On the other hand, we call the remaining observable signals *external*. We use these notions for the corresponding alphabets, too. One can easily prove that timed condition/event systems are condition/event systems.

LEMMA 2.16. *For any timed condition/event system* T, $\mathcal{S}_T$ *is a condition/event system.* □

2.5. Composition of Timed Condition/Event Systems. Timed condition/event systems can be composed using a feedback and a cascade operator in the same way as condition/event systems. In the full paper [14] we show that Theorem 2.7 and Theorem 2.10 can be extended to timed condition/event systems.

3. Timed Automata. *Timed automata* (TAs) [2] are finite state automata extended by real-valued variables. Semantically, timed automata allow two kinds of transitions, namely *discrete* and *time-pass transitions*. The discrete transitions are specified by the edges between the control locations and guarded by conditions on the variables. A discrete transition can only be taken when the values of the variables satisfy its guard. Moreover, when a discrete transition is taken, some of the variables may be reseted. While control resides at a control location of the automaton time can pass and the values of the variables increase by the amount of time that passed. Therefore, these real-valued variables are called *clocks*.

The verification problem for timed automata has been intensively investigated and many interesting logics have been identified for which this problem is decidable [1, 3, 5, 6, 19]. Also the synthesis problem for timed automata is decidable [20].

In this section we define *timed words* as well as *timed automata* which recognize sets of timed words. Since timed condition/event systems do not include any acceptance condition we only consider *safety timed automata* [11].

3.1. Timed Languages. Let Σ be an alphabet. The behavior of a real-time system corresponds to a timed word over Σ. As we are interested in a *dense-time* model, we choose the set $\mathbb{R}_{\geq 0}$ of non-negative reals as time domain.

DEFINITION 3.1. *A time sequence $\tau = (\tau_i)_{i \in \omega}$ is an infinite sequence of time values $\tau_i \in \mathbb{R}_{\geq 0}$ that satisfies the following conditions:*

- Monotonicity: *τ increases monotonically; that is, $\tau_{i+1} > \tau_i$, for every $i \in \omega$.*
- Divergence: *τ diverges, that is, for every $t \in \mathbb{R}_{\geq 0}$ there is $i \in \omega$ such that $\tau_i \geq t$.*

A timed word over an alphabet Σ is a pair (σ, τ), where σ is an infinite word in $(2^{\Sigma}_{\emptyset})^{\omega}$ and τ is a time sequence. A timed language over Σ is a set of timed words over Σ. □

The intuitive interpretation of a timed word (σ, τ) is that at time point τ_i we observe the symbols in σ_i.

3.2. Safety Timed Automata. Let $\mathcal{V}$ be a set of real-valued variables called *clocks*. A *constraint* γ over $\mathcal{V}$ is a boolean combination of formulas of the form $x \# c$, where $x \in \mathcal{V}$, $\# \in \{<, \leq, >\}$, and $c \in \mathbb{N}$. Let $\mathcal{C}(\mathcal{V})$ denote the set of constraints over $\mathcal{V}$. A *valuation* over $\mathcal{V}$ is a function $\nu : \mathcal{V} \to \mathbb{R}_{\geq 0}$. The satisfaction relation $\nu \models \gamma$ between valuations and constraints is defined as usual. Given a valuation ν and a set $R \subseteq \mathcal{V}$, we denote by $\nu[R \mapsto 0]$ the valuation ν' which associates with each clock in R the value 0 and coincides with ν on all the other clocks. For $t \in \mathbb{R}_{\geq 0}$ we denote by $\nu + t$ the valuation ν' such that $\nu'(x) = \nu(x) + t$, for all $x \in \mathcal{V}$. Moreover, we denote by ν_0 the clock valuation which maps every clock to 0. We are now ready to define safety timed automata.

DEFINITION 3.2. *A safety timed automaton (TA) over an alphabet Σ is given by a tuple $A = (\mathcal{Q}, q_0, \mathcal{X}, \mathcal{E}, Urg)$, where*

- $\mathcal{Q}$ *is a finite set of locations,*
- $q_0 \in \mathcal{Q}$ *is the initial location,*

- $\mathcal{X}$ *is a finite set of* clocks,
- $\mathcal{E} \subseteq \mathcal{Q} \times \mathcal{C}(\mathcal{X}) \times 2^{\Sigma}_{\emptyset} \times 2^{\mathcal{X}} \times \mathcal{Q}$ *is a set of* edges, *and*
- $Urg \subseteq \mathcal{E}$ *is a set of* urgent edges. □

An edge $(q, \gamma, \sigma, \xi, q')$ stands for a transition from location q to location q' which is guarded by the constraint γ, labeled by σ, and which resets the clocks in ξ. Intuitively, an urgent transition has a higher priority than a non-urgent transition and also higher than time passing, i.e., when urgent and non-urgent transitions are enabled at the same time, then one of the urgent transitions is taken. Moreover, time is not allowed to pass beyond a time point at which an urgent transition is enabled.

A *state* of a timed automaton A is a pair (q, ν) where q is a location of A and ν is a valuation of the clocks of A. Let Ξ_A denote the set consisting of the states of A. To define the semantics of safety timed automata we associate to every timed automaton A a labeled transition system T_A having the same states as A. Therefore, we introduce the following definitions.

DEFINITION 3.3. *A labeled transition system is given by a tuple* $T = (\mathcal{X}, L, q_0, \rightarrow)$, *where*

- $\mathcal{X}$ *is a set of* states,
- L *is a set of* labels,
- $q_0 \in \mathcal{X}$ *is the* initial state, *and*
- $\rightarrow \subseteq \mathcal{X} \times L \times \mathcal{X}$ *is the* transition relation.

A run r *of* T *over a word* $(l_i)_{i \in \omega}$ *is a sequence* $(q'_i)_{i \in \omega}$ *such that* $q_0 = q'_0$ *and* $q'_i \xrightarrow{l_i} q'_{i+1}$, *for every* $i \in \omega$. *The* language of T, *denoted by* $\mathcal{L}(T)$, *is the set of words* α *such that there exists a run of* T *over* α. □

To relate timed automata and transition systems we need to introduce following definition. Let A be a timed automaton and $L = 2^{\Sigma}_{\emptyset} \times \mathbb{R}_{>0}$. The relation $\rightsquigarrow \subseteq \Xi_A \times L \times \Xi_A$ is defined as follows: $(q, \nu) \xrightarrow{(\sigma, \delta)} (q', \nu')$ iff there is an edge $(q, \gamma, \sigma, \xi, q')$ in A such that the following conditions hold.

- $\nu + \delta$ satisfies the constraint γ and
- $\nu' = (\nu + \delta)[\xi \mapsto 0]$.

We use the relation $\rightsquigarrow$ to define the semantics of timed automata.

DEFINITION 3.4. *With every timed automaton A we associate a labeled transition system* $T_A = (\Xi_A, L, (q_0, \nu_0), \rightarrow)$, *where* $L = 2^{\Sigma}_{\emptyset} \times \mathbb{R}_{>0}$ *is the set of labels of* T_A *and the transition relation* $\rightarrow \subseteq \Xi_A \times L \times \Xi_A$ *is defined as follows:* $(q, \nu) \xrightarrow{(\sigma, \delta)} (q', \nu')$ *iff there is an edge* $e = (q, \gamma, \sigma, \xi, q')$ *in A such that the following conditions are satisfied:*

- $(q, \nu) \xrightarrow{(\sigma, \delta)} (q', \nu')$,
- *if* $e \in Urg$, *then there is no* $(q, \gamma', \sigma', \xi', q'') \in Urg$, *valuation ν'' and* $\delta' < \delta$ *such that* $(q, \nu) \xrightarrow{(\sigma', \delta')} (q'', \nu'')$, *and*
- *if* $e \notin Urg$, *then there is no* $(q, \gamma', \sigma', \xi', q'') \in Urg$, *valuation ν'' and* $\delta' \leq \delta$ *such that* $(q, \nu) \xrightarrow{(\sigma', \delta')} (q'', \nu'')$.

□

We define the language $L(A)$ of a timed automaton A as the set of timed words $(\sigma_i, t_i)_{i \geq 0}$ such that there exists $(\delta_i)_{i \geq 0}$ with $(\sigma_i, \delta_i)_{i \geq 0} \in T_A$ and $t_i = \Sigma_{j \leq i} \delta_j$.

Later we will apply the standard notion of bisimulation [23, 21] to transition systems to compare timed automata. Let $T = (\mathcal{Q}, L, q_0, \rightarrow_T)$ and $T' = (\mathcal{Q}', L, q_0', \rightarrow_{T'})$ be two given labeled transition systems.

DEFINITION 3.5. *A symmetric relation* $R \subseteq (\mathcal{Q} \times \mathcal{Q}') \cup (\mathcal{Q}' \times \mathcal{Q})$ *is called a* bisimulation *between* T *and* T', *if for every* $q, \bar{q} \in \mathcal{Q}$, $q' \in \mathcal{Q}'$, *and* $l \in L$ *with* $(q, q') \in R$ *the following condition is satisfied:*

- *Whenever* $q \xrightarrow{l}_T \bar{q}$ *there exists a state* $\bar{q}'$ *such that* $q' \xrightarrow{l}_{T'} \bar{q}'$ *and* $(\bar{q}, \bar{q}') \in R$.

□

The largest bisimulation between T and T' (which exists by Tarski's theorem on fixpoints) is denoted by $\sim$. We say that T and T' are *bisimilar*, denoted by $T \sim T'$, if $q_0 \sim q_0'$. We say that two timed automata A and B are *timed bisimilar*, if $T_A \sim T_B$.

Composing timed automata. Timed automata are composed using the parallel operator $\|$. Timed automata A and A' over alphabets Σ and Σ' synchronize on common events when put in parallel. The formal semantics of $A \parallel A'$, where A and A' have disjoint sets of clocks, is given by the timed automaton $B = (\mathcal{Q} \times \mathcal{Q}', (q_0, q_0'), \mathcal{X} \cup \mathcal{X}', \mathcal{E}_B, \mathrm{Urg}_B)$ over the alphabet $\Sigma \cup \Sigma'$ such that $e = ((q_1, q_1'), \gamma \wedge \gamma', \sigma \cup \sigma', \xi \cup \xi', (q_2, q_2')) \in \mathcal{E}_B$ iff $e_1 = (q_1, \gamma, \sigma, \xi, q_2) \in \mathcal{E}$, $e2 = (q_1', \gamma', \sigma', \xi', q_2') \in \mathcal{E}'$, and $\sigma \cap L' = \sigma' \cap L$. Moreover, $e \in \mathrm{Urg}_B$ iff $e_1 \in \mathrm{Urg}_1$ or $e_2 \in \mathrm{Urg}_2$.

4. From Timed Condition/Event Systems to Timed Automata.
In this section, we show that timed condition/event systems can be effectively transformed into timed automata while preserving the same real-time behavior. To do so, we present a function Ψ that transforms timed condition/event systems into timed automata. A theoretical consequence of this result is that timed automata are at least as expressive as TCESs, i.e. every system that can be modeled by a TCES can also be modeled by a timed automaton. Here, we take language inclusion as our criterion for comparing expressiveness. A practical approach of this result is that existing tools, like KRONOS [22], UPPAAL [4], and HyTech [10], for the analysis of timed automata, can now be used to analyze TCESs. The transformation Ψ we present is, however, not very efficient since it transforms a TCES into a timed automaton which has much more discrete states. Therefore, we present a more efficient transformation Ψ' which avoids this increase of discrete states whenever possible. The relationship between both transformations is that they produce for a given TCES two timed automata that are timed bisimilar. It is also worth to mention that the presented transformations also allow to reduce a reachable problem for TCESs, that is, given a TCES and a discrete state whether there is a run of the given TCES that reaches this discrete state, into a reachability problem for timed automata. There are tools that can solve the latter problem efficiently.

Relating timed words and TCES-behaviors. Since the behavior of a TCES is defined as a relation associating to input signals a set of output signals whereas the language of a TA is a set of timed words, we first have to relate both concepts. This is done by the function β, which assigns to each timed word $w = (\sigma_i, t_i)_{i \in \omega}$ a set of behaviors such that for each behavior $s \in \beta(w)$ the following conditions are true:

- for all $t \in [0, t_0)$ we have $s(t) = \sigma_0$ and
- for all $t \in [t_i, t_{i+1})$, $i \geq 0$, we have $s(t) = \sigma_i$.

The mapping β is pointwisely extended to sets of behaviors.

The basic transformation. The transformation function Ψ from TCES into timed automata and its correctness are illustrated in Fig. 4.1. That is, if B is a timed condition/event system and $L(\Psi(B))$ is the language of the resulting timed automaton $\Psi(B)$, then the resulting relation $\beta(L(\Psi(B)))$ equals the relation S_B generated by B, i.e. $\beta(L(\Psi(B))) = S_B$. In [17] we illustrate the analysis of timed condition/event systems by tools for timed automata using the railroad crossing example.

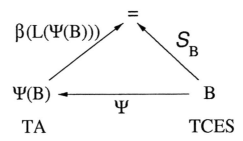

FIG. 4.1. *Transformation from Timed Condition/Event Systems to Timed Automata*

Formally, we can state the following result:

THEOREM 4.1. *There exists an effective function Ψ such that for every timed condition/event system T, we have $\beta(L(\Psi(T))) = S_T$.* □

In the sequel, we present the transformation function Ψ and explain its correctness. First of all, the transformation Ψ has the following characteristics: For each c/e timer θ of the timed condition/event system there exists exactly one clock x in $\Psi(T)$. This clock x is reset if and only if θ is reset. Furthermore, Ψ transforms T with the set of states Q into a timed automaton A with the set of states $Q \times U \cup \{q_{ini}\}$, because in A it is always necessary to remember the last external condition symbol in U to imitate the behavior of T. The additional state $\{q_{ini}\}$ is necessary to build A where initially every condition symbol is possible as it is in T. A major step in the transformation is to determine the guards of the transitions in A. This is realized by the function $cons_\theta$ mapping condition and event symbols in $Int_\theta \cup Ala_\theta$ to clock constraints. For each $a \in Int_\theta \cup Ala_\theta$, the constraint $cons_\theta((a, x))$ is in the table below.

To understand this translation note that, since s_u is a piecewise function,

$$cons_\theta((a,x)) = \begin{cases} x \leq T^1 & \text{if } a = \text{``}\theta < T^{1}\text{''} \\ x > T^m & \text{if } a = \text{``}\theta \geq T^{m}\text{''} \\ x = T^j & \text{if } a = \text{``}\theta = T^{j}\text{''} \\ T^j < x \leq T^{j+1} & \text{if } a = \text{``}T^j \leq \theta < T^{j+1}\text{''} \\ \bigwedge_{j=1}^{m} x \neq T^j & \text{if } a = 0 \end{cases}$$

TABLE 4.1

Definition of $cons_\theta$

we have $s_u(t^-) = u^-$ iff there exists an interval I_t left from t such that for each $t' \in I_t$, $s_u(t') = u^-$.

Moreover, consider a time point t in a run r of a TCES. Then, we have $r(t) \in f(r(t^-), s_u(t^-), s_v(t))$. In order to determine the condition output $s_y(t) = g(r(t), s_u(t))$ for some timer θ we have to determine $s_u(t)$. Therefore, we define a function $next_\theta : (Int_\theta \times Ala_\theta \times Res_\theta) \to Int_\theta$ determining the timer condition in t for a given timer condition in t^- and the timer events in t. For a given set of thresholds $\{T^1, \ldots, T^m\}$ the function $next_\theta$ is determined by Table 4.2, where "*" abbreviates that any possible value is allowed.

u	v	z	$next_\theta(u, v, z)$
*	*	"$\theta := 0$"	"$\theta < T^{1}$"
*	0	0	u
"$\theta < T^{1}$"	"$\theta = T^1$"	0	"$T^1 \leq \theta < T^{2}$" if $m > 1$
"$\theta < T^{1}$"	"$\theta = T^1$"	0	"$\theta \geq T^{1}$" if $m = 1$
"$T^j \leq \theta < T^{j+1}$"	"$\theta = T^{j+1}$"	0	"$T^{j+1} \leq \theta < T^{j+2}$" if $m \geq j+2$
"$T^j \leq \theta < T^{j+1}$"	"$\theta = T^{j+1}$"	0	"$\theta \geq T^{j+1}$" if $m < j+2$

TABLE 4.2

Definition of $next_\theta$

The label of a transition in the constructed timed automaton is the set of symbols determined by the external signals of the timed condition/event system at the time point t, where the corresponding state transformation, given by f, takes place. Now, we define Ψ explicitly.

DEFINITION 4.2. *Consider a TCES* $T = (U, V, Y, Z, D, \Theta)$, *where* $D = (U, V, Q, Y, Z, f, g, h, q_0)$ *is the DCES and* $\Theta = \{\theta_i \mid 1 \leq i \leq n\}$ *is the set of clocks. We define* $\Psi(T) = (Q, q_{ini}, \mathcal{X}, \mathcal{E}, Urg)$ *by*

- $Q = (Q \times U) \cup \{q_{ini}\}$, $\mathcal{X} = \{x_1, \cdots, x_n\}$, *and*

- $\mathcal{E}$ *and Urg are given by*
  - $e = (q_{ini}, \bigwedge\limits_{i=1}^{n} x_i < T_i^1, \sigma_0, \emptyset, (q_0, u_0)) \in \mathcal{E}$ *and* $e \notin Urg$, *where* $\sigma_0 = \{u_0, \mathbf{0}_V, y_0, \mathbf{0}_Z\}$, $u_0 \in U$, *and* $y_0 = g(q_0, \vec{u}_0) \in Y$, $\vec{u}_0 = (u_0, \text{``}\theta_1 < T_1^1\text{''}, \cdots, \text{``}\theta_n < T_n^1\text{''}) \in U^+$,
  - $e = ((q, u_0), \gamma, \sigma, \xi, (q', u_0')) \in \mathcal{E}$ *if there exists*
    * $\vec{u} = (u_0, u_1, \cdots, u_n) \in U^+$,
    * $\vec{u}' = (u_0', u_1', \cdots, u_n') \in U^+$, *and*
    * $\vec{v} = (v_0, v_1, \cdots, v_n) \in V^+$,
  such that the following requirements are satisfied:
    1. $q' \in f(q, \vec{u}, \vec{v})$,
    2. $\gamma = \bigwedge\limits_{i=1}^{n} cons_{\theta_i}(u_i, x_i) \wedge \bigwedge\limits_{i=1}^{n} cons_{\theta_i}(v_i, x_i)$,
    3. $\sigma = \{u_0', v_0, g(q', \vec{u}'), h(q, q', \vec{v})_0\}$,
    4. $\xi = \{x_i \in \mathcal{X} \mid h(q, q', \vec{v})_i \neq 0\}$.
    5. $u_i' = next_{\theta_i}(u_i, v_i, h(q, q', \vec{v})_i)$ *for all* $i = 1, \cdots, n$
  Moreover, $e \in Urg$, *if and only if there exists* $i \in \{1, \cdots, n\}$ *such that* $v_i \neq \mathbf{0}$.

$\square$

By the transformation Ψ we obtain a timed automaton the states of which except q_{ini} are in the Cartesian product of the set of control locations of the timed condition/event system and the external input condition alphabet. In general, this is not necessary because often we cannot distinguish two condition symbols in the sense that they have the same effect on f and g. Thus, the state space can be reduced to a product of control locations with equivalent classes of condition symbols. To obtain a more efficient transformation we define an equivalence on condition symbols.

DEFINITION 4.3. *For every state* $q \in \mathcal{Q}$ *in a given TCES we call two condition symbols* $u, u' \in U$ *equivalent at* q, *denoted by* $u \simeq_q u'$, *if for all* $u_\theta \in \Pi_{i=1}^{n} Int_i$ *the following requirements are satisfied:*
- *for all* $\vec{v} \in V^+$, $f(q, (u, u_\theta), \vec{v}) = f(q, (u', u_\theta), \vec{v})$, *and*
- $g(q, (u, u_\theta)) = g(q, (u', u_\theta))$. $\square$

Let $U|_{\simeq q}$ denote the set of all equivalent classes of condition symbols for a state q. We define another transformation Ψ' from timed condition/event systems to timed automata exactly as before, but in this case we restrict the states of the timed automaton to $(\bigcup_{q \in \mathcal{Q}}(\{q\} \times U|_{\simeq q})) \cup \{q_{ini}\}$ and define its transition relation on states $(q, u_{\simeq q})$, where $u_{\simeq q} \in U|_{\simeq q}$. In comparison to the first transformation Ψ, we reduce the number of resulting states by summarizing all states (q, u^i), $i \in \mathbb{N}$, where all u^i and u^j are equivalent, into one state $(q, u_{\simeq q})$. $\Psi(\mathcal{T})$ and $\Psi'(\mathcal{T})$ are related by the following lemma.

LEMMA 4.4. *For a timed condition/event system* $\mathcal{T}$, *the timed automata* $\Psi(\mathcal{T})$ *and* $\Psi'(\mathcal{T})$ *are timed bisimilar, i.e.* $\Psi(\mathcal{T}) \sim \Psi'(\mathcal{T})$. $\square$

Returning to the verification problem, we see that language inclusion for timed condition event systems $\mathcal{T}$ and $\mathcal{T}'$ can be checked directly for their corresponding timed automata $\Psi(\mathcal{T})$ and $\Psi(\mathcal{T}')$, respectively. However, to check reachability that is not straightforward to apply, since the state space of the resulting timed automata is not just the set of control location $\mathcal{Q}$, but its Cartesian product with the external input condition alphabet. Thus, we have to check whether the pair consisting of location and external input condition symbol is reachable. This leads to the following: For a given timed condition/event system $\mathcal{T}$ a control location $q \in \mathcal{Q}$ is reachable, if and only if there exists an external input condition symbol $u \in U$ such that (q, u) is reachable in $\Psi(\mathcal{T})$, respectively $\Psi'(\mathcal{T})$.

   5. Example. To illustrate timed condition/event systems, their composition and transformation to timed automata we consider the laboratory batch plant example [18], the so-called Evaporator System. The system is shown in Figure 5.1, where the following production sequence takes place: "A salt solution is filled into tank 1 T1 via valve V12 and then evaporated until a desired concentration is reached. During evaporation, the condenser C1 is in operation and captures the steam coming from T1. When the desired concentration is reached, the material is drained from T1 into tank 2 T2 via valve V15 as soon as T2 becomes empty. A post-processing step takes place in T2, before the material can be pumped out of T2 to a subsequent part of the plant via valve V18."

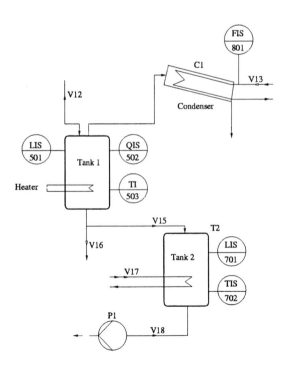

FIG. 5.1. *The Evaporator System*

We suppose that in the undisturbed case the operation sequence described above is ensured by the controller and direct our interest to the problem of appropriate control reaction to disturbances. In particular, we look at the consequences of a cooling breakdown in the condenser. This failure can lead to a dangerously high pressure in the condenser tube, if the evaporating is continued. On the other hand, when the heater in T1 is switched off, the pressure in C1 will not rise anymore. We assume that the material in T1 becomes solid after a certain time when it cools down and cannot be drained into T2 via V15. This situation is of course not desired. As a consequence, the controller should not switch off the heater immediately after a cooling breakdown. But, if T2 is still full, switching off the heater must be delayed to ensure that T1 can be drained via V15 before the material becomes solid. However, a controller should start draining T2 via V18 as soon as a cooling breakdown occurs, so that no time is lost.

In the sequel we give a model of the evaporator system as a composition of timed condition/event systems. Moreover, for the sake of illustration, we give the result of the transformation of section 4 when applied to one of the components of the system.

5.1. Specification. We first specify the evaporator system as the composition of the TCESs modules *Tank1*, *Solution1*, *Heater*, *Tank2*, *Solution2*, *Condenser*, *Pressure*, and *Controller*. To represent TCESs a graphical description is used which is quite similar to that used for input/output automata. First, each state is labeled with a possible output condition in that state. Second, each transition is labeled with $(ic, ie)/oe$, where ic is an input condition, ie is an input event and oe is an output event. Sometimes, when there is no ic or no ie we simply omit the parenthesis and write only the remaining components. The same holds if there is no oe. In this case we also omit the slash symbol. Moreover, if in a state the label of an input or output symbol of a transition from that state is arbitrary we shortly write '*'. It represents each possible symbol of the corresponding alphabet.

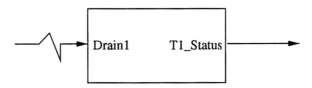

Tank1 and Solution1. The block diagram of the *Tank1* module is shown in Figure 5.2. It has input event alphabet $Drain1 = \{drain1\}$ and output condition alphabet $T1\_Status = \{e1, f1\}$. The graphical representation of *Tank1* is shown in Figure 5.3. The set of states is $\mathcal{Q} = \{empty, full\}$. The module *Tank1* describes the filling and draining processes of T1. At the beginning, *Tank1* is *empty* and can spontaneously get filled by going to *full*. It can stay there or go back to *empty* when it receives the event "*drain1*" i.e. T1 was drained.

Being *empty* and receiving *"drain1"* it remains *empty*. *Tank1* is a pure discrete condition/event system. There is no timer.

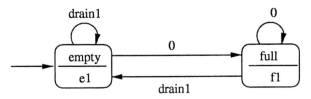

FIG. 5.3. *Tank 1*

The graphical representation of *Solution1* is shown in Figure 5.4. It has input event alphabet $H\_Off = \{h\_off\}$, input condition alphabet $T1\_Status =$

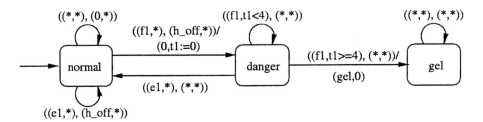

FIG. 5.4. *Solution 1*

$\{e1, f1\}$ and output event alphabet $Gel = \{gel\}$. Moreover, we use a timer $t1$ with threshold vector (4) in order to measure the time passed. So, the label of a transition takes the form $((T1\_Status, \text{Int}_{t1}), (H\_Off, \text{Ala}_{t1}))/(Gel, \text{Res}_{t1})$, where $\text{Int}_{t1} = \{\text{"}t1 < 4\text{"}, \text{"}t1 \geq 4\text{"}\}$, $\text{Ala}_{t1} = \{\text{"}t1 = 4\text{"}, 0\}$, and $\text{Res}_{t1} = \{\text{"}t1 := 0\text{"}, 0\}$, are the intervals, alarm and reset sets of the timer $t1$, respectively. *Solution1* describes the different states of the salt solution inside *Tank1*. At the beginning, the salt solution in T1 is normally heated, state *normal*. However, if the status of *Tank1* is full, condition *"f1"*, and the heater was switched off, the module goes to *danger*. The timer $t1$ is reset. In *danger*, *Solution1* has 4 time units to go back to *normal*, if *Tank1* was in *"e1"*. If these 4 time units passed before *Tank1* could be drained, then *Solution1* goes into *gel*, i.e. the salt solution gelatinize.

Notice that *Tank1* and *Solution1* have the alphabet $T1\_Status$ in common, and that $T1\_Status$ is an output condition alphabet from *Tank1* and an input condition alphabet from *Solution1*, such that we can compose both modules by the cascade interconnection operator: $S_1 = Tank1 \rightarrow Solution1$. Moreover, since $T1\_Status$ does not need to be visible outside this composition we hide it. One obtains a module with input alphabets *Drain1*, H_Off and output alphabet *Gel*.

Tank 2 and Solution 2. Similarly to *Tank1* the *Tank2* module describes the two possible statuses of tank 2, T2, namely, *empty* and *full*. The status of *Tank2* can be changed from *empty* to *full* if T1 is drained, event *"drain1"*. On the other hand, it can change from *full* to *empty* just when T2 was successfully drained, that is, it receives the event *"empty2"*.

Assuming that T2 has 10 time units to be successfully drained if an emergency situation occurs, the module *Solution2* exactly describes that, if a failure in the whole system occurs T2 has to be emergency drained within 10 time units; otherwise, an overflow occurs. *Solution2* has input event alphabet *Emergency* = {*emer_drain*}, input condition alphabet *T2_Status* = {*e2, f2*} and output event alphabet *Empty2* = {*empty2*}. Moreover, we use a timer *t2* with threshold vector (10) in order to measure the time passed after the emergency has occurred.

Tank2 and *Solution2* can be composed by cascade interconnection of both modules and subsequent feedback of the resulting module, i.e. $S_2 = (Tank2 \rightarrow Solution2) \hookleftarrow$.

Heater. This module is shown in Figure 5.5. It has input event alphabet

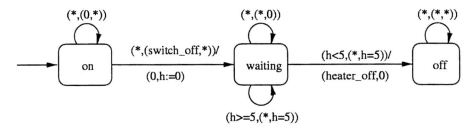

FIG. 5.5. *Heater*

Switch = {*switch_off*}, output event alphabet *H_Off* = {*heater_off*} and timer *h* with threshold vector (5). Assuming that the heater is switched off with a delay of 5 time units the module Heater exactly describes this process. Here, after receiving *switch_off* the module delays the time to switch off the heater by 5 time units. The heater is switched off by the transition from *waiting* to *off*. The event *heater_off* is sent.

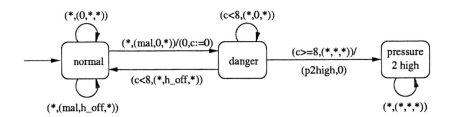

FIG. 5.6. *Pressure*

Condenser and Pressure. *Condenser* is a discrete condition event system with only an output event alphabet *Mal* = {*mal*}. It describes the situation that in C1 a failure can spontaneously occur, event *"mal"*. On the other hand, the module *Pressure* describes the process that, if such a failure occurs in C1 (event "*mal*") the heater must be switched off within 8 time units. Otherwise, the pressure in C1 will be too high. *Condenser* and *Pressure* can be composed by cascade interconnection of both modules, i.e. $S_3 = Condenser \rightarrow Pressure$. Now, up to the Controller module all other modules have been described and connected. The already formalized modules build the whole system. This can be built by $S = (Heater \rightarrow S_1) \rightarrow S_3) \rightarrow S_2$.

Controller. We would like to develop a controller to prevent under any circumstances that the pressure in C1 will become too high, the material in T1 will gelatinize, and there is an overflow in T2. In other words, the Controller module must ensure that the states *gel* in *Solution1*, *pressure2high* in *Pressure*, and *overflow* in *Solution2* are unreachable. One module which meets such requirements is shown in Figure 5.8. In that figure we use a hierarchical representation of states like the one used in statecharts. So, for instance, the box involving the states *normal*, *st1*, *st2*, *st3*, and *st6* is a super state. That means, that each transition occurring from that super state is a transition occurring from each state involved by this super state. The same also holds for transitions coming into the super state. For a symbol a the notation $\hat{a}$ represents all symbols of the corresponding alphabet except a.

Transformation. The full specification, complete transformation, and the results of the verification of the evaporator system are given in the full paper [14]. Here, we only give the transformation of section 4 when applied to the timed condition/event system *Heater*. We obtain the timed automaton shown in Figure 5.7. In that graphical representation we omit the synchronization symbols $0_{Switch}, 0_{H\_Off}$ and also the set of them $\{0_{Switch}, 0_{H\_Off}\}$. Urgent transitions are shown as dashed arrows. Note that since both transitions from state *waiting* to state *off* are urgent the automaton cannot stay in *waiting* beyond 5.

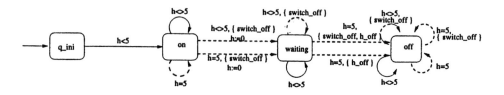

FIG. 5.7. *Timed Automaton Transformation of Module Heater*

6. Conclusion. In this paper we showed that timed condition/event systems can be efficiently transformed into timed automata allowing this way for

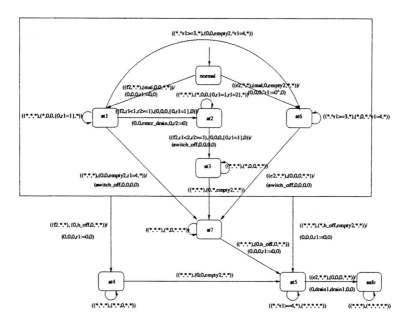

FIG. 5.8. *Controller*

automatic verification using tools as [22, 10, 4]. Currently, we are developing a tool which includes a graphical interface for the description of block diagrams of timed condition/event systems. This tool uses the transformation given in the present paper to transform the described system into a timed automaton which is then analyzed by one of the tools [22, 10, 4]. We are also studying a compositional approach for the verification of timed condition/event systems.

REFERENCES

[1] R. ALUR, C. COURCOUBETIS, AND D. DILL, *Model Checking for Real-Time Systems*, in LICS'90, 1990, pp. 414–425.

[2] R. ALUR AND D. DILL, *A Theory of Timed Automata*, Theoretical Computer Science, 126 (1994), pp. 183–235.

[3] R. ALUR, T. FEDER, AND T. HENZINGER, *The Benefits of Relaxing Puntuality*, Journal of the ACM, 43 (1996), pp. 116–146.

[4] J. BENGTSSON, K. LARSEN, F. LARSSON, P. PETTERSSON, AND W. YI, *UPPAAL — A Tool Suite for Automatic Verification of Real-Time Systems*, in Hybrid Systems III, LNCS 1066, Springer–Verlag, 1996, pp. 232–243.

[5] A. BOUAJJANI AND Y. LAKHNECH, *Temporal Logic + Timed Automata: Expressiveness and Decidability*, in CONCUR'95, LNCS 962, Springer–Verlag, 1995, pp. 531–546.

[6] A. BOUAJJANI, Y. LAKHNECH, AND S. YOVINE, *Model Checking for Extended Timed Temporal Logics*, in FTRTFT'96, LNCS 1135, Springer–Verlag, 1996, pp. 306–326.

[7] S. ENGELL AND I. HOFFMANN, *Modular Hierarchical Models of Hybrid Systems*, in 35th

IEEE Conf. on Decision and Control, Kobe, Japan, 1996.

[8] S. ENGELL, S. KOWALEWSKI, B. KROGH, AND J. PREUSSIG, *Condition/Event Systems: A Powerful Paradigm for Timed and Untimed Discrete Models of Technical Systems*, in EUROSIM'95, 1995.

[9] H.-M. HANISCH AND M. RAUSCH, *Synthesis of Supervisory Controllers Based on a Novel Representation of Condition/Event Systems*, in IEEE Int. Conf. on Systems, Man., and Cybernetics, Vancouver, Canada, 1995.

[10] T. HENZINGER, P.-H. HO, AND H. WONG-TOI, *HyTech : The Next Generation*, in RTSS'95, 1995, pp. 56–65.

[11] T. HENZINGER, X. NICOLLIN, J. SIFAKIS, AND S. YOVINE, *Symbolic Model Checking for Real-Time Systems*, Information and Computation, 111 (1994), pp. 193–244.

[12] I. HOFFMANN, S. KOWALEWSKI, J. PREUSSIG, AND O. STURSBERG, *Towards Systematic Derivation of Timed and Hybrid Automata from Continuous Models*, in Hybrid Systems III, vol. 1066 of LNCS, Springer-Verlag, 1996.

[13] L. HOLLOWAY, *Time Measures and State Maintainability for a Class of Composed Systems*, in WODES'96, Edinburgh, UK, 1996, pp. 24–30.

[14] R. HUUCK, Y. LAKHNECH, B. LUKOSCHUS, L. URBINA, S. ENGELL, S. KOWALEWSKI, AND J. PREUSSIG, *Integrating Timed Condition/Event Systems and Timed Automata to the Verification of Hybrid Systems*, tech. report, Institut für Informatik, Christian–Albrechts Universität zu Kiel, 1998.

[15] S. KOWALEWSKI, *Modulare diskrete Anlagenmodellierung zum systematischen Steuerungsentwurf*, PhD thesis, Fachbereich Chemietechnik, Universität Dortmund, 1995.

[16] S. KOWALEWSKI, S. ENGELL, M. FRITZ, R. GESTHUISEN, G. REGNER, AND M. STOBBE, *Modular Discrete Modelling of Batch Processes by Means of Condition/Event Systems*, in Analysis and Design of Event–Driven Operations in Process Systems, London, 1995.

[17] S. KOWALEWSKI, S. ENGELL, J. PREUSSIG, R. HUUCK, Y. LAKHNECH, AND L. URBINA, *Analyse zeitbewerteter Bedingungs/Ereignis-Systeme mittels Echtzeitautomaten-Tools*, in EKA'97, Braunschweig, Germany, 1997.

[18] S. KOWALEWSKI AND J. PREUSSIG, *Timed Condition/Event Systems: A Framework for Modular Discrete Models of Chemical Plants and Verification of their Real–Time Discrete Control*, in LNCS 1055, Springer–Verlag, 1996, pp. 225–240.

[19] Y. LAKHNECH, *Specification and Verification of Hybrid and Real-Time Systems*, PhD thesis, Institut für Informatik und Praktische Mathematik, Christian-Albrechts-Universität zu Kiel, 1996.

[20] O. MALER, A. PNUELI, AND J. SIFAKIS, *On the Synthesis of Discrete Controllers for Timed Systems*, in LNCS 900, E. Mayr and C. Puech, eds., Springer Verlag, 1995, pp. 229–242.

[21] R. MILNER, *Communication and Concurrency*, Prentice Hall, 1989.

[22] A. OLIVERO AND S. YOVINE, *KRONOS: A Tool for Verifying Real–Time Systems. User's Guide and Reference Manual*, VERIMAG, Grenoble, France, 1993.

[23] D. PARK, *Concurrency and Automata on Infinite Sequences*, in 5th GI Conference, LNCS 104, Springer-Verlag, 1981.

[24] R. SREENIVAS AND B. KROGH, *On Condition/Event Systems with Discrete State Realizations*, in Discrete Event Dynamic Systems: Theory and Applications 1, Kluwer Academic, Boston, USA, 1991, pp. 209–236.

[25] T. WILKE, *Automaten und Logiken zur Beschreibung zeitabhängiger Systeme*, PhD thesis, Institut für Informatik und Praktische Informatik der Universität zu Kiel, 1994.

AUTOMATIC DERIVATION OF PATH AND LOOP ANNOTATIONS IN OBJECT-ORIENTED REAL-TIME PROGRAMS*

JAN GUSTAFSSON[†] AND ANDREAS ERMEDAHL [‡]

Abstract. This paper presents a new method for deriving path and loop annotations automatically for object-oriented real-time programs. Such annotations are necessary when the worst case execution time (*WCET*) of programs is to be calculated. Normally these annotations must be given manually by the programmer.

By automating the the generation of annotations the user is relieved from a task that can be quite difficult and highly critical. If, for example, a programmer gives a too optimistic annotation for a loop, a tool may calculate a too short *WCET*. This may invalidate subsequent analysis, leading to that a real-time system may violate its real-time properties.

The method is based on the notion of abstract interpretation, and is illustrated by showing the analysis of an example in Smalltalk.

The paper also discusses alternatives to the semantic analysis used in the method. It is shown that syntactic analysis suffices in some cases, and that it can be used to reduce the calculation cost for loops.

1. Introduction. To be able to guarantee the correct timely behaviour needed in hard real-time systems, the execution time of the software in the system must be known prior to execution. As the execution time of most programs varies, depending on input data and the system state, the worst case execution time, *WCET*, is used as a least upper limit on the execution time. For programs with some complexity, it can be hard to find the input data that causes the *actual* worst case execution time, $WCET_A$. Therefore, measurement is not considered a feasible method in the general case. Instead, static analysis, which from the source code derives $WCET_C$ (the *calculated* worst case execution time), has been proposed by many researchers (see for example [21, 22, 5, 16, 23, 1]). $WCET_C$ should be as *tight* approximation of $WCET_A$ as possible to avoid waste of resources. Still, it must be *safe*, i.e., $WCET_C \geq WCET_A$.

However, a common drawback of these methods is that *manual annotations* are required. Manual annotations are extra information in the program, given to the $WCET_C$ tool. The annotations can be written as comments in a special format, or in an extension to the used language. The following example from [21] shows an extension of the C syntax used to give annotations for the maximum number of iterations of for-loops.

The expression constr_expr is given by the programmer and is calculated statistically by the compiler to yield the maximum number of iterations of

---

*This work was supported by The National Board for Industrial and Technical Development (DOORS project, 93–3180) and ASTEC (Advanced Software Technology, a competence center at Uppsala University).

† Dept. of Computer Engineering, Mälardalens University, Box 883 S-721 23 Västerås, Sweden (jgn@mdh.se).

‡ Dept. of Computer Systems,Uppsala University, Box 325,S-751 05 Uppsala, Sweden (ebbe@docs.uu.se).

```
FOR (expr1; expr2; expr3) MAX_COUNT(constr_expr)
    statement1
[ON_OVERRUN(statement2)]
```

FIG. 1.1. *Example of syntax for manual loop annotations*

statement1, to be used by the $WCET_C$ tool. The number of iterations is also supervised during run-time, and if overrun occurs, statement2 is executed. The upper-case letters mark that this is an extension to the normal C syntax.

There are typically three types of manual annotations:

a) The *maximum number of iteration count* for loops. Calculating the iteration count is impossible in the general case, since the problem is equivalent to the well-known, undecidable, halting problem.

b) The *maximum depth of recursive function calls* for the same reason as in a). However, recursion is usually not allowed in real-time programs.

c) Information of *dependent program parts*. In this way, false paths (non-executable paths) can be identified and excluded from the analysis, thereby making tighter $WCET_C$ calculation possible. Examples of this type of annotation can be found in [19].

But to give these manual annotations is not always a simple task. It is easy to find small examples where, e.g., the maximum number of iterations in a loop is hard to calculate, and where the dependencies are complicated (see section 3 for an example). The main problems are that:

• To give manual annotations means *extra work*. The programmer has to figure out the worst behaviour in his loops and to find false paths.

• To give manual annotations is *error-prone*. An incorrect annotation may lead to one of two unpleasant situations:

  1. A too big (untight) $WCET_C$, causing overreservation of resources.
  2. Or worse, a too small (unsafe) $WCET_C$, causing risk for missed deadlines, with possible catastrophic consequences.

The idea of our new method is introduce an analysis that finds the annotations *automatically*, as they are inherent in the semantics of the program. Termination of the analysis is guaranteed by defining a *time budget* for the program. The analysis can be seen as a first phase of a $WCET_C$ calculation. The derived annotations are used by a following phase, an object-code analysis, which also considers modern hardware architectures with caches and pipelines.

In our analysis of a program we will use *data flow analysis* to find possible variable values at different points in the program. Using this information we can find false paths and calculate minimum and maximum iterations in loops. We will not consider recursion in this paper, but the method can be applied to recursion as well.

The method has been studied by the authors for a subset of C [7]. We show by a small example in Smalltalk how the method may be extended to object-oriented languages. As shown in the example in section 3, also sizes of collections (data structures in Smalltalk) and other useful information for execution time calculation can be extracted. One of the goals of the method is to be a part of execution time calculations for RealTimeTalk (RTT), which is a Smalltalk dialect for hard real-time systems, developed at Mälardalens University [9].

The remainder of the paper is organised as follows: In section 2, the new method is introduced. In section 3 we present an illustrative example. Section 4 describes related work in the area of program analysis. Section 5 discusses ways to make loop analysis more efficient using syntactic loop analysis. Section 6 makes some conclusions, and finally, section 7 gives ideas for future work.

2. Analysis of Smalltalk programs. Smalltalk is a "pure" object-oriented programming language where everything is an object. The syntax is built on three basic mechanisms: assignments, message passing and return expressions. Smalltalk supports single inheritance and polymorphism and is dynamically typed. For a presentation of Smalltalk, we refer to [13].

When analyzing Smalltalk programs we are interested in the values of variables at different points in the program. We call these points *control points*, denoted by $c_0, c_1, \cdots, c_m$. With each control point c_i we associate the program code p_i, which is the rest of the code to be analyzed at that point. For the following three Smalltalk expressions we may insert control points as shown below:

```
                        [c_0]
a := 5.                 [c_1]
mySet := Set new.       [c_2]
mySet add: a.           [c_3]
```

With each control point c_i we also associate one or more *states*, σ_i^j, each of which holds the possible values of the variables at the corresponding control point at program execution. We distinguish between different passings j of a control point, since it can be passed several times in e.g., a loop.

The *concrete semantics* (meaning) of a program p_0 is defined by a transition system over sets of *configurations*, γ (we are using the terminology of [18]). A configuration is either *intermediate*, $\gamma = \langle p_i, \sigma_i \rangle$, or *final*, $\gamma = \sigma$. The transition relation "$\Rightarrow$" is defined using rules of structural operational semantics.

The semantics of a program is defined transitively in terms of "$\Rightarrow$" so that

$$\mathcal{P}[\![p_0]\!]\sigma_0 = \begin{cases} \sigma & \text{if } \{\langle p_0, \sigma_0 \rangle\} \overset{*}{\Rightarrow} \{\sigma\} \\ \bot & \text{otherwise.} \end{cases}$$

For the initial state σ_0 a program p_0 *terminates* iff there is a finite sequence of configuration sets $\{\gamma_0\} = \{\langle p_0, \sigma_0 \rangle\} \Rightarrow \ldots \Rightarrow \{\langle \varepsilon, \gamma_k \rangle\} \Rightarrow \{\gamma_k\}$, where ε represents an "empty" program, i.e., the analysis is finished. If γ_k is a final configuration, the program has terminated *successfully*. If γ_k is an intermediate configuration, we have a *stuck* configuration, meaning there is no transition possible. This is probably due to an error in the program (like "method not found"). If the sequence is infinite, the program does not terminate (indicated with $\perp$).

We analyze sets of configurations, because some of our transitions yield more than one configuration. See figure 2.3 and figure 2.6.

If each variable in the initial state, σ_0, is assigned to one single value, like $\sigma_0 = [a \mapsto 1, b \mapsto 4]$, the evaluation of the rules will correspond to a "normal" execution of the program.

For our analysis, we will define an *abstract state* where variables can be assigned to *split intervals* of integers or floats, like $\sigma_0 = [a \mapsto 1..3, b \mapsto 2.0..4.0 \lor 7.0]$. We can have polymorphic variables, like $\sigma_1 = [c \mapsto 0..3 \lor 9.0]$, meaning that c is either an integer with value 1, 2 or 3, or a float with value 9.0. We can have collections (data structures) of variables, like the following collection of two elements: $\sigma_2 = [d \mapsto \{3..6 \lor 9.0, 11..20\}]$. This syntax means that the first element of d is either an integer with the value 3, 4, 5 or 6, or a float with value 9.0, and the second is an integer with a value between 11 and 20 (inclusive). This restricted domain can in a straight-forward manner be extended to other types of data and collections.

For each concrete semantic rule in the programming language, a corresponding *abstract rule* is defined. For example, our abstract version of the '+' operator must handle split intervals of integers and reals instead of single ones.

The cost (time and memory) needed to express and calculate the exact states is often too big. The representation can then be simplified by a safe approximation. For example, $a \mapsto 1 \lor 3 \lor .. \lor 99$ can be replaced by 1..99. The approximation must be safe (possible values must not be removed), tight (as few extra values as possible), and efficient (in terms of analysis calculations). We will of course face a trade-off between cost of computation and quality of results.

Abstract interpretation techniques [6] can be used to define a correct relation between the abstract and the concrete domains.

2.1. Analysis of sequences. For each expression in a sequence, the state is updated with the corresponding abstract rule. If a message send is performed, the invoked method is analysed and the return values are stored in the state.

For example, consider the program in figure 2.1. Here we identify the control points c_0, c_1, c_2 and c_3 respectively, where c_0 denotes the start of the program.

$$[c_0]$$
```
a := 5.        [c_1]
b := b - 2.    [c_2]
a := a + b.    [c_3]
```

FIG. 2.1. *Smalltalk sequence*

A concrete and an abstract evaluation of the sequence can be seen in figure 2.2. We have in the concrete evaluation assumed that $a = 1$ and $b = 4$ in the initial state. In the abstract evaluation we have $a = 1..3$ and $b = 2..4 \lor 7$ as the initial state. The abstract values are either input values or values calculated during analysis of the previous code. If nothing is known about the values, they are assumed to be ⊤, e.g., for an integer any value in the interval *minint..maxint*, which is the smallest and the largest integer value possible, respectively, for the current language implementation and hardware configuration. Note that the abstract evaluation corresponds to a set of concrete evaluations and that each concrete evaluation corresponds to one execution.

$$\sigma_0 = [a \mapsto 1, b \mapsto 4] \qquad\qquad \sigma_0 = [a \mapsto 1..3, b \mapsto 2..4 \vee 7]$$
$$\sigma_1 = [a \mapsto 5, b \mapsto 4] \qquad\qquad \sigma_1 = [a \mapsto 5, b \mapsto 2..4 \vee 7]$$
$$\sigma_2 = [a \mapsto 5, b \mapsto 2] \qquad\qquad \sigma_2 = [a \mapsto 5, b \mapsto 0..2 \vee 5]$$
$$\sigma_3 = [a \mapsto 7, b \mapsto 2] \qquad\qquad \sigma_3 = [a \mapsto 5..7 \vee 10, b \mapsto 0..2 \vee 5]$$

(a) Concrete   (b) Abstract

FIG. 2.2. *Different evaluations of the Smalltalk sequence*

If the selector is implemented by more than one method (polymorphism), all are analysed, and the resulting states are merged (see section 2.4).

2.2. Analysis of selection constructs. Selection in Smalltalk is accomplished with ifTrue-constructs. The idea is to perform the analysis of the two alternate paths in an ifTrue-construct in *two* states, as shown in the rule in figure 2.3.

$$\{\langle (\texttt{C}) \ \texttt{ifTrue:} \quad [\texttt{E1}] \ \texttt{ifFalse:} \quad [\texttt{E2}] . \quad \texttt{P}, \ \sigma \rangle\} \Rightarrow \{\langle \texttt{E1}. \quad \texttt{P}, \ \sigma^t \rangle, \langle \texttt{E2}. \quad \texttt{P}, \ \sigma^f \rangle\}$$
where
$$\sigma^t = \mathcal{C}[\![\texttt{C}]\!]\sigma$$
$$\sigma^f = \mathcal{C}[\![\text{not } \texttt{C}]\!]\sigma$$

FIG. 2.3. *Rule for* ifTrue-*constructs*

The rest of the code in the program is denoted with P. The expression E1 is evaluated in the state where C is true, σ^t, and E2 is evaluated where C is false, σ^f. A condition can be seen as a constraint to be applied on the variables in a given state. The construct $\mathcal{C}[\![\texttt{C}]\!]\sigma$ constrains a state σ with the condition C to yield the constrained state.

2.2.1. False paths. If the abstract value of a variable in a state is empty (i.e., ⊥), the corresponding path is considered as false. This is the way our method finds false paths.

Figure 2.4 contains an example of an false path. The program has a path that is false for *all* input data (assuming that S1 and S2 does not change the value of a).

```
(a > 10) ifTrue:  [S1] ifFalse: [S2].
(a > 5)  ifTrue:  [S3] ifFalse: [S4]
```

FIG. 2.4. *Example 1 of false paths*

We see that the path passing the expressions S1 and S4 is a false path, since $a > 10$ implies $a > 5$. Please note that the program does *not* contain dead code, since the statements S1 and S4 are executed in other paths.

We can also have false paths which depend on input data. For example, in the program in figure 2.5, the path passing the expression a := a + 1 is false, since the state where this statement should be evaluated is empty. In this case, we must assume that a previous analysis has resulted in a possible value range where $a \geq 2$. In this example, the false paths analysis also identifies dead code, since the expression a := a + 1 never will be executed.

```
"a := 5..10."
(a < 2) ifTrue: [a := a + 1]
```

FIG. 2.5. *Example 2 of false paths*

2.3. Analysis of loop constructs. The core idea is to transform loops into ifTrue-constructs. For example, consider the whileTrue-expression. We will analyse it according to the rule in figure 2.6.

$$\{\langle [C] \text{ whileTrue: } [S]. P, \sigma \rangle\} \Rightarrow$$
$$\{\langle S. [C] \text{ whileTrue: } [S]. P, \sigma^t \rangle, \{\langle P, \sigma^f \rangle\}$$
$$\text{where}$$
$$\sigma^t = \mathcal{C}[\![C]\!]\sigma$$
$$\sigma^f = \mathcal{C}[\![\text{not } C]\!]\sigma$$

FIG. 2.6. *Rule for whileTrue-constructs*

The ifTrue-construct generates two states each time it is analysed, as defined in the previous section. After each iteration we will have:

1. The state in which the loop will continue, σ^t.
2. The state in which the loop will terminate, σ^f.

We can find minimum and maximum number of iterations by keeping track of the iteration count. This can be made by introducing a loop counter for each loop during analysis, which is set to 0 before the loop and which is incremented each iteration. We can record the following two events:

- Minimum occurs where $\sigma^f \neq \bot$ for the first time in the next iteration.
- Maximum occurs where $\sigma^t = \bot$ for the first time in the next iteration.

When $\sigma^f = \bot$ the loop *must* continue. So, when $\sigma^f \neq \bot$ for the first time, it *may* terminate, and the minimum number of iterations has been identified.

Similarly, when $\sigma^t \neq \bot$, the loop *may* continue. So, when $\sigma^t = \bot$ for the first time, it *must* terminate, and the maximum number of iterations has been identified.

Since we are using approximations in our analysis, as mentioned earlier, the states used during analysis may contain values that are not possible in a real execution. This may lead to a loop state σ^f becoming $\neq \perp$ too early in the analysis, leading to a too low minimum number of iterations. Similarly, the loop state σ^t may become $= \perp$ too late, leading to a too high maximum number of iterations. Still, the computed values are safe.

A loop is "rolled out" until it terminates, or until the time budget is exceeded (see section 2.5). An example is provided in section 3.

2.4. Merging of states. Each ifTrue-construct will double the number of states when it is analysed, and every whileTrue-expression will double the number of states each iteration, as explained above. To avoid exponential complexity explosion, states can be *merged* at certain points, so the analysis can continue from *one* state instead of several. Merging is allowed when all configurations are at the same control point.

$$\{\langle p, \sigma^1 \rangle, \langle p, \sigma^2 \rangle, \cdots, \langle p, \sigma^n \rangle\} \Rightarrow \{\langle p, \sigma \rangle\}$$
$$\text{where}$$
$$\sigma = \sigma^1 \oplus \sigma^2 \oplus \cdots \oplus \sigma^n$$

FIG. 2.7. *The effect of merging*

The value of a variable in the merged state $\sigma = \sigma^1 \oplus \sigma^2$ is the union of its values in σ^1 and σ^2. Collections are merged elementwise. The merging may lead to overestimation of possible values, depending on how states are represented and where and how merging is performed. As a first heuristics, we have decided to merge configurations at four points in the analysis:

1. After polymorphic message sending.
2. After each loop iteration.
3. When a loop has terminated.
4. When a method has terminated.

In this way we will avoid a state explosion, to the price of introducing some pessimism, both in terns of overestimation and that false paths are only discovered on one level of code within methods or loop bodies. As always, we have a trade-off between quality of results and calculation costs.

In the example in section 3, merging is done after each loop iteration, and when the loop has terminated. Merging points are marked with $\oplus$ in the figures 3.2 and 3.4.

2.5. Termination of the analysis. To guarantee termination of the analysis we will use the fact that a real-time program must terminate within a given time [15]. This *time budget*, T_{budget}, should be a realistic upper time limit for the program on a given hardware. The time budget may be calculated during the design phase and can be seen as part of the specification of the program. It is the only "annotation" needed by the method. Note that our time annotation is different from the annotations of other methods. Erroneous path or loop annotations may lead to a wrong $WCET_C$, but an erroneous T_{budget} may, in the worst case, only lead to a failure of the analysis, not to an incorrect result.

Each construct or program block has an associated time interval $t_{minc}..t_{maxc}$, its minimum and maximum execution time. This time is calculated from the corresponding assembler code. With our own compiler for RTT, we have full knowledge of the generated code. If the hardware uses caches, pipelines etc., the time intervals will increase. In this case the time budget may have to be increased.

For each analysed construct, the corresponding time interval will be added to an accumulated time for the analyzed path. The longest path, with its interval $T_{minc}..T_{maxc}$, is compared to the time budget during the analysis. If $T_{maxc} \leq T_{budget}$ holds when the analysis is finished, we can guarantee that the program will not exceed its time budget. If $T_{maxc} > T_{budget}$, the program may not terminate within the time budget, and the analysis should stop.

3. Example. The Smalltalk program in fig. 3.1 will be analysed by our the method. The program uses the **SmallInteger** class with the methods <=, <, + and *, the **Float** class with the methods + and *, the **OrderedCollection** class with the method **add**, assignments, the **True** and **False**-classes for selection constructs (**ifTrue:ifFalse:**) and a loop construct (**whileTrue:**). The example contains a selection within a loop, where a collection is filled with variables of different types. The example does not illustrate inheritance or recursion.

We will compare the analysis results to the real results, in terms of overestimations of numbers, sizes, and values. We assume that the initial values are $n = 1..10$ and $x = 2.0..7.0$.

```
"n := 1..10. x := 2.0..7.0. Initially"        [c0]
myOC := OrderedCollection new.                [c1]
[n <= 5] whileTrue: "Start of loop" [         [c2]
    (n < 3)  ifTrue: [                        [c3]
        myOC add: (n * (n + 1))] "Integer"    [c4]
             ifFalse: [                        [c5]
        myOC add: (x * (x + 2))]. "Float"      [c6]
    n := n + 2.                                [c7]
    x := x + 1.                                [c8]
    ]. "End of loop"                           [c9] [c10] [c11]
```

FIG. 3.1. *The example program*

In the program we have inserted control points after each expression plus two extra for merging:

- c_9 for merging of the loop body ($\sigma_9^j = \sigma_8^{jt} \oplus \sigma_8^{jf}$). In the example, σ_i^{jf} denotes the environment at control point c_i at loop iteration j, with a false selection condition. Similarly, σ_i^{jt} denotes the same control point and loop iteration with a true selection condition.

Iter.	Loop cond.	If cond.	Control point	σ	n	x	myOC	Note
0			c_0	σ_0	1..10	2.0..7.0		
0			c_1	σ_1	1..10	2.0..7.0	{}	
1	f		c_{10}	σ_{10}^1	6..10	2.0..7.0	{}	1. min # iter = 0
1	t		c_2	σ_2^1	1..5	2.0..7.0	{}	
1	t	t	c_3	σ_3^{1t}	1..2	2.0..7.0	{}	
1	t	t	c_4	σ_4^{1t}	1..2	2.0..7.0	{2..6}	
1	t	t	c_7	σ_7^{1t}	3..4	2.0..7.0	{2..6}	
1	t	t	c_8	σ_8^{1t}	3..4	3.0..8.0	{2..6}	
1	t	f	c_5	σ_5^{1f}	3..5	2.0..7.0	{}	
1	t	f	c_6	σ_6^{1f}	3..5	2.0..7.0	{8.0..63.0}	
1	t	f	c_7	σ_7^{1f}	5..7	2.0..7.0	{8.0..63.0}	
1	t	f	c_8	σ_8^{1f}	5..7	3.0..8.0	{8.0..63.0}	
1	t		c_9	σ_9^1	3..7	3.0..8.0	{2..6 ∨ 8.0..63.0}	2. $\sigma_9^1 = \sigma_8^{1f} \oplus \sigma_8^{1t}$
2	f		c_{10}	σ_{10}^2	6..7	3.0..8.0	{2..6 ∨ 8.0..63.0}	
2	t		c_2	σ_2^2	3..5	3.0..8.0	{2..6 ∨ 8.0..63.0}	
2	t		c_3	σ_3^{2t}	⊥			3. $\sigma_3^{2t} = \bot$
2	t	f	c_5	σ_5^{2f}	3..5	3.0..8.0	{2..6 ∨ 8.0..63.0}	
2	t	f	c_6	σ_6^{2f}	3..5	3.0..8.0	{2..6 ∨ 8.0..63.0, 15.0..80.0}	
2	t	f	c_7	σ_7^{2f}	5..7	3.0..8.0	{2..6 ∨ 8.0..63.0, 15.0..80.0}	
2	t	f	c_8	σ_8^{2f}	5..7	4.0..9.0	{2..6 ∨ 8.0..63.0, 15.0..80.0}	
2	t		c_9	σ_9^2	5..7	4.0..9.0	{2..6 ∨ 8.0..63.0, 15.0..80.0}	4. $\sigma_9^2 = \sigma_8^{2f} \oplus \bot$
. 3	f		c_{10}	σ_{10}^3	6..7	4.0..9.0	{2..6 ∨ 8.0..63.0, 15.0..80.0}	
3	t		c_2	σ_2^3	5	4.0..9.0	{2..6 ∨ 8.0..63.0, 15.0..80.0}	
3	t		c_3	σ_3^{3t}	⊥			5. $\sigma_3^{3t} = \bot$
3	f	f	c_5	σ_5^{3f}	5	4.0..9.0	{2..6 ∨ 8.0..63.0, 15.0..80.0}	
3	f	f	c_6	σ_6^{3f}	5	4.0..9.0	{2..6 ∨ 8.0..63.0, 15.0..80.0, 24.0..99.0}	
3	f	f	c_7	σ_7^{3f}	7	5.0..10.0	{2..6 ∨ 8.0..63.0, 15.0..80.0, 24.0..99.0}	
3	f	f	c_8	σ_8^{3f}	7	5.0..10.0	{2..6 ∨ 8.0..63.0, 15.0..80.0, 24.0..99.0}	
3	f		c_9	σ_9^3	7	5.0..10.0	{2..6 ∨ 8.0..63.0, 15.0..80.0, 24.0..99.0}	6. $\sigma_9^3 = \sigma_8^{3f} \oplus \bot$
4	t		c_2	σ_2^4	⊥	5.0..10.0	{2..6 ∨ 8.0..63.0, 15.0..80.0, 24.0..99.0}	7. max # iter = 3
4	f		c_{10}	σ_{10}^4	7	5.0..10.0	{2..6 ∨ 8.0..63.0, 15.0..80.0, 24.0..99.0}	
4			c_{11}	σ_{11}^4	6..10	2.0..10.0	{} ∨ {2..6 ∨ 8.0..63.0} ∨{2..6∨ 8.0..63.0, 15.0..80.0} ∨{2..6 ∨ 8.0..63.0, 15.0..80.0, 24.0..99.0}	8. result after analysis: $\sigma_{11}^4 = \sigma_{10}^1 \oplus \sigma_{10}^2 \oplus \sigma_{10}^3 \oplus \sigma_{10}^4$

FIG. 3.2. *Abstract evaluation of the example program*

n (start)	n (end)	x (start)	x (end)	Iter.	myOC (end)
1	7	2.0..7.0	5.0..10.0	3	{2, 15.0..80.0, 24.0..99.0}
2	6	2.0..7.0	4.0..9.0	2	{6, 15.0..80.0}
3	7	2.0..7.0	4.0..9.0	2	{8.0..63.0, 15.0..80.0}
4	6	2.0..7.0	3.0..8.0	1	{8.0..63.0}
5	7	2.0..7.0	3.0..8.0	1	{8.0..63.0}
6	6	2.0..7.0	2.0..7.0	0	{}
7	7	2.0..7.0	2.0..7.0	0	{}
8	8	2.0..7.0	2.0..7.0	0	{}
9	9	2.0..7.0	2.0..7.0	0	{}
10	10	2.0..7.0	2.0..7.0	0	{}
Total:	6..10		5.0..10.0	0..3	{} ∨ {8.0..63.0}∨ {6, 15.0..80.0}∨ {8.0..63.0, 15.0..80.0}∨ {2, 15.0..80.0, 24.0..99.0}

FIG. 3.3. *Actual possible environments after execution*

- c_{11} for merging of all environments (at c_{10}) where the loop has terminated ($\sigma_{11}^4 = \sigma_{10}^1 \oplus \sigma_{10}^2 \oplus \sigma_{10}^3 \oplus \sigma_{10}^4$).

Figure 3.2 shows the analysis of the example program. From left to right, the columns show the iteration count, the values of the loop and selection conditions, the control point, the environment and the abstract values of n, x and myOC.

- Note 1 marks the minimum number of iterations (0) in the loop. It is found where $\sigma^f \neq \perp$ the first time in the next iteration.
- Note 2, 4 and 6 marks merging of the loop body.
- Note 3 and 5 marks false paths (when the selection condition true yields $\sigma^t = \perp$ in the loop body at iteration 2 and 3).
- Note 7 marks the termination of the loop. It is found when the true loop condition yields an empty environment, i.e., $\sigma_2^4 = \perp$, implying that the maximum number of iterations in the loop is 3.

Figure 3.4 shows the evaluation graphically, from the start state σ_0 to the resulting state σ_{11}^4. The index of the merging function $\oplus$ refers to one of the four types of merging described in section 2.4.

The purpose of the example is to show that the analysis gives results which can be used, e.g., to annotate the program graph. When we compare the result of the analysis (note 8 in figure 3.2) to the real values (in figure 3.3), we can conclude the following:

1. *Number of iterations in loops.* Minimum number of iterations is 0 and maximum is 3. No overestimation is made in the analysis.

2. *False paths and dead code.* We have found false paths (in iterations 2 and 3) but no dead code (since the code is executed in iteration 1).

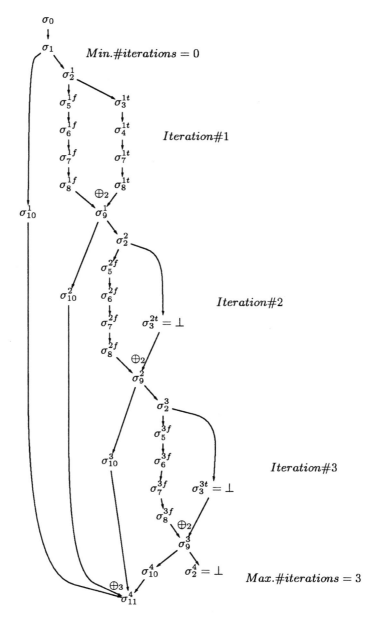

FIG. 3.4. *Graph showing the abstract evaluation*

3. *Size of collections.* Minimum size of myOC is 0 and maximum is 3 elements. No overestimation is made in the analysis.

4. *Number of different types in polymorphic collections.* We have two (safe)

overestimations. First, only one integer does not occur. In the maximum case, the analysis gives one integer and two floats, or three floats. This is the second overestimation, since the latter case does not occur.

5. *Possible values for all variables in each control point in the program.* The variables n and x are estimated correctly. However, the collection myOC is (safely) overestimated, since none of the collections {2..5, 15.0..80.0} and {3..6, 15.0..80.0, 24.0..99.0} occur after execution.

The results in point 1 and 2 are useful in $WCET_C$ calculation, as mentioned in section 1. The results in point 3 and 4 can be useful if the code in figure 3.5 follows the example program.

```
myOC do: [:el | "For each element do"
 (el < 100) ifTrue: [
    el := el^2] " take the square"
 ifFalse: [
    el := el^3]. "or take the cube"
].
```

FIG. 3.5. *Program fragment*

In the $WCET_C$ calculation of the code, the size of myOC is useful (for number of iterations) and the type of the elements (since floats take more time to calculate than integers). Finally, the result in point 5 gives values useful in subsequent analysis.

4. Related Work. The purpose of the method described in this paper is to calculate annotations to be used in $WCET_C$ calculation. This is accomplished by static program analysis based on abstract interpretation. This seems to be a novel idea, even though there is an extensive body of research in the program analysis area, but with other aims, like compiler optimizations, program proofs, and language construction.

The method in this paper derives an approximation of variable values in the control points of Smalltalk/RTT programs. A number of researchers have done similar analyses for other languages, like C and Pascal (see below). No one has analysed Smalltalk in this way, however.

4.1. Abstract Interpretation. Cousot and Cousot laid the theoretical framework for abstract interpretation in [6]. Abstract interpretation can be seen as a non-standard semantics, in which the domain of values is replaced by a domain of descriptions of values, and in which the operators are given a corresponding non-standard interpretation. A number of researchers have used methods based on abstract interpretation in program analysis, primarily in the context of compiler optimizations. Their efforts have been to find value ranges by static analysis to yield more effective and smaller programs.

Harrison showed as early as 1977 [14], albeit not using the abstract interpretation framework, that interval range analysis could be used to statically calculate possible values for variables. The results could be used to eliminate redundant tests, choose data representation, and more.

In a more recent paper, [24], Verbrugge et. al. uses abstract interpretation to statically analyze the full C language (including pointers, functions and recursion) to yield a range for each variable at each point.

Bourdoncle uses abstract interpretation and interval range analysis for "abstract debugging" [4]. He tries to find potential errors in programs by calculating values of variables. In this way, he can identify possible division by 0, indeces out of bounds, and more. He has developed a prototype tool, Syntox, which analyses Pascal programs.

Patterson describes an analysis similar to the above used for static branch prediction in [20]. The results from his analysis are useful in compiler optimizations, especially for instruction scheduling, cache optimizations and register allocation. Although he doesn't refer to Cousot and Cousot, the method is very similar to abstract interpretation with interval range analysis. The value range representation is more detailed than the common interval $l..u$, however. Patterson uses split intervals, where each part interval, beside a lower bound l and an upper bound u, also has a probability and a stride (arithmetic step size).

His method can find some kinds of false paths, namely those where dead code is found (like the one in figure 2.5). It cannot find false paths like the one in figure 2.4, because his method merges values after each if-statement.

His method tries to optimize loop analysis by comparing the operations made on variables in loops to different templates. If simple increments are found, for example, the template can be used to derive the final value range from the initial value and the increments.

It should be clear from the paper that we use a different method than the above-mentioned methods based on abstract interpretation. In those methods, a loop is seen as a system of equations, where the union of the input and output values of the loop are used as input to the loop. The loop is then "iterated" until a fixed-point is found. This means that in each control point in the loop, we have the *union* of the possible values of all iterations of the loop. (The technique is described in more detail in, e.g., [4]). In our method, the loop is "rolled out" (see for example the rule in figure 5.1), and each loop iteration is analysed *separately*. We will calculate the possible values of the values in the control points of each iteration of the loop. In this way, we will have a much more exact approximation, albeit to a higher calculation cost.

4.2. Symbolic Execution. There are also a few methods based on *symbolic execution*. For example, Altenbernd can find false paths automatically for some simple cases (see [1]). Forsyth uses symbolic execution, program annotations and a notion of execution modes in [10]. With his method, false paths can be excluded and the $WCET_C$ values that are calculated are sensitive to both input data and program modes. However, both Altenbernds and Forsyths methods rely on manual annotations.

5. Complexity of Loop Analysis. One problem that program analysis has to face is the potential risk of "getting stuck" in loops. The approach used in the method presented in this paper will analyse each loop iteration that is possible during run-time, and for each iteration create two states. It is obvious that there is a risk that a tool could be too slow and memory gobbling to be used for programs containing complex, nested loops with many iterations.

5.1. Widening/Narrowing Techniques. A common way to solve this in similar methods, is to use *widening/narrowing* techniques, as devised by Cousot and Cousot, and used in e.g., [4]. The idea is first to use a widening function that gives a safe (upper) approximation of the fixed points of the loop values. Next, a narrowing function is used to find a safe approximation of the least fixed point. The right widening and narrowing functions can give a significant speed-up of the convergence of the loop analysis.

Now, there are some problems with the widening/narrowing approach, which makes it unsuitable for our method:

- As we don't use fixpoint computations for loops, the widening/narrowing method doesn't fit into our current approach.

- It is not easy to find the right widening and narrowing functions. They must be carefully selected "by hand" and may be hard to include in a general tool.

- The narrowing step normally only narrows down the loop index. Other variables calculated in the loop are often pushed up to infinity by the widening function, and are never narrowed down by the narrowing function. This is far too crude for our analysis, if we need those values in the subsequent analysis.

5.2. Syntactic Loop Analysis. Another approach would be to try to to find the number of iterations in loops by *syntactic analysis* (to differ from *semantic loop analysis*, the main topic of this paper). There are actually some simple cases where it is possible to statically decide the minimum and maximum number of iterations from the syntax of the loop construct. There are even unterminating loop constructs which we can identify. This is similar to what Patterson is doing in [20]. Blieberger is studying this problem in [3], where he defines a new kind of loop, *discrete loops*, which are more general than for-loops, but still analyzable.

Of course, syntactic analysis cannot handle all cases, so we have to rely on semantic analysis in the general and more complex cases. Syntactic analysis should be regarded as an optimization of the analysis.

General *while-loops* are complex to analyze, but there is a number of simple cases analyzable by syntactic analysis. Let us first look at a general while-loop in Smalltalk (figure 5.1).

The block containing the loop body will be invoked as long as the condition block yields the value **true**.

```
[condition] whileTrue:
   [loop body]
```

FIG. 5.1. *Smalltalk while-loop*

There are of course an abundance of cases that a tool has to recognize and deal with. We will just look at a few, to get an idea of what is possible. Assume k and c are integer constants, $c > 0$ and that the integer loop variable i has the initial value i_0 before entering the following loop:

```
(i < k) whileTrue:   [i := i+c]
```

A mathematical analysis based on the semantics of the whileTrue-expression gives the following *recurrence equation* when $i_0 < k$:

$$i = i_0;$$
$$i_{n+1} = i_n + c;$$

Note that n denotes the number of iterations in the loop, because a new value for i is calculated once for each loop iteration.

A recurrence equation describes a value in terms of earlier ones, plus a boundary value. Recurrences are thoroughly described in [11]. The recurrence equation above has an **open form**, i.e., one has to compute all previous valus to yield the current value. A solution to a recurrence has a **closed form** which gives the value by a single computation. The solution to the recurrence above is simply

$$i_n = i_0 + nc$$

giving the following result for the two possible cases, after solving for n in the second case:

$$n = 0 \text{ and } i = i_0 \text{ if } i_0 \geq k$$
$$n = \lceil \tfrac{k-i_0}{c} \rceil \text{ and } i = i_0 + nc \text{ if } i_0 < k.$$

So we can calculate the number of iterations exactly and quickly in this special case, assuming we can recognize it in a tool. If the loop body contains other code than just manipulating the loop variable (as it should do in a real program), the following must not occur within the loop body for the result to hold:

1. The execution encounters a return expression.

2. The index is manipulated.

3. There are program errors (like "method not found") that causes the program to fail.

4. The execution loops forever in an non-terminating loop.

The first and second requirements are relatively easy to check by a tool. The third requirement can be fulfilled by a type inference/type checker for Smalltalk (see for example [12]). The fourth requirement can be handled if the inner loop is analyzable by syntactic analysis. If it has to be analysed by semantic loop analysis (according to section 2.3), it must be analyzed in each iteration of the outer loop, and little speed-up is gained.

As we don't execute the body in a syntactic loop analysis, we will not get the possible values of the variables updated in the body (except for the value of the condition expression or loop index). This is of course a serious drawback of the analysis, if we need those values for the analysis after the loop or for inner loops.

However, we can calculate the values for those variables by syntactic loop analysis, if we can find a formula for their values as we leave the loop. This is possible if the variables are updated in the same way that we can handle for the loop variable. (This is similar to the notion of *induction variables* in compiler theory: a variable is called an induction variable of a loop if it is incremented or decremented by some constant every time it changes value [2]).

We can also find non-terminating loops by syntactic analysis. A simple example of this is the following loop:

$$(i > k) \text{ whileTrue: } [i := i+c]$$

giving the following result, after a similar analysis as above:

$$n = 0 \text{ and } i = i_0 \text{ if } i_0 \leq k$$
$$n = \perp \text{ and } i = \perp \text{ if } i_0 > k.$$

As above, the assumptions 1 – 4 above has to be checked in a non-trivial loop body for the result to hold.

6. Conclusions. We have presented a new method which can be used to derive annotations for paths and loops automatically. The purpose of the method is to relieve the real-time programmer from the diffucult and error-prone task of determining annotations manually. The method also gives a number of spin-off results, like safe estimations of possible values of variables, sizes and contents of collections, and discovery of dead code.

The method is demonstrated for a subset of Smalltalk. We have omitted recursion and most classes and primitives that are included in a Smalltalk implementation. We are convinced that our method can be extended to cover also these parts of Smalltalk. We can not allow the class hierarchy to be changed during runtime, however, since this could change the semantics of the programs.

Because the method is based on the general notion of abstract interpretation, it can be adapted to other object-oriented languages, like C++, Ada95 and Java. A potential problem is state growth during analysis of complex loops. In order to limit the calculation cost, we have described some ways to make approximations. We have also pointed out a method, syntactic loop analysis, that can be used to make analysis of simple loops more efficient.

7. Future work. Future work includes defining a detailed abstract semantics for the analysis, based on a concrete semantics of Smalltalk [17], and to develop a prototype tool. Special consideration will be taken to complexity and how the method scales.

An interesting question is: how are hard real-time programs written "out there" in the real world? How complicated constructs are the programmers really using? Do they avoid certain features that make programs harder to analyze? What aspects of $WCET_C$ calculation should we give priority to?

The authors are conducting an investigation in Swedish industry to find out what the reality looks like. An inquiry has been answered by 50+ companies working with software for embedded systems (see [8]). The main goal of the investigation was to find out how the companies calculate $WCET_C$ today, and their attitude towards a $WCET_C$ tool (what functions should be included etc.). A part of the questionnaire included questions about the C language; could certain language constructs be removed to gain more analyzable programs? The inquiry is followed up by a number of interviews with software designers and programmers. We think that we can discern two different streams in the real-time programming area.

- The first is a trend towards simple and highly modulized software, especially for embedded systems and smaller control systems. The real-time operating system allows the software to be broken down in many small, simple and relatively independent modules. Potentially dangerous features like recursion, function pointers and dynamic allocation of memory (in C) are avoided or even forbidden. Complex while-loops are avoided and replaced by simpler for-loops with a fixed number of iterations.

- The second is a trend towards more and more complex real-time systems and applications, still with hard real-time demands. We can see this trend in larger control systems, multi-media and games.

To start with, we will concentrate on software of the first type. In such systems, complexity is a smaller problem than in the second type. Maybe, syntactic analysis may even be sufficient for parts of the loop analysis.

Further investigation will show how these trends develop and inspire new ideas for the program analysis and our $WCET_C$ calculation research.

REFERENCES

[1] P. Altenbernd. On the false path problem in hard real-time programs. In *Proceedings of the Eight Euromicro Workshop on Real-Time Systems*, pages 102–107, June 1996.

[2] A. V. Aho, R. Sethi, and J. D. Ullman. *Compilers – Principles, Techniques, and Tools*, chapter 10, Code optimizations. Addison - Wesley, 1986.

[3] J. Blieberger. Discrete loops and worst case performance. *Computing Languages*, 20(3):193–212, 1994.

[4] F. Bourdoncle. Abstract debugging of high-order imperative languages. In *Proceedings of SIGPLAN'93 Conference on Programming Language design and Implementation*, pages 46–55, 1993.

[5] R. Chapman, A. Burns, and A. Wellings. Integrated program proof and worst-case timing analysis of SPARK Ada. In *ACM Sigplan Workshop on Language, Compiler and Tool Support for Real-Time Systems*, June 1994.

[6] P. Cousot and R. Cousot. Abstract interpretation: A unified model for static analysis of programs by construction or approximation of fixpoints. In *4th ACM Symp. on Principles of Programming Languages*, pages 238–252, 1977.

[7] A. Ermedahl and J. Gustafsson. Deriving annotations for tight calculation of execution time. In *EuroPar'97, workshop 20, Real-Time Systems and Constraints, Passau, Germany*, Aug 1997.

[8] A. Ermedahl and J. Gustavsson. Enkät om realtids industrins syn på verktyg för exekveringstidsanalys, (inquiry towards the real-time industry of its view of tools for execution time analysis). Technical report, Department of Computer Systems, Uppsala University, Sweden, 1997. In swedish.

[9] C. Eriksson, J. Mäki-Turja, K. Post, M. Gustafsson, J. Gustafsson, K. Sandström, and E. Brorson. An overview of RTT - a design framework for real-time systems. *The Journal of Parallel and Distributed Computing*, 36, 1996.

[10] C. Forsyth. Implementation of the worst-case execution analyser. *York Software Engineering Ltd*, 1992.

[11] R. L. Graham, D. E. Knuth, and O. Patashnik. *Concrete Mathematics – A foundation for Computer Science*. Addison - Wesley, 1989.

[12] Jan Gustafsson, Kjell Post, Jukka Mäki-Turja, and Ellus Brorsson. Benefits of type inference for an object-oriented real-time language. In *WOORTS'95, the Workshop on Object-Oriented Real-Time Systems at the Seventh IEEE Symposium on Parallel and Distributed Processing, San Antonio, Texas, USA*, Oct 1995.

[13] A. Goldberg and D. Robson. *Smalltalk 80, The Language*. Addison - Wesley, 1989.

[14] W. Harrison. Compiler analysis of the value range of variables. *IEEE Transactions on Software Engineering*, SE-3, 1977.

[15] C. Liu and J. Leyland. Scheduling algorithms for multiprogramming in hard real-time environment. *Journal of the ACM*, pages 46 – 61, Jan 1973.

[16] Y-T.S. Li and S. Malik. Performance analysis of embedded software using implicit path enumeration. In *ACM Workshop on Lang., Comp. and Tools for RTS*, May 1995.

[17] J. Mäki-Turja, K. Post, and J. Gustafsson. An operational semantics for Smalltalk. Department of Computer Engineering, Mälardalen University, Sweden, Feb 1997.

[18] H. R. Nielson and F. Nielson. *Semantics with Applications*. John Wiley & Sons, 1992.

[19] C.Y. Park. Predicting program execution times by analyzing static and dynamic program paths. *The Journal of Real-Time System*, 5:31–62, 1993.

[20] J. R. C. Patterson. Accurate static branch prediction by value range propagation. In *SIGPLAN'95 Conference on of Programming Language Design and Implementation (PLDI'95)*, pages 67–78, 1995.

[21] P. Puschner and C. Koza. Calculating the maximum execution time of real-time programs. *The Journal of Real-Time Systems*, 1(2):159 –176, Sep 1989.

[22] C.Y. Park and A.C. Shaw. Experiments with a program timing tool based on a source-level timing schema. *Proceeding of 11th IEEE Real-Time Systems Symposium*, pages 72–81, Dec 1990.

[23] P. Puschner and A. Schedl. Computing maximum task execution times with linear programming techniques. Technical report, Report, Techn. Univ., Inst. für Technische Informatik, Vienna, April 1995.

[24] C. Verbrugge, P. Co, and L. Hendren. Generalized constant propagation i C. In *Proceedings of the 6th International Conference on Compiler Construction, CC'96*, April 1996.

INTEGRATED SCHEDULING OF TASKS AND MESSAGES IN DISTRIBUTED REAL-TIME SYSTEMS*

G. MANIMARAN[†], SHASHIDHAR MERUGU[‡], ANAND MANIKUTTY[§], AND C. SIVA RAM MURTHY[¶]

Abstract. The demand for more and more complex real-time applications which require high computational needs with timing constraints, and geographical distribution of computational entities (tasks) of these applications, have led to the choice of distributed systems as a natural candidate for supporting such real-time applications, due to their potential for high performance and reliability. The distributed real-time system considered here consists of uniprocessor or multiprocessor nodes connected through a multihop network. Scheduling of tasks in such a system involves scheduling of dynamically arriving tasks within a node (*local scheduling*), migration of tasks across the network (*global scheduling*) if it is not possible to schedule them locally, and (iii) scheduling of messages on communication links (*message scheduling*) to support inter-task communication and task migration. Most of the existing schemes on scheduling in distributed real-time systems have addressed each of these issues in isolation. Moreover, these schemes consider the load on the processors at a node as the basis to migrate tasks from a heavily loaded node (sender) to a lightly loaded node (receiver). We believe that the identification of a receiver node should be based not only on the load on its processors, but also on the availability of a path, which satisfies the bandwidth required for the task migration, from the sender to that receiver. In this paper, we present an integrated framework for scheduling dynamically arriving real-time tasks in distributed real-time systems. Our proposal consists of (i) algorithms for global scheduling and (ii) interactions among the three schedulers in a way to improve the schedulability of the system. The effectiveness of the proposed framework has been evaluated through simulation by comparing it with existing schemes.

1. Introduction. Distributed real-time systems are natural candidates for real-time applications due to their potential for high performance and reliability. The distributed real-time system considered here consists of uniprocessor or multiprocessor nodes connected through a multihop network. Tasks arrive at each node dynamically (aperiodic tasks) and possibly communicate with tasks in other nodes by message passing. Each task has a deadline before which its execution must be completed and each message has an end-to-end deadline before which it should reach its destination node. Scheduling in distributed real-time systems involves scheduling of tasks within a node (*local scheduling*), migration of tasks to other nodes (*global scheduling*) if it is not possible to schedule them locally, and scheduling of messages on communication links (*message scheduling*).

---

*This work was supported by the Department of Science and Technology, New Delhi.

†Dept. of Computer Science and Engineering, Indian Institute of Technology Madras, Chennai 600036 (gmani@bronto.iitm.ernet.in).

‡College of Computing, Georgia Institute of Technology Atlanta, GA 30332-0280 (merugu@cc.gatech.edu).

§Dept. of Computer Sciences, University of Wisconsin Madison, WI 53706 (manikuti@cs.wisc.edu).

¶Dept. of Computer Science and Engineering, Indian Institute of Technology Madras, Chennai 600036 (murthy@iitm.ernet.in).

The problem of local scheduling [2, 9, 11] is to determine when and on which processor a given task executes. For scheduling tasks in a node, all the tasks arrive at the task scheduler (which does local scheduling) from where they are distributed to other processors in the node for execution. The task scheduler dynamically determines the feasibility of scheduling newly arriving tasks without jeopardizing the guarantees that have been provided for the previously scheduled tasks. The communication between the task scheduler and the processors is through *dispatch queues*. Each processor has its own dispatch queue. The task scheduler runs in parallel with the processors, scheduling the newly arriving tasks, and periodically updating the dispatch queues [10, 14].

Three important components of a global scheduling algorithm are its *transfer policy, location policy*, and *information policy* [16]. The transfer policy at a node determines whether the node is in a suitable state to participate in a task transfer either as a sender or as a receiver. Many proposed transfer policies are *threshold* based [6, 15]. The location policy at a node determines where a task should be transferred. Most of the existing location policies find a suitable receiver node through *polling*. The major drawbacks of this approach are: 1) the delay involved in probing the nodes and 2) a suitable receiver may not be identified within the polling limit if the system has few lightly loaded nodes. This causes the missing of tasks' deadlines. Location policies are broadly classified as *sender-initiated* [12, 15, 17, 19], in which potential senders search for suitable receivers, *receiver-initiated* [3], in which potential receivers search for suitable senders, and *symmetrically initiated* [6], in which both senders and receivers search for complementary nodes. The information policy decides when information about the states of other nodes in the system is collected, what information is collected, and where it is collected from. There are three types of information policies: 1) demand driven 2) periodic and 3) state-change driven. Focussed addressing, bidding, and flexible algorithms proposed in [17] are demand-driven policies. The buddy set algorithm proposed in [15] is state-change driven.

The message scheduler at a node is responsible for scheduling aperiodic messages, which require a delay bound on message delivery, among communicating tasks which are executing on different nodes. Also, it schedules messages, which constitute a task, during task transfer from a heavily loaded node to a lightly loaded node so that they reach their destination with bounded delay. To guarantee time-constrained communication of messages, real-time channels are to be established with specified traffic characteristics and performance requirements. The traffic characteristics include parameters such as maximum message rate, maximum message size, and maximum burst size and parameters such as maximum end-to-end delay and jitter, and maximum loss rate constitute the performance requirements. There are two distinct phases involved in handling real-time channels: channel establishment and run-time message scheduling. The channel establishment phase involves the selection of a route for the channel satisfying traffic characteristics and performance requirements. In [4], a scheme for establishing a real-time channel has been discussed. The real-time channel establishment procedure with associated schedulability check and run-time scheduling of messages in a multihop network is given in [5]. Algorithms for distributed scheduling of real-time tasks in multiple-access and multihop networks are proposed in [13] and [1], respectively. Unlike ours, these algorithms consider periodic tasks whose schedule is constructed off-line.

The objective of any distributed real-time scheduling algorithm is to meet the deadlines of dynamically arriving tasks. The performance metric used to evaluate the effectiveness of a scheduling algorithm is the *guarantee ratio* defined as the ratio of the number of tasks guaranteed to meet their deadline to the number of tasks arrived. The goal of this work is to maximize the guarantee ratio. The scheduling algorithm should be efficient in the sense that it should offer better guarantee ratio with a minimal scheduling cost.

None of the above and other known works consider the impact of the message scheduler on the task scheduler and vice-versa in distributed real-time task scheduling. The main contribution of our work is to bring out the possible interactions between these two schedulers and other modules such as transfer policy, location policy, and information policy of a node, and to study the effect of these interactions in improving the guarantee ratio.

The rest of the paper is organized as follows. In section 2, we discuss our approach to the distributed real-time scheduling problem. In Section 3, we describe the motivation for interaction among various components and the kinds of interactions we propose for improving the guarantee ratio. The simulation results are presented in Section 4, and finally, in Section 5, some concluding remarks are made.

2. Our Approach to the Distributed Scheduling. In this section, we present our approach to the distributed real-time scheduling problem which involves the following:

1. *Task scheduler:* a variation of myopic scheduling algorithm [11] (scheduling algorithm used in the Spring kernel) has been used for local scheduling.
2. *Message scheduler:* a rate-based scheduler similar to Hierarchical Round Robin (HRR) [18] has been used for message scheduling.
3. *Information Policy:* a new Maekawa set [7] based state exchange protocol has been proposed.
4. *Transfer Policy:* a new adaptive load determination algorithm has been proposed.
5. *Location Policy:* a new heuristic algorithm has been proposed which takes into account the states of both the nodes and links of the network, and existing connection status from (or through) the current node.
6. *Interactions:* a set of interactions between the message scheduler and transfer policy, and the message scheduler and location policy has been proposed.

The schematic of a node in the distributed real-time system is shown in Fig. 1. In the rest of the section, we discuss the functionality of the modules of a node. The interactions between these modules are discussed in the next section.

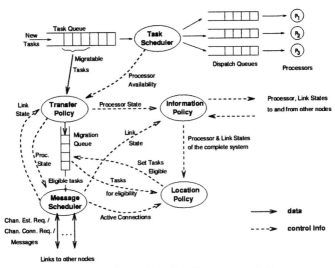

FIG. 1. *Schematic of a node in the distributed real-time system.*

2.1. State of a Node. Most of the existing work consider the state of the node only in terms of the load on the processors, for task transfer. This has the following potential problem: when a node is heavily loaded, it finds a suitable receiver based on its location policy and then transfers a task to it. If none of the routes to the receiver node is able to provide the required real-time channel for the task transfer, then the identified receiver node cannot be a receiver. Also, even if there is a routing path, it might be costlier than the routing path to some other possible receiver which has not been considered. This may result in missing of task deadlines.

The above problem motivates us to define the state of a node as the combination of the load on its processors as well as that on its links. The load on the processors (*processor state*) can be in any of the following states:

- LIGHT state: the processors are idle most of the time without tasks for execution.
- HEAVY state: the processors are always busy executing tasks and the task queue has many tasks with tight laxities.
- MEDIUM state: neither in LIGHT state nor in HEAVY state.

Similarly, the load on the links (*link state*) can be in any of the following states:

- LIGHT state: the message scheduler can accept incoming channel establishment requests.
- HEAVY state: the message scheduler cannot accept the incoming channel establishment requests.
- MEDIUM state: the message scheduler can either accept or reject incoming channel establishment requests depending on the processor state.

The channel establishment requests are made either for transferring tasks or for sending aperiodic messages between tasks running on different nodes. A node is qualified to be a receiver for task transfer from a sender only when its processor state is LIGHT and the link states along the route (including its link state) from the sender node to the receiver node is either in LIGHT or in MEDIUM state. A node is said to be in HEAVY state if its processor state is HEAVY irrespective of its link state.

2.2. Task Scheduler. The myopic algorithm, proposed in [11] for scheduling aperiodic tasks with resource constraints, is a heuristic search algorithm which operates on a set of tasks. A variation of myopic algorithm [9] has been used for local scheduling that works as follows:

1. Order the tasks in non-decreasing order of deadline (d_i) in the task queue.
2. Start with an empty partial schedule. (i.e., no task in the schedule).
3. Determine whether the current schedule is strongly feasible (check if first K tasks meet their deadlines when considered independently).
4. If found to be feasible,

(a) Compute heuristic function $(H = d_i + W * EST(T_i))$ for the first K tasks, where W is an input parameter and $EST(T_i)$ is the earliest start time of task T_i.

(b) Choose the task with the best (smallest) H value to extend the schedule.
5. else

(a) Backtrack to the previous search level.

(b) Extend the schedule with the task having next best H value.
6. Repeat steps (3-5) until a termination condition is met.

The termination conditions for the algorithm are either (a) a complete feasible schedule has been found, or (b) maximum number of backtracks or H function evaluations has been reached, or (c) no more backtracking is possible.

2.3. Information Policy. Here, we propose a new information policy algorithm for distributed real-time task scheduling. This algorithm is based on the Maekawa set used in distributed mutual exclusion algorithm [7]. In the algorithm, the sender does not probe nodes for receiving a task. Instead it collects information about potential receivers in advance. This is essential in real-time systems since probing nodes is a time consuming process and hence the chances of a task missing its deadline due to probing is high. The Maekawa set has been chosen to give equal responsibility to every node in state information exchange, using minimal number messages, with decentralized control.

2.3.1. Data Structures. Each node maintains the following three sets for efficient information policy:

- Request set: Set of nodes to which the current node requests for state information.
- Inform set: Set of nodes to which the current node informs its state.
- Status set: Set of nodes whose state is maintained by the current node.

The Request set is constructed using finite projective plane method and the size of the set is $\sqrt{N}$ [7], where N is the number of nodes. The Inform set is the same as the Request set. The Status set is the set of all nodes in whose

Request set the present node lies. In Maekawa sets, for any two nodes i and j, one of the following holds: (i) the Inform sets overlap - the Request sets of either node overlaps with the Inform set of the other node and hence the mutual state information exchange occurs in two steps and (ii) both nodes lie in the other's Request set - hence, mutual state information exchange occurs in one step. Thus, the information policy algorithm intends to capture the complete state of the system for deciding the best receiver node to transfer a task from a heavily loaded node (i.e., the sender) in a very short duration of time (at most two steps) and simultaneously keeps the number of state exchange messages small.

2.3.2. State Exchange Protocol. Nodes exchange state messages containing the state of both their processors and links [8]. This aids in identifying an actual receiver node overcoming the problems stated in Section 2.1. We use the following protocol which depends on the processor state:

- LIGHT state: Inform(LIGHT) message is sent to its Inform set nodes. The current node informs its Inform set that the processor state of the node is in LIGHT state and hence the node can receive task(s). It also informs the state of its links. If the Inform(LIGHT) message does not reach a node in the Inform set within the periodic interval, they record the state of the current node as MEDIUM or HEAVY in their Status sets. A message may not reach its destination either due to its current node being in MEDIUM/HEAVY state or due to failures in intermediate nodes/links.
- MEDIUM state: Request(node state) message is sent to its Request set nodes. The current node requests its Request set nodes about their state which will be used when the current node becomes HEAVY. Reply(node state) is received from its Request set nodes. This is in response to the Request(node state) message from the current node. It is important to note that once the current node receives the responses from all of its Request set nodes, it has complete knowledge about all the node states of the distributed system.
- HEAVY state: Establish real-time channel to a receiver node and transfer a set of tasks to it. Tear down the channel once the tasks have been migrated.
  Since the information policy collected the state information of other nodes when its processor state was MEDIUM, anticipating that the node might enter HEAVY state, it has complete state information *in advance* which can be used to find the best receiver quickly. This is crucial in the context of real-time scheduling since no time is wasted to find the receiver once the current node has become HEAVY. Once the receiver has been found, a channel can be established and task transfer takes place. The channel is torn down on completion of task transfer.

2.4. Transfer Policy. The transfer policy decides which tasks are to be migrated and when they are to be migrated. To achieve this, it needs to deter-

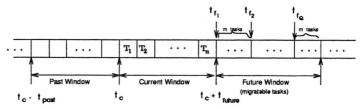

FIG. 2. *Task queue as viewed by the transfer policy.*

mine the processor state which depends on (a) the current load on the processors, (b) the past load within a time interval, and (c) the future estimate of the load. Having decided the processor state, the transfer policy uses the link state of the node for moving the tasks to the migration queue. This is discussed in detail in Section 3.1. The computation of the processor state is based on the heuristic described below.

The task queue of the myopic algorithm is divided into three regions, namely, *past window*, *current window*, and *future window* as in Fig. 2. Let t_c be the time at which the current window begins, i.e., the present time. T_p is the set of tasks in the past window which have been feasibly scheduled by the scheduler between times $(t_c - t_{past})$ and t_c. T_c is the set of tasks whose deadline is between t_c and $(t_c + t_{future})$. T_f is the set of FUT_WIN_SIZ tasks with deadline greater than $(t_c + t_{future})$. t_{past}, t_{future}, and FUT_WIN_SIZ are input parameters. Let $T_{f1}, T_{f2}, ..., T_{fQ}$ be equal partitions of the set T_f whose cardinalities are m, except possibly T_{fQ}, where m is the number of processors in the current node and $Q = \lceil |T_f|/m \rceil$. t_{f1} is the estimated start time of the tasks in the first partition T_{f1} and is computed as:

$$(2.1) \qquad t_{f1} = t_c + \frac{C_{av} * |T_c|}{m}$$

where C_{av} is the average worst case computation time of a task. Then, the estimated start time of the tasks in the k-th partition is computed as:

$$(2.2) \qquad t_{fk} = t_{f(k-1)} + C_{av}, \quad 2 \leq k \leq Q$$

The overall laxity (urgency), L_{index}, of the tasks in the current node is defined in terms of laxity of tasks in the past and future windows, which is defined as:

$$(2.3) \quad L_{index} = \frac{\sum_{\tau_i \in T_p} (d_i - f_i)}{|T_p|} + W\_LDF * \left(\sum_{k=1}^{Q} \frac{\sum_{\tau_i \in T_{fk}} (d_i - t_{fk} - c_i)}{|T_{fk}|} \right) / Q$$

where d_i, f_i, and c_i are the deadline, finish time, and worst case computation time of task τ_i, respectively. W_LDF is an input parameter which represents the weight associated with the future load estimation. The state of the processors in a node is defined as:

$$proc\ state = \begin{cases} LIGHT & \text{if } L_{index} \leq L_{low} \\ MEDIUM & \text{if } L_{low} < L_{index} < L_{high} \\ HEAVY & \text{if } L_{index} \geq L_{high} \end{cases}$$

where L_{low} and L_{high} are the input parameters denoting low and high threshold values of laxity. Based on the processor state and the link state, the transfer policy decides to move tasks from the task queue to the migration queue. The number of tasks M moved is calculated as follows:

$$(2.4) \qquad M = min \left\{ \frac{FW\_SIZ * (L_{index} - L_{avg})}{|L_{index}|}, FW\_SIZ \right\}$$

where $L_{avg} = (L_{high} + L_{low})/2$. The set of tasks chosen is the first M tasks in the future window in the increasing order of laxity. The transfer policy is invoked just before the invocation of the task scheduler. The execution time of the transfer policy is assumed to be very small compared to the execution time of the task scheduler.

The state of every outgoing link is defined as:

$$link\ state = \begin{cases} LIGHT & \text{if } B_{index} \leq B_{low} \\ MEDIUM & \text{if } B_{low} < B_{index} < B_{high} \\ HEAVY & \text{if } B_{index} \geq B_{high} \end{cases}$$

where B_{index} is the fraction of the total bandwidth of a link currently being utilized, and B_{low} and B_{high} denote the low and high threshold values of bandwidth utilized in a link, respectively.

2.5. Location Policy. Due to space limitation, we briefly mention the essence of our location policy. The function of the location policy is to identify suitable receivers for the tasks in the migration queue based on the node and link states of the entire distributed system (obtained from the information policy) and the currently active task migration channels from the current node (obtained from the message scheduler) to other nodes. The location policy does the following:

1. It picks up one or more tasks from the migration queue and identifies LIGHT receiver nodes for them with associated routing path. During this process it might decide to send group of tasks to the same destination if the receiver node state permits so. Sending a group of tasks to the same destination eliminates the channel establishment for subsequent tasks.

2. It marks the tasks as eligible and places them into the migration queue after filling information related to task transfer such as destination node, routing path to the destination node, and the task grouping identification. The tasks with all these information filled are called *eligible tasks* for migration.

2.6. Message Scheduler. The tasks in the migration queue which are marked eligible by the location policy are considered for transfer by the message scheduler. The HRR [18] scheduling policy has been used for message scheduling. Before transferring a task from a sender to a receiver, a real-time channel has to be established with a required Quality of Service (QoS) specified by the source node in terms of delay bound and the traffic is characterized as periodic with associated rate. Source routing (which is computed by the location policy) has been used during channel establishment. During channel establishment, the call admission test has been carried out, i.e., we check whether the sum of the utilization[1] of the link by all the channels passing through the link is less than or equal to one. Once the channel has been established, the data transfer (task migration) begins with the data rate specified at the time of channel establishment. After migrating the task, the channel is torn down.

2.7. Real-time Channel Requirements.

- Permanent real-time channels for state exchange messages which are used as part of the information policy. These are multicast channels among the nodes as determined by the Maekawa set.

- Permanent real-time channels with variable bandwidth (over time) for exchanging aperiodic messages which are generated on completion of aperiodic tasks. These channels are among all pairs of nodes with some approximate performance requirements. The performance parameters of a channel such as message generation rate (which decides the bandwidth requirement) are varied dynamically by observing the message traffic on the channel over a period of time. Here, we do not discuss the problem of dynamically varying the bandwidth of a channel.

- Non-permanent channel for migrating a task from a heavily loaded node to a lightly loaded node. This channel is torn down after the task is migrated.

3. Interaction Among Modules of a Node. In this section, we bring out the motivation for interaction among various modules and discuss the kinds of interactions that will improve the guarantee ratio.

3.1. Interaction Between Message Scheduler and Transfer Policy. The motivation for interaction between the message scheduler (MS) and transfer policy (TP) [8] is given below and the effect of interaction is given in Fig. 3.

1. Due to lack of interaction between location policy and message scheduler, the transfer policy might move unguaranteed tasks from the task queue (TQ) to the migration queue (MQ) without knowing the link state. If the link happens to be heavily loaded, the message scheduler would not be able to transfer the tasks which would result in missing of task deadlines. Instead, if the transfer policy had not moved those tasks from the task queue, they possibly would have been scheduled successfully in the local node itself.

2. Similarly, due to lack of interaction, the call admission control (CAC) of the message scheduler may accept incoming channel requests even if the processor state of the node to which it belongs is in HEAVY state. This

---

[1]ratio of service time of a message to its period

would saturate the link usage such that task migration is not possible from the current node. This will also result in missing of deadlines.

Action by	Proc. state	Link state	Action taken
	HEAVY	LIGHT	move tasks from TQ to MQ
Transfer	HEAVY	HEAVY	don't move tasks
Policy	LIGHT	–	don't move tasks
	MEDIUM	–	don't move tasks
	HEAVY	–	reject incoming channel requests
	MEDIUM	LIGHT	accept/reject is decided by CAC
Message	MEDIUM	MEDIUM	reject incoming channel requests
Scheduler	MEDIUM	HEAVY	reject incoming channel requests
	LIGHT	–	accept/reject is decided by CAC

FIG. 3. *Effect of interaction between message scheduler and transfer policy.*

3.2. Interaction Between Message Scheduler and Location Policy. The location policy uses information, obtained from the message scheduler about the active connections from the current node, for deciding whether some of the tasks in the migration queue can be transferred, using already established migration channels. This reduces the channel establishment time which is very crucial in the context of real-time systems. The message scheduler establishes channels for the eligible tasks in the migration queue, if required, for the destinations decided and using the routing path specified by the location policy.

The chances of more than one heavily loaded node transferring tasks to the same lightly loaded node, even if there are many lightly loaded nodes in the system, are very small due to the fact that the sender establishes channel to a receiver node before transferring task to it. If the receiver node has changed state because of a successful channel establishment from one sender, it can always reject the channel requests from other senders. The rejected senders try their next best receivers for their task transfer, and so on, provided the tasks meet their deadline by transferring to other nodes.

4. Simulation Studies. We have conducted extensive simulations to study the effectiveness of our distributed real-time scheduling framework. In our evaluation, we have also studied the significance of making use of link state information and interactions among components. For simulation, we have considered a distributed system of 9 nodes connected as a 3×3 mesh topology. Each node comprises of 8 processors used for executing tasks. The inter-arrival rate of the tasks is based on a pseudo-random distribution whose mean is obtained by the formula $A * b^i$ for the ith node, where $A > 0, b > 1, i = 0, 1, 2, 3, ..$ [12]. The values of A, b, feasibility check window size and the average laxity have been taken as 3, 1.3, 18 and 4, respectively (if they are not specified, otherwise). The average single hop time has been taken as 15 time units and each link is assumed to have a total bandwidth of 30 units. The minimum and maximum bandwidth required per connection is 6 and 10 units, respectively. The curves in these figures (Figs. 4-7) correspond to the following schemes :

1. *No Migration* : Each node schedules its tasks locally and there is no migration at all.

2. *Random* : The selection of a destination for migration of a task is random. Here, the state exchange among nodes does not take place.

3. *Focussed* : In this scheme [17], the location policy considers only the processor(s) state of the nodes in selecting a potential receiver for migration of tasks. Each node has the knowledge of the status of the entire system (information policy) obtained by the periodic state exchange policy based on Maekawa sets or some other means.

4. *Our Algorithm* : This is a full-fledged scheme that makes use of Maekawa set based information policy, interactions between message scheduler and global scheduling policies, processor and link states for identifying the receiver node.

In a real-time system, while evaluating the effectiveness of different algorithms, it is necessary to equate the scheduling costs of different algorithms. In our experiments, this is achieved by adding the worst case computation time of the algorithm under evaluation to the worst case computation time of every task. That is, a task takes more time to execute when a more complex scheduling algorithm is used, compared to its execution time when a less complex scheduling algorithm is used. The different parameters considered in the simulation are specified in the following table.

Parameter	Explanation
Task Laxity	laxity parameter which decides the deadline of tasks
Task Load	amount of system wide computation demand per processor per unit time
Proc. per Node	number of processors per node
Bandwidth	bandwidth of each of the links

From the graphs plotted in Figs. 4-7, it can be observed that the proposed scheme performs better than the other three algorithms for all the parameters varied. The simulation results indicate that the guarantee ratio can be improved by a large extent by making the modules of a node interact and using the states of both the processors and links for taking global scheduling decisions. The following trends are observed for variation of different parameters:

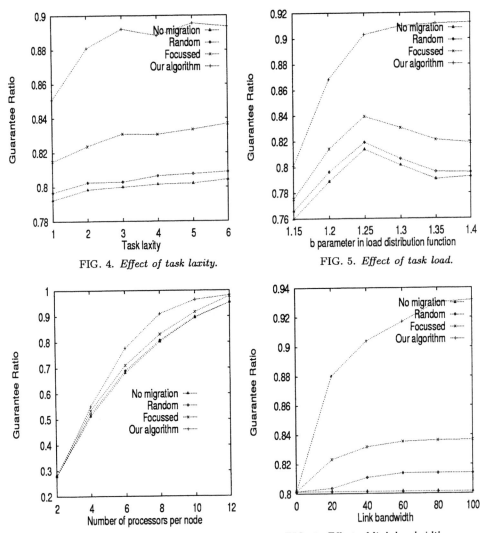

FIG. 4. *Effect of task laxity.*

FIG. 5. *Effect of task load.*

FIG. 6. *Effect of number of processors.*

FIG. 7. *Effect of link bandwidth.*

1. *Task Laxity:* The guarantee ratio of the system increases with the increase in the average laxity of the tasks arrived (Fig. 4). The algorithms which consider interactions are able to show considerable improvement for even lower laxity values. At higher laxity values, the migration is very effective since the heavy nodes can easily transfer their excess tasks which can be scheduled at the light nodes.

2. *Task Load:* Here, we have studied the variation in the arriving pattern of the tasks by varying the value of b (Fig. 5). Initially, we observe an increase in the guarantee ratio since the heavy nodes become lighter and are able to schedule more tasks. However, after a point, the guarantee ratio decreases because the system on the whole becomes heavier and

there will be a certain number of tasks that are always rejected.

3. *Proc. per Node:* This is to study the scalability of the framework. The guarantee ratio of the system increases with the increase in the number of processors available to execute the tasks at each node (Fig. 6). Since the arrival rate of the tasks is the same, the increase in the number of processors makes the nodes lighter. These curves tend to converge at either extreme, because at those points the load on all the nodes is uniform and migration is not effective.

4. *Bandwidth of the Links:* We observe that an increase in the bandwidth of the links increases the guarantee ratio of the system as many connections can be established for migrating tasks (Fig. 7).

5. Conclusions. In this paper, we have highlighted the significance of considering states of both processors and links for taking global scheduling decisions, and proposed interactions among local, global, and message schedulers, which were not found in earlier works. We have conducted extensive simulation studies to demonstrate the effectiveness of these proposals. Our studies reveal that (i) migration always improves the guarantee ratio, (ii) interactions among schedulers result in better guarantee ratio than non-interaction, and (iii) identification of a receiver node, for task transfer, based on the knowledge of both processor and link states improves the guarantee ratio.

REFERENCES

[1] T.F. ABDELZAHER AND K.G. SHIN, *Optimal combined task and message scheduling in distributed real-time systems,* In Real-Time Systems Symp., (1995), pp.162-171.

[2] M.L. DERTOUZOS AND A.K. MOK, *Multiprocessor on-line scheduling of hard real-time tasks,* IEEE Trans. Software Engg., 15(12) (1989), pp.1497-1506.

[3] D. FERGUSON, Y. YEMINI, AND A. NIKALAOU, *Microeconomic algorithms for load balancing in distributed computer systems,* International Conf. on Distributed Computing Systems, (1988), pp.491-499.

[4] D. FERRARI AND D.C. VERMA, *A scheme for real-time channel establishment in wide-area networks,* IEEE J. Select. Areas Commun., 8(4) (1990), pp.368-379.

[5] D.D. KANDLUR, K.G. SHIN, AND D. FERRARI, *Real-time communication in multihop networks,* IEEE Trans. Parallel and Distributed Systems, 5(10) (1994), pp.1044-1056.

[6] P. KRUEGER AND N.G. SHIVARATRI, *Adaptive location policies for global scheduling,* IEEE Trans. Software Engg., 20(6) (1994), pp.432-444.

[7] M. MAEKAWA, *A $\sqrt{N}$ algorithm for mutual exclusion in decentralised systems,* ACM Trans. Computer Systems, 2(2) (1985), pp.145-158.

[8] G. MANIMARAN, M. SHASHIDHAR, ANAND MANIKUTTY, AND C. SIVA RAM MURTHY, *Integrated scheduling of tasks and messages in distributed real-time systems,* In Proc. IEEE Joint International Workshop on Parallel and Distributed Real-Time Systems, (1997), pp.64-71.

[9] G. MANIMARAN AND C. SIVA RAM MURTHY, *An efficient dynamic scheduling algorithm for multiprocessor real-time systems,* IEEE Trans. Parallel and Distributed Systems, 9(3), (1998), pp.312-319.

[10] G. MANIMARAN, C. SIVA RAM MURTHY, MACHIRAJU VIJAY, AND K. RAMAMRITHAM, *New algorithms for resource reclaiming from precedence constrained tasks in multiprocessor real-time systems,* Journal of Parallel and Distributed Computing, 44(2) (1997), pp.123-132.

[11] K. RAMAMRITHAM, J. A. STANKOVIC, AND P.-F. SHIAH, *Efficient scheduling algorithms for real-time multiprocessor systems*, IEEE Trans. Parallel and Distributed Systems, 1(2) (1990), pp.184-194.

[12] K. RAMAMRITHAM, J.A. STANKOVIC, AND W. ZHAO, *Distributed scheduling of tasks with deadlines and resource requirements*, IEEE Trans. Computers, 38(8) (1989), pp.1110-1123.

[13] K. RAMAMRITHAM, *Allocation and scheduling of precedence-related periodic tasks*, IEEE Trans. Computers, 6(4) (1995), pp.412-420.

[14] C. SHEN, K. RAMAMRITHAM, AND J.A. STANKOVIC, *Resource reclaiming in multiprocessor real-time systems*, IEEE Trans. Parallel and Distributed Systems, 4(4) (1993), pp.382-397.

[15] K.G. SHIN AND Y.G. CHANG, *Load sharing in distributed real-time systems with state-change broadcasts*, IEEE Trans. Computers, 38(8) (1989), pp.1124-1142.

[16] N.G. SHIVARATRI, P. KRUEGER, AND M. SINGHAL, *Load distributing for locally distributed systems*, IEEE Computer, (10) (1992), pp.33-44.

[17] J.A. STANKOVIC, K. RAMAMRITHAM, AND S. CHENG, *Evaluation of a flexible task scheduling algorithm for distributed hard real-time systems*, IEEE Trans. Computers, 34(12) (1985), pp.1130-1143.

[18] H. ZHANG, *Service disciplines for guaranteed performance service in packet-switching networks*, Proc. IEEE, 83(10) (1995), pp.1374-1396.

[19] S. ZHOU, *A trace-driven simulation study of dynamic load balancing*, IEEE Trans. Software Engg., 14(9) (1988), pp.1327-1341.

REAL-TIME SCHEDULING IN VIDEO SYSTEMS

E.A. DE KOCK*, E.H.L. AARTS*†, AND G. ESSINK*

Abstract. We consider the problem of mapping video algorithms onto systems of high-performance video signal processors with hard real-time constraints. The mapping problem under consideration is computationally hard due to the many constraints that need to be satisfied. We present a compact mathematical formulation which identifies the decision variables and the constraints that are involved. We demonstrate that the mapping problem is NP-hard in the strong sense. The insight resulting from the mathematical formulation leads to a solution approach in which the problem is decomposed into subproblems called delay management, partitioning, and scheduling. These subproblems are handled with well-known techniques from the literature such as network flow, local search, and constraint satisfaction.

1. Introduction. At Philips Research a programmable video signal processor system has been developed to support flexible video algorithm development and evaluation by means of real-time execution. Vissers et al. [23] provide an overview of the hardware architecture, the programming trajectory, and the applications. Programming is done by mapping a specification, given by a signal flow graph, onto a given network of processors. The mapping problem can be viewed as a feasibility problem in which operations must be assigned to processors and start times must be found such that a set of time, processor, and communication constraints is met.

Similar mapping problems in the field of video processing have been reported by Yeung & Rabaey [25] and Bove & Watlington [5]. The scheduling issues in this field have a typical strictly periodic nature; see Korst [14] and Verhaegh [21]. However, the general concepts such as memory management, partitioning, and scheduling apply to any distributed or parallel system. In each specific situation one needs to develop clear problem definitions in order to recognize these general concepts and to apply well-known solution strategies from the literature such as network flow, local search, and constraint satisfaction techniques.

In this paper we concentrate on a mathematical formulation of the video signal processor mapping problem. The mapping problem contains many constraints that originate from the video signal processor architecture under consideration. The purpose of the paper is to demonstrate that these constraints can be modeled systematically in such a way that the decision variables and the relations between memory management, partitioning, and scheduling become transparent.

The organization of the paper is as follows. In Section 2, we discuss the video signal processor architecture under consideration leading to a model of the target system. In Section 3, we discuss the specification of video algorithms in the form of signal flow graphs. In Section 4, we present a formulation of the mapping problem. In Section 5, we show that the problem is NP-hard in the

---

*Philips Research, Prof. Holstlaan 4, 5656 AA Eindhoven, The Netherlands, E-mail: kock@natlab.research.philips.com,

†Eindhoven University of Technology, P.O. Box 513, 5600 MB Eindhoven, The Netherlands.

strong sense. In Section 6, we present an overview of the developed solution approach. In Section 7, finally, we summarize some conclusions.

2. Video Signal Processor Systems. Video signal processor systems typically contain a number of interconnected video signal processors that interact with surrounding systems; see Figure 2.1. We abstract from these surround-

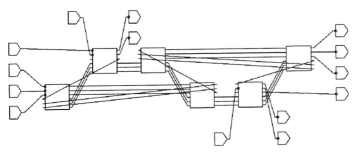

FIG. 2.1. *Graphical representation of an example of a video signal processor system. Squares represent video signal processors with inputs on the left and outputs on the right, pentagons represent input and output processors, and lines represent interconnections.*

ing systems by assuming that input processors produce incoming sample streams and that output processors consume outgoing sample streams. Examples of input and output processors are analog-to-digital converters and digital-to-analog converters. The interconnections between the processors are fixed and directed from processor inputs to processor outputs. Each processors input is connect to at most one processor output.

Internally, the video signal processors contain processing elements that are connected to a switch matrix. Both the processing elements and the switch matrix are programmable. There are four types of processing elements, i.e., arithmetic and logic elements (ALEs), memory elements (MEs), buffer elements (BEs), and output elements (OEs); see Figure 2.2. The processing elements are pipelined which means that they start a new instruction in each clock cycle. The computation results are transferred back to the switch matrix or, in case of output elements, to the outputs. The instructions are stored in program memories and the computation results are stored in programmable delay elements called silos.

The program memories are loaded with instructions via a serial download. The instructions control the switch matrix, the silos, and the cores of the processing elements. After initialization, the programs are executed cyclostatically, which means that each instruction is executed unconditionally and that the programs are executed cyclically. This guarantees real-time execution of any algorithm.

The silos consist of a random access memory and some address calculation logic. The storage capacity of the random access memory is thirty-two words. Data from the switch matrix is written cyclically in the random access memory,

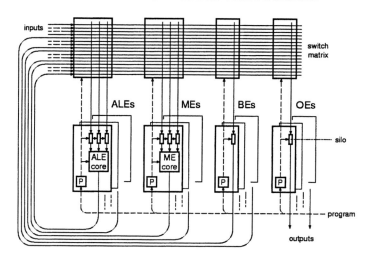

FIG. 2.2. *Video signal processor architecture.*

so the lifetime of data in a silo is thirty-one clock cycles. The read address is calculated by a modulo subtraction of the write address and the required delay length.

Beside these common resources, the various processing element types contain distinct resources which are shown in Figure 2.3. Arithmetic and logic elements

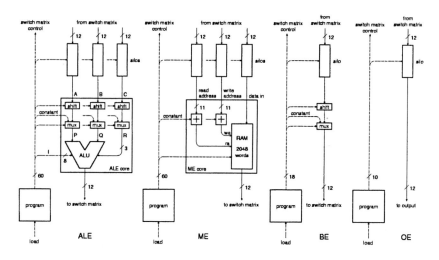

FIG. 2.3. *Processing element architectures.*

contain an arithmetic and logic unit which has a data depended instruction set. This instruction set consists of additions, subtractions, logical operations, comparisons, and multiplications. It is symmetrical so for each instruction there exists a symmetrical variant. Hence, it is always possible to maintain the functionality while swapping the contents of the two data inputs. The arithmetic and logic elements also contain programmable barrel shifters and multiplexers. The barrel shifters are used to execute arithmetical and logical shifts and the multiplexers are used to select operands from either the switch matrix or the program memories. Buffer elements also contain these barrel shifters and multiplexers. Memory elements contain a random access memory with two data ports and either one or two address ports; Figure 2.3 only shows a dual address ported memory element. Single address ported memory elements (ME1s) start at most one read or write instruction per clock cycle, while dual address ported memory elements (ME2s) can start both a read and a write instruction per clock cycle. Memory elements also contain adders which are positioned in front of the address ports to add offsets from the program memory to the addresses from the switch matrix. Dual address ported memory elements furthermore contain additional address calculation logic such that they can be used like first-in-first-out buffers. This featuring is called compact silo. In compact silos the write address is incremented each instruction cycle whereas in silos the write address is incremented in each clock cycle. The storage capacity occupied by a compact silo equals $2^{\lceil {}^2\log(n+1)\rceil}$ words from the random access memory where the integer n represents the total number of samples that must be stored. For more information about the compact silo feature the reader is referred to Dijkstra et al. [7].

The number of pipeline stages varies for each processing element type and for each input; see Table 2.1. Each pipeline stage takes one clock cycle to

TABLE 2.1
Number of pipeline stages.

input nr.	ALE	ME1	ME2	BE	OE
0	4	4	4	3	1
1	4	3	6		
2	5		3		

complete. For dual address ported memory elements that execute read and write instructions in parallel holds that the read instruction accesses the random access memory before the write instruction but that both accesses occur in the single clock cycle of the last pipeline stage.

The above-mentioned video signal processor architecture has been used for two IC versions that are called VSP1 and VSP2. The characteristics of both ICs are listed in Table 2.2.

In VSP1 each processing element has a program memory and a program counter, but in VSP2 buffer elements and output element share program memories and program counters in order to save IC area. The instruction width of arithmetic and logic elements and memory elements equals sixty bits while the instruction width of buffer elements and output elements equals eighteen and ten bits, respectively; see Figure 2.3. So three buffer elements share one program memory of sixty bits width. In the same way six output elements share

TABLE 2.2
VSP1 and VSP2 characteristics.

	VSP1	VSP2
Technology	1.2μ CMOS	0.8μ CMOS
Transistors	206,000	1,150,000
Clock	27 MHz	54 MHz
Max. program length	16	32
# ALEs	3	12
# MEs	2	4
ME storage capacity	512×12 bit	2048×12 bit
ME memory style	single port	dual port
# BEs	-	6
# inputs	5	6
# outputs (= OEs)	5	6

one program memory of sixty bits width. This saves nine program counters in total, but as a consequence the programs of the processing elements that share a program memory must have the same length. For more information about VSP1 and VSP2 the reader is referred to Van Roermund et al. [19] and Veendrick et al. [22], respectively.

The following two definitions formally describe the processing element types and the processor types. Throughout this paper, the symbol $\mathbb{IN}$ denotes the set of non-negative integers and the symbol $\mathbb{IN}_n$ denotes the set $\{0,...,n-1\}$ of the n smallest non-negative integers .

DEFINITION 2.1 (Processing Element Types). *The set* $T_p = \{\text{ALE, ME1, ME2, BE, OE, IN, OUT}\}$ *defines the set of processing element types. With this set we associate the functions*

- X_p *which defines the set of input port numbers for each* $t \in T_p$ *as*

$$X_p(t) = \begin{cases} \mathbb{IN}_0 & \text{if } t \in \{\text{IN}\} \\ \mathbb{IN}_1 & \text{if } t \in \{\text{BE, OE, OUT}\} \\ \mathbb{IN}_2 & \text{if } t \in \{\text{ME1}\} \\ \mathbb{IN}_3 & \text{if } t \in \{\text{ALE, ME2}\}, \end{cases}$$

- Y_p *which defines the set of output port numbers for each* $t \in T_p$ *as*

$$Y_p(t) = \begin{cases} \mathbb{IN}_0 & \text{if } t \in \{\text{OUT}\} \\ \mathbb{IN}_1 & \text{if } t \in T_p \setminus \{\text{OUT}\}, \end{cases}$$

- e *which defines the execution time for each* $t \in T_p$ *and each* $n \in X_p(t)$ *as listed in Table 2.1 for the nonzero values, and*
- s_p *which defines the storage capacity for each* $t \in T_p$ *as listed in Table 2.2 for the nonzero values.* □

DEFINITION 2.2 (Processor Types). *The set* $T_v = \{\text{VSP1, VSP2, INPUT, OUTPUT}\}$ *defines the set of processor types. With this set we associate the functions*

- X_v which defines the set of input port numbers for each $t \in T_v$ as

$$X_v(t) = \begin{cases} \text{IN}_5 & \text{if } t = \text{VSP1} \\ \text{IN}_6 & \text{if } t = \text{VSP2} \\ \text{IN}_0 & \text{if } t = \text{INPUT} \\ \text{IN}_1 & \text{if } t = \text{OUTPUT}, \end{cases}$$

- Y_v which defines the set of output port numbers for each $t \in T_v$ as

$$Y_v(t) = \begin{cases} \text{IN}_5 & \text{if } t = \text{VSP1} \\ \text{IN}_6 & \text{if } t = \text{VSP2} \\ \text{IN}_1 & \text{if } t = \text{INPUT} \\ \text{IN}_0 & \text{if } t = \text{OUTPUT}, \end{cases}$$

- N_v which defines the set of processing element numbers for each $v \in T_v$ and $p \in T_p$. The nonempty sets are denoted by IN_n where the integer n is listed in Table 2.2 or equals 1 for $N_v(\text{INPUT}, \text{IN})$ and $N_v(\text{OUTPUT}, \text{OUT})$, and
- l which defines the program capacity for each $t \in T_v$ as listed in Table 2.2 for the finite values. □

The two succeeding definitions formally state the set of processors and the set of processing elements.

DEFINITION 2.3 (Processors). *The set* **V** *defines the set of processors. With this set we associate the functions*

- $t_v : \mathbf{V} \to T_v$ which defines the processor type for each $v \in \mathbf{V}$, and
- $t_i : \mathbf{V} \times \mathbf{V} \to \text{IN}$ which defines the transport time between two processors. □

DEFINITION 2.4 (Processing Elements). *The set* $\mathbf{P} = \{(v, t, n) \in \mathbf{V} \times T_p \times \text{IN} \mid n \in N_v(t_v(v), t)\}$ *defines the set of processing elements. With this set we associate the function*

- $t_p : \mathbf{P} \to T_p$ which defines the processing element type for each $p \in \mathbf{P}$. □

We model a video signal processing system as a directed graph in which the nodes represent the processors and the arcs represent the interconnections between the processors. Each input port is connected to at most one output port. With each video signal processing system we can associate a processing element graph in which the nodes represent the processing elements of the system and the arcs indicate the connections between the processing elements.

DEFINITION 2.5 (VSP System). *A pair (V, I) defines a video signal processing system, where*

- $V \subset \mathbf{V}$ defines a finite set of processors, and
- $I \subset Y \times X$ defines a finite set of interconnections, where $Y = \{(v, n) \in V \times \text{IN} \mid n \in Y_v(t_v(v))\}$ denotes the set of output ports and $X = \{(v, n) \in V \times \text{IN} \mid n \in X_v(t_v(v))\}$ denotes the set of input ports, such that for all $(y_1, x_1), (y_2, x_2) \in I$ holds

$$x_1 = x_2 \Rightarrow y_1 = y_2.$$ □

DEFINITION 2.6 (Processing Element Graph). *Given a VSP system* (V, I). *Then a pair* (P, C) *defines a processing element graph, where*

- $P = \{(v, t, n) \in \mathbf{P} \mid v \in V\}$ *defines a finite set of processing elements, and*
- $C = \{((v, t, n), (v', t', n')) \in P \times P \mid (t \in \{\text{OE, IN, OUT}\} \wedge ((v, n), (v', n'')) \in I) \vee (t \notin \{\text{OE, IN, OUT}\} \wedge v = v')\}$ *defines a finite set of connections.*

With each connection, we associate a transport time which is given by the function

- $t : C \to \mathbb{N}$ *which defines the transport time for each connection* $c = (p, p') \in C$, *where* $p = (v, t, n)$ *and* $p' = (v', t', n')$, *such that if* $t_p(p) \in \{\text{OE, IN, OUT}\}$ *then* $t(c) = t_i(v, v')$, *and otherwise* $t(c) = 0$. $\square$

3. Signal Flow Graphs. Signal flow graphs contain nodes that represent operations and they contain arcs that represent precedences between operations. The operations are periodic which means that they must be executed repeatedly at regular intervals in time. Signal flow graphs typically are repeated on successive input samples to which we refer by means of input operations. We refer to output samples by means of output operations. Signal flow graphs are multi-rate if the operations have different periods so that the time between two successive executions is different for various parts of the signal flow graph; see Figure 3.1.

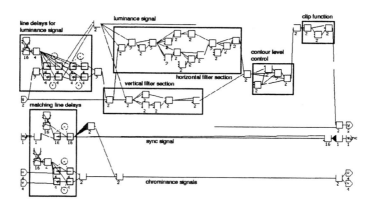

FIG. 3.1. *Graphical representation of an example of a multi-rate signal flow graph. Squares represent periodic operations with inputs on the left and outputs on the right, pentagons represent input and output operations, and lines represent precedences. The numbers denote the periods of the operations.*

Signal flow graphs describe the functional behavior of video algorithms in terms of video signal processor instructions. The operations in a signal flow graph correspond with instructions for the functional units in the cores of the processing elements, i.e., the barrel shifters, the multiplexers, the arithmetic and logic units, the adders, and the random access memories. Signal flow graphs do not contain instructions to control switch matrices, silos, and compact silos.

In order to model the use of random access memories, signal flow graphs contain memories. Each memory has a storage capacity and contains operations with read and write instructions that operate on that storage capacity.

The precedences in a signal flow graph correspond with the relations between the operations. Each precedence relates executions of one operation to executions of another operation. There are two types of precedences called data precedences and no-value precedences. Data precedences connect an operation output to an operation input and specify a periodic data flow. No-value precedences interconnect operations in the same memory and specify the order of read and write accesses.

The following two definitions formally state the operation type and the set of operations. Throughout this paper, the symbol $\mathbb{Z}$ denotes the set of integers and the symbol $\mathbb{Z}_+$ denotes the set of positive integers.

DEFINITION 3.1 (Operation Types). *The set $T_o = \{$alu, constant, shift, pass, read, write, in, out$\}$ defines the set of operation types. With this set we associate the functions*

- *X_o which defines the set of input port numbers for each $t \in T_o$ as*

$$X_o(t) = \begin{cases} \mathbb{N}_0 & \text{if } t \in \{\text{constant, in}\} \\ \mathbb{N}_1 & \text{if } t \in \{\text{shift, pass, read, out}\} \\ \mathbb{N}_2 & \text{if } t \in \{\text{write}\} \\ \mathbb{N}_3 & \text{if } t \in \{\text{alu}\}, \text{ and} \end{cases}$$

- *Y_o which defines the set of output port numbers for each $t \in T_o$ as*

$$Y_o(t) = \begin{cases} \mathbb{N}_0 & \text{if } t \in \{\text{write, out}\} \\ \mathbb{N}_1 & \text{if } t \notin \{\text{write, out}\}. \end{cases} \qquad \square$$

DEFINITION 3.2 (Operations). *The set $\mathbf{O}$ defines the set of operations. With this set we associate the functions*

- *$t_o : \mathbf{O} \to T_o$ which defines the operation type of each $o \in \mathbf{O}$, and*
- *$p : \mathbf{O} \to \mathbb{Z}_+$ which defines the period of each $o \in \mathbf{O}$.* $\square$

We model the production and consumption of data between operations by data precedences that run from output ports to input ports. Formally, the set of data precedences is described as follows.

DEFINITION 3.3 (Data Precedences). *The set $\mathbf{R} = Y \times X \times (\mathbb{Z}_+ \times \mathbb{Z} \times \mathbb{Z})$ defines the set of data precedences, where $Y = \{(o, n) \in \mathbf{O} \times \mathbb{N} \mid n \in Y_o(t_o(o))\}$ denotes the set of output ports and $X = \{(o, n) \in \mathbf{O} \times \mathbb{N} \mid n \in X_o(t_o(o))\}$ denotes the set of input ports, such that for all $((o, n), (o', n'), (p, b, b')) \in \mathbf{R}$ holds*

$$p(o)|p \wedge p(o')|p. \qquad \square$$

A data precedence $((o, n), (o', n'), (p, b, b'))$ indicates that the production of the $(\frac{p}{p(o)}k + b)$th execution of port (o, n) is consumption of the $(\frac{p}{p(o')}k + b')$th execution of port (o', n').

Next, we introduce the set of memories. Each memory has a size that indicates its storage capacity. The address space ranges from zero to its size.

Throughout this paper, the symbol $\mathcal{P}$ denotes the power set, i.e., the set of all subsets.

DEFINITION 3.4 (Memories). *The power set* $\mathbf{M} = \mathcal{P}(\{o \in \mathbf{O} \mid t_o(o) \in \{\text{read}, \text{write}\}\})$ *defines the set of memories. With this set we associate the function*

- $s_o : \mathbf{M} \to \mathbb{Z}_+$ *which defines the size for each* $m \in \mathbf{M}$. $\qquad\square$

We define additional precedence relations between operations to model the order of read and write accesses on memories.

DEFINITION 3.5 (No-Value Precedences). *The set* $\mathbf{S} = \mathbf{O} \times \mathbf{O} \times (\mathbb{Z}_+ \times \mathbb{Z} \times \mathbb{Z})$ *defines the set of no-value precedences such that for all* $(o, o', (p, b, b')) \in S$ *holds*

$$p(o)|p \wedge p(o')|p. \qquad\qquad\square$$

A no-value precedence $(o, o', (p, b, b'))$ indicates that the $(\frac{p}{p(o)}k + b)$th execution of operation o is completed before the $(\frac{p}{p(o')}k + b')$th execution of operation o' is completed. If we assume that operations o and o' operate on the same memory, then the $(\frac{p}{p(o)}k + b)$th access of operation o takes place before the $(\frac{p}{p(o')}k + b')$th access of operation o'.

Precedences can define the same relation between two operations. If that is the case then these precedences are called equivalent.

DEFINITION 3.6 (Precedence Equivalence). *Given are two precedences* $r_1, r_2 \in \mathbf{R} \cup \mathbf{S}$, *where* $r_1 = (y_1, x_1, (p_1, b_1, b'_1))$ *and* $r_2 = (y_2, x_2, (p_2, b_2, b'_2))$. *Then* r_1 *and* r_2 *are said to be equivalent if and only if* $y_1 = y_2$, $x_1 = x_2$, $p_1 = p_2$, $b_1 - b'_1 = b_2 - b'_2$, *and* $b_1 \equiv b_2 (\text{mod} \frac{p}{p(o)})$. *This is denoted by* $r_1 = r_2$. $\qquad\square$

We model a signal flow graph as a directed graph in which the nodes represent operations and the arcs represent precedences. Each input port consumes at most one sample per execution. Formally, this is stated as follows.

DEFINITION 3.7 (Signal Flow Graph). *A 4-tuple* (O, R, S, M) *defines a signal flow graph, where*

- $O \subset \mathbf{O}$ *defines a finite set of operations,*
- $R \subset \{((o, n), (o', n'), (p, b, b')) \in \mathbf{R} \mid o, o' \in O\}$ *defines a finite set of data precedences such that for all* $r_1, r_2 \in R$ *where* $r = ((o_1, n_1), (o', n'), (p_1, b_1, b'_1))$ *and* $r_2 = ((o_2, n_2), (o', n'), (p_2, b_2, b'_2))$ *satisfying* $r_1 \neq r_2$ *holds*

$$b'_1 \not\equiv b'_2 \quad (\text{mod } \gcd(\frac{p_1}{p(o')}, \frac{p_2}{p(o')})),$$

- $S \subset \{(o, o', (p, b, b')) \in \mathbf{S} \mid o, o' \in O\}$ *defines a finite set of no-value precedences, and*
- $M \subset \mathbf{M}$ *defines a finite set of memories such that* M *is a partition of* $\{o \in O \mid t_o(o) \in \{\text{read}, \text{write}\}\}$. $\qquad\square$

We complete this section with two signal flow graph transformations. The purpose of these transformations is to change the flow rate and the flow path within signal flow graphs without changing the functionality in order to map the signal flow graphs onto a video signal processor system. To formulate these transformations, we introduce the following partial ordering.

DEFINITION 3.8 (Precedence Division). *Given are two precedences* $r_1, r_2 \in$ $\mathbf{R} \cup \mathbf{S}$, *where* $r_1 = (y_1, x_1, (p_1, b_1, b_1'))$ *and* $r_2 = (y_2, x_2, (p_2, b_2, b_2'))$. *Then* r_1 *is said to divide* r_2 *if and only if* $y_1 = y_2$, $x_1 = x_2$, $p_1 | p_2$, $b_1 - b_1' = b_2 - b_2'$, *and* $b_1 \equiv b_2 (\mod \frac{p_2}{p(o)})$. *This is denoted by* $r_1 | r_2$ *or by* $r_1 |_k r_2$ *if the fraction* $k = p_2/p_1$ *is of interest.* ☐ The equivalence relation of Definition 3.6 partitions each precedence set $R \subseteq \mathbf{R} \cup \mathbf{S}$ in equivalence classes. Each precedence $r = (y, x, (p, b, b')) \in R$ defines a class $R_r = \{r' \in R \mid r' = r\}$. The partial ordering of Definition 3.8 partitions each equivalence class R_r into k equivalence classes $R_r^k(i) = \{r' \in R_r \mid r' = (y, x, (kp, b + i\frac{p}{p(o)}, b' + i\frac{p}{p(o')}))\}$ where $0 \le i < k$. The two transformations are formulated in the following two definitions. Examples of the transformations are shown in Figure 3.2 and Figure 3.3.

DEFINITION 3.9 (Flow Rate Transformation). *Given is a signal flow graph* (O, R, S, M). *The flow rate transformation replaces one data precedence* $r \in R$ *by* k *data precedences* $r_i \in \mathbf{R}_r^k(i)$, *where* $0 \le i < k$. *The inverse flow rate transformation replaces* k *data precedences* $r_i \in R_r^k(i)$, *where* $0 \le i < k$, *by one data precedence* $r \in \mathbf{R}_r$. ☐

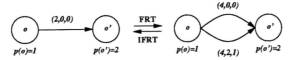

FIG. 3.2. *Example of a flow rate transformation.*

DEFINITION 3.10 (Flow Path Transformation). *Given are a signal flow graph* (O, R, S, M), *an operation* $o' \in \mathbf{O}$ *satisfying* $t_o(o') = \text{pass}$, *and data precedences* $\hat{r}_i = ((o, n), (o_i', n_i'), (p(o'), b, b_i'))$, $\hat{r}_0' = ((o, n), (o', 0), (p(o'), b, 0))$, *and* $\hat{r}_i' = ((o', 0), (o_i', n_i'), (p(o'), 0, b_i'))$, *for all* $1 \le i \le k$. *The flow path transformation inserts* o' *in* O *and replaces* k *data precedences* $r_1, ..., r_k$, *where* $r_i \in \mathbf{R}_{\hat{r}_i}$ *for all* $1 \le i \le k$, *by* $k + 1$ *data precedences* $r_0', ..., r_k'$, *where* $r_j' \in \mathbf{R}_{\hat{r}_j'}$ *for all* $0 \le j \le k$. *The inverse flow path transformation deletes* o' *from* O *and replaces* $k + 1$ *data precedences* $r_0', ..., r_k'$, *where* $r_j' \in \mathbf{R}_{\hat{r}_j'}$ *for all* $0 \le j \le k$, *by* k *data precedences* $r_1, ..., r_k$, *where* $r_i \in \mathbf{R}_{\hat{r}_i}$ *for all* $1 \le i \le k$. ☐

4. Problem Formulation. To formulate the mapping problem we introduce four assignments that are called processing element assignment, silo assignment, delay assignment, and time assignment, respectively.

A processing element assignment assigns each operation to a processing element on which it is executed. We assume that each operation is always executed on the same processing element.

DEFINITION 4.1 (Processing Element Assignment). *Given are a signal flow graph* (O, R, S, M) *and a processing element graph* (P, C). *Then a function* $\alpha : O \to P$ *is called a processing element assignment.* ☐ To formulate the feasibility constraints on a processing element assignment, we introduce four

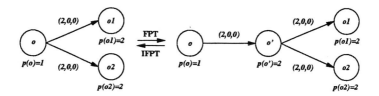

FIG. 3.3. *Example of a flow path transformation.*

derived assignments that are called type assignment, period assignment, memory assignment, and path assignment, respectively. A type assignment assigns each operation to a processing element type. It is feasible if each operation is assigned to a processing element type that can execute that type of operation.

DEFINITION 4.2 (Type Assignment). *Given are a signal flow graph (O, R, S, M), a processing element graph (P, C), and a processing element assignment $\alpha : O \to P$. Then the function $\tau : O \to T_\mathrm{p}$ is called a type assignment and is defined for all $o \in O$ by*

$$\tau(o) = t_\mathrm{p}(\alpha(o)).$$

A type assignment τ is called feasible if and only if the type constraints are satisfied which state that for all $o \in O$ holds

$$\tau(o) \in \begin{cases} \{\text{ALE}\} & \text{if } t_o(o) \in \{\text{alu}\} \\ \{\text{ALE}, \text{BE}\} & \text{if } t_o(o) \in \{\text{constant}, \text{shift}\} \\ \{\text{ME1}, \text{ME2}\} & \text{if } t_o(o) \in \{\text{read}, \text{write}\} \\ \{\text{ALE}, \text{BE}, \text{ME2}, \text{OE}\} & \text{if } t_o(o) \in \{\text{pass}\} \\ \{\text{IN}\} & \text{if } t_o(o) \in \{\text{in}\} \\ \{\text{OUT}\} & \text{if } t_o(o) \in \{\text{out}\}. \end{cases} \qquad \square$$

A period assignment assigns a period to each processing element which indicates the length of its program. It is feasible if the program length does not exceed the capacity of the corresponding program memory.

DEFINITION 4.3 (Period Assignment). *Given are a signal flow graph (O, R, S, M), a processing element graph (P, C), and a processing element assignment $\alpha : O \to P$. Then the function $\gamma : P \to \mathbb{N}$ is called a period assignment and is defined for all $p = (v, t, n) \in P$ by*

$$\gamma(p) = \begin{cases} \mathrm{lcm}\{p(o) \mid \alpha(o) = (v, t, n)\} & \text{if } t_v(v) \neq \text{VSP2} \lor t \neq \{\text{BE}, \text{OE}\} \\ \mathrm{lcm}\{p(o) \mid \exists_{n' \in \mathbb{N}_3} \alpha(o) = (v, t, n')\} & \text{if } t_v(v) = \text{VSP2} \land t = \text{BE} \land n \in \mathbb{N}_3 \\ \mathrm{lcm}\{p(o) \mid \exists_{n' \notin \mathbb{N}_3} \alpha(o) = (v, t, n')\} & \text{if } t_v(v) = \text{VSP2} \land t = \text{BE} \land n \notin \mathbb{N}_3 \\ \mathrm{lcm}\{p(o) \mid \exists_{n' \in \mathbb{N}_5} \alpha(o) = (v, t, n')\} & \text{if } t_v(v) = \text{VSP2} \land t = \text{OE} \end{cases}$$

A period assignment γ is called feasible if and only if the period constraints are satisfied which state that for all $p = (v, t, n) \in P$ holds

$$\gamma(p) \leq l(t_v(v)). \qquad \square$$

A memory assignment assigns each memory to a set of processing elements. It is feasible if each memory is assigned to precisely one processing element and if the storage capacity of each processing element is not be exceeded.

DEFINITION 4.4 (Memory Assignment). *Given are a signal flow graph (O, R, S, M), a processing element graph (P, C), and a processing element assignment $\alpha : O \rightarrow P$. Then the function $\mu : M \rightarrow \mathcal{P}(P)$ is called a memory assignment and is defined for all $m \in M$ by*

$$\mu(m) = \{\alpha(o) \mid o \in m\}.$$

A memory assignment μ is called feasible if and only if the memory constraints are satisfied which state that for all $m \in M$ holds

$$|\mu(m)| = 1,$$

and for all $p \in P$ holds

$$\sum_{m \in M, \mu(m) = \{p\}} s_o(m) \leq s_p(t_p(p)). \qquad \square$$

A path assignment assigns a pair of processing elements to each data precedence that represents the data path for that precedence. It is feasible if each data precedence is assigned to a data path that belongs to the set of connections in the processing element graph.

DEFINITION 4.5 (Path Assignment). *Given are a signal flow graph (O, R, S, M), a processing element graph (P, C), and a processing element assignment $\alpha : O \rightarrow P$. Then the function $\pi : R \rightarrow P^2$ is called a path assignment and is defined for all $r = ((o, n), (o', n'), (p, b, b')) \in R$ by*

$$\pi(r) = (\alpha(o), \alpha(o')).$$

A path assignment π is called feasible if and only if the path constraints are satisfied which state that for all $r \in R$ holds

$$\pi(r) \in C. \qquad \square$$

The feasibility of a processing element assignment is now formally stated as follows.

DEFINITION 4.6 (Feasible Processing Element Assignment). *Given are a signal flow graph (O, R, S, M), a processing element graph (P, C), and a processing element assignment $\alpha : O \rightarrow P$. Then the processing element assignment α is called feasible if and only if the processing element constraints are satisfied which state that the corresponding type assignment τ, period assignment γ, memory assignment μ, and path assignment π are feasible.* $\qquad \square$

A silo assignment assigns each data precedence to a silo number. In combination with the processing element assignment it uniquely assigns each data precedence to a silo in which the data is stored. A silo assignment is feasible if the input ports of the operations match with the input ports of the processing elements, i.e., data ports must be assigned to data ports, read address ports must be assigned to read address ports, and write address ports must be assigned to write address ports.

DEFINITION 4.7 (Silo Assignment). *Given is a signal flow graph (O, R, S, M), a processing element graph (P, C), and a feasible processing element assignment $\alpha : O \to P$. Then a function $\lambda : R \to \mathbb{N}_3$ is called a silo assignment. A silo assignment λ is called feasible if and only if for all $r = ((o, n), (o', n'), (p, b, b')) \in R$ holds that if $\tau(o') = $ ALE then*

$$n' \in \mathbb{N}_2 \Leftrightarrow \lambda(r) \in \mathbb{N}_2,$$

and otherwise

$$\lambda(r) = \begin{cases} n' & \text{if } \tau(o') \neq \text{ME2} \vee t_o(o') = \text{read} \\ n' + 1 & \text{if } \tau(o') = \text{ME2} \wedge t_o(o') = \text{write} \\ n' + 2 & \text{if } \tau(o') = \text{ME2} \wedge t_o(o') = \text{pass.} \end{cases} \qquad \square$$

A delay assignment assigns a delay to each operation that indicates the latency between the consumption and production of data. The delay is expressed in number of executions. The latency in clock cycles therefore equals the product of the amount of delay and the period of the operation. A delay assignment is feasible if the delay of each operation can be implemented on the core of the processing element on which it is executed. This can only be done on dual ported memory elements by means of the compact silo feature. Furthermore, the storage capacity of each processing element may not be exceeded.

DEFINITION 4.8 (Delay Assignment). *Given is a signal flow graph (O, R, S, M), a processing element graph (P, C), and a feasible processing element assignment $\alpha : O \to P$. Then a function $\delta : O \to \mathbb{N}$ is called a delay assignment. A delay assignment δ is called feasible if and only if the delay constraints are satisfied which state that for all $o \in O$ holds*

$$\delta(o) > 0 \Leftrightarrow t_o(o) = \text{pass} \wedge \tau(o) = \text{ME2},$$

and for all $p \in P$ for which an $o \in O$ exists that satisfies $\alpha(o) = p$ and $\delta(o) > 0$ holds

$$\sum_{m \in M, \mu(m) = \{p\}} s_o(m) + 2^{\lceil 2 \log(1 + \sum_{o \in O, \alpha(o) = p} \delta(o)) \rceil} \leq s_p(t_p(p)). \qquad \square$$

A time assignment assigns each operation to a time slot in which its first execution is completed. In combination with the processing element assignment and the silo assignment it uniquely assigns start times to all input ports.

DEFINITION 4.9 (Time Assignment).   *Given is a signal flow graph*
(O, R, S, M). *Then a function* $\sigma : O \to \mathbb{Z}$ *is called a time assignment.*   □ To
formulate the feasibility constraints on a time assignment, we introduce three
derived assignments called phase assignment, read assignment, and write assignment. A phase assignment assigns each operation to a phase that indicates in
which instruction cycles it is executed. It is feasible if the executions of the
operations on the same processing elements do not overlap in time or can be
executed in parallel.

DEFINITION 4.10 (Phase Assignment).   *Given are a signal flow graph*
(O, R, S, M), *a processing element graph* (P, C), *a feasible processing element*
assignment $\alpha : O \to P$, *and a time assignment* $\sigma : O \to \mathbb{N}$. *Then the function*
$\phi : O \to \mathbb{N}$ *is called a phase assignment and is defined for all* $o \in O$ *by*

$$\phi(o) = \sigma(o) \bmod p(o).$$

A phase assignment ϕ *is called feasible if and only if the phase constraints are*
satisfied which state that for all $o, o' \in O$ *satisfying* $\alpha(o) = \alpha(o')$ *holds*

$$\phi(o) \not\equiv \phi(o') \quad (\bmod \ \gcd(p(o), p(o')))$$

or

$$\tau(o) = \tau(o') = \text{ME2} \wedge \{t_o(o), t_o(o')\} = \{\text{read}, \text{write}\}.$$ □

Read and write assignments assign each data precedence to read and write
times that indicate the time of consumption and production of the first sample,
respectively. They are feasible if the read and write accesses on the silos do not
overlap in time. Since the value of a feasible silo assignment does not affect the
timing of read accesses, feasibility with respect to the phase constraints implies
feasibility with respect to the read constraints. For completeness, however, we
also formulate the read constraints.

DEFINITION 4.11 (Read and Write Assignment).   *Given are a signal flow*
graph (O, R, S, M), *a processing element graph* (P, C), *a feasible processing ele-*
ment assignment $\alpha : O \to P$, *a feasible silo assignment* $\lambda : R \to \mathbb{N}_3$, *a feasible*
delay assignment $\delta : O \to \mathbb{N}$, *and a time assignment* $\sigma : O \to \mathbb{N}$. *Then the*
function $\rho : R \to \mathbb{Z}$ *is called a read assignment and the function* $\omega : R \to \mathbb{Z}$ *is*
called a write assignment and are defined for all $r = ((o, n), (o', n'), (p, b, b')) \in R$
by

$$\rho(r) = \sigma(o') + b'p(o') - e(\tau(o'), \lambda(r)),$$

and

$$\omega(r) = \sigma(o) + (b + \delta(o))p(o) + t(\pi(r)).$$

A read assignment ρ *and a write assignment* ω *are called feasible if and only if the*
read constraints are satisfied which state that for all data precedences $r_1, r_2 \in R$

where $r_1 = ((o_1, n_1), (o_1', n_1'), (p_1, b_1, b_1'))$ and $r_2 = ((o_2, n_2), (o_2', n_2'), (p_2, b_2, b_2'))$ that satisfy $r_1 \neq r_2$, $\alpha(o_1') = \alpha(o_2')$, and $\lambda(r_1) = \lambda(r_2)$ holds

$$\rho(r_1) \not\equiv \rho(r_2) \quad (\text{mod } \gcd(p_1, p_2)),$$

and the write constraints are satisfied which state that if $(o_1, n_1) \neq (o_2, n_2)$ then

$$\omega(r_1) \not\equiv \omega(r_2) \quad (\text{mod } \gcd(p_1, p_2)). \qquad \square$$

A time assignment is feasible if the resulting execution cycles and silo accesses do not overlap in time and if it preserves the precedence relations. For the data precedences this implies that the time between production and consumption must not exceed the available buffering time. For the no-value precedences this implies that the order of read and write operations must not be violated.

DEFINITION 4.12 (Feasible Time Assignment). *Given are a signal flow graph (O, R, S, M), a processing element graph (P, C), a feasible processing element assignment $\alpha : O \to P$, a feasible silo assignment $\lambda : R \to \mathbb{N}_3$, a feasible delay assignment $\delta : O \to \mathbb{N}$, and a time assignment $\sigma : O \to \mathbb{Z}$. Then the time assignment σ is called feasible if and only if the corresponding phase assignment ϕ, read assignment ρ, and write assignment ω are feasible, the data precedence constraints are satisfied which state that for all $r = ((o, n), (o', n'), (p, b, b')) \in R$ satisfying $\tau(o') \in \{\text{IN}, \text{OUT}\}$ holds*

$$\rho(r) = \omega(r),$$

and for all other $r \in R$ holds

$$0 < \rho(r) - \omega(r) < 32,$$

and the no-value precedence constraints are satisfied which state that for all $(o, o', (p, b, b')) \in S$ satisfying $t_o(o) = \text{read}$, $t_o(o') = \text{write}$, and $\tau(o) = \tau(o') = \text{ME2}$ holds

$$\sigma(o) + bp(o) \leq \sigma(o') + b'p(o),$$

and for all other $(o, o', (p, b, b')) \in S$ holds

$$\sigma(o) + bp(o) < \sigma(o') + b'p(o). \qquad \square$$

We can now formally state the mapping problem as follows.

DEFINITION 4.13 (Mapping). *Given are a signal flow graph (O, R, S, M) and a processing element graph (P, C). Find a transformation of the given signal flow graph into $(\mathcal{O}, \mathcal{R}, S, M)$, a feasible processing element assignment $\alpha : \mathcal{O} \to P$, a feasible silo assignment $\lambda : \mathcal{R} \to \mathbb{N}_3$, a feasible delay assignment $\delta : \mathcal{O} \to \mathbb{N}$, and a feasible time assignment $\sigma : \mathcal{O} \to \mathbb{Z}$, if they exist.* $\qquad \square$

5. Complexity Analysis. In this section, we show that the mapping problem is NP-hard in the strong sense. The proof of this theorem is taken from Korst [14] who shows that the problem of constructing a constrained processor assignment that uses a minimum number of processors for given set of strictly periodic operations and a given time assignment is NP-hard in the strong sense.

THEOREM 5.1. *Mapping is NP-hard in the strong sense.*

Proof. For a given instance of the mapping problem we can verify in polynomial time whether the signal flow graph $(\mathcal{O}, \mathcal{R}, S, M)$ is a transformation of (O, R, S, M) and whether the assignments α, λ, δ, and σ are feasible. Hence, the mapping problem is in NP.

To prove that mapping is NP-hard we use the following polynomial time reduction from graph coloring which is known to be NP-hard (see Karp, [11]). The graph coloring problem can be defined as follows. Given are a graph (V, E) and a positive integer K. Find a function $f : V \to \mathbb{N}_K$ such that for all $\{v_i, v_j\} \in E$ holds $f(v_i) \neq f(v_j)$, if one exists.

Given an arbitrary instance of graph coloring as defined above, we construct a corresponding instance of the mapping problem such that a function f exists if and only if a transformed signal flow graph $(\mathcal{O}, \mathcal{R}, S, M)$ and feasible assignments α, λ, δ, and σ exist. We take the $n(n-1)/2$ smallest prime numbers that are larger than n where $n = |V|$. According to the prime number theorem (Niven & Zuckerman, [18]), the largest of these prime numbers has magnitude $O(n^2 \log(n))$. We denote these numbers by π_{ij} for all $1 \leq i < j \leq n$ and we define $\pi_{ij} = \pi_{ji}$ for all $j < i$. For each $v_i \in V$ we define an operation $o_i \in O$ with $t_o(o_i) = \text{in}$ and

$$p(o_i) = \prod_{\{v_i,v_j\}\notin E, v_i \neq v_j} \pi_{ij}.$$

Note that for all $v_i, v_j \in V$ satisfying $v_i \neq v_j$ holds that if $\{v_i, v_j\} \in E$ then $\gcd(p(o_i), p(o_j)) = 1$ and if $\{v_i, v_j\} \notin E$ then $\gcd(p(o_i), p(o_j)) = \pi_{ij}$. Furthermore, we define the remainder of the signal flow graph by $R = S = M = \emptyset$ and we define a trivial transformation by $\mathcal{O} = O$ and $\mathcal{R} = R$. Finally, we associate with each $k \in \mathbb{N}_K$ a processor $v'_k \in \mathbf{V}$ and a processing element $p_k = (v'_k, \text{IN}, 0) \in P$, and we define $C = \emptyset$. As a result of these definitions, the silo assignment λ and the delay assignment δ are trivial and all constraints, except the phase constraints, are trivially satisfied.

Suppose the function f colors graph (V, E) with K colors. Then we can construct a feasible processing element assignment and a feasible time assignment as follows. Choose for each $o_i \in O$ $\alpha(o_i) = p_{f(v_i)}$ and choose $\sigma(o_i) = i$. Then for all $o_i, o_j \in O$ satisfying $o_i \neq o_j$ and $\alpha(o_i) = \alpha(o_j)$ holds $0 < |\phi(o_i) - \phi(o_j)| < n$ and $\gcd(p(o_i), p(o_j)) = \pi_{ij} > n$, since $\{v_i, v_j\} \notin E$, which satisfies the phase constraints.

Suppose we have a feasible processing element assignment α and a feasible time assignment σ. Then we can construct a feasible coloring f by taking $f(v_i) = k$ where $\alpha(o_i) = p_k$, since $\gcd(p(o_i), p(o_j)) \neq 1$ and $\{v_i, v_j\} \notin E$, if two operations o_i and o_j satisfying $o_i \neq o_j$ are assigned to the same processing element, i.e., $\alpha(o_i) = \alpha(o_j)$.

The magnitude of the largest integer in the constructed instance of the mapping problem is polynomial in the size of the instance, which means that the mapping problem is NP-hard in the strong sense.   □

6. Solution Approach. Since the mapping problem is NP-hard in the strong sense we cannot expect to find an algorithm that solves the mapping problem in polynomial time. In order to handle the mapping problem we propose a decomposition into three subproblems called delay management, partitioning, and scheduling which are more commonly known from the literature. The literature describes good solution techniques to handle these subproblems, although they are also NP-hard in the strong sense.

The purpose of delay management is to allocate memory capacity for the storage of intermediate data such that the life times do not exceed the maximal storage time of the silos. More precisely, one must find a signal flow graph transformation, a delay assignment, and a time assignment that satisfy the precedence constraints. The solution strategy for the delay management problem is based on a decomposition into delay minimization and delay assignment. In the delay minimization step one determines a preliminary time assignment using network flow techniques, see Ahuja et al. [3], to minimize the total storage requirement. The delay minimization problem is a special case of the dual of the minimum cost flow problem in which the completion times of the operations correspond to the potentials of the nodes. In the delay assignment step one allocates memory using bin packing heuristics, see Coffman et al. [6], to determine a signal flow graph transformation and a delay assignment. The capacities of the processing elements correspond to the capacities of the bins and the frequencies of the operations correspond to the sizes of the items. The bin packing heuristics intent to minimize the maximum utilization of the processing elements. For more information about the delay management problem and its solution approach, the reader is referred to Smeets et al. [20]. Related work on storage minimization is presented by Bilsen et al. [4].

The purpose of partitioning is to distribute the operations over the processors and to route the data flow through the system such that the processing capacities and the communication capacities are not exceeded. More precisely, one must find a signal flow graph transformation and a processing element assignment that satisfy the path constraints. The solution strategy for the partitioning problem is based on hierarchical bipartitioning which decomposes the single multi-way partitioning problem into multiple bipartitioning problems. This decomposition tackles the routing problem. In the bipartitioning step one minimizes the amount of communication using local search techniques, see Aarts & Lenstra [2]. The solution space is restricted to solutions with a feasible processing element utilization. One explores the solution space by means of a variable-depth search algorithm, see Kernighan & Lin [12], using sequences of two-exchanges. The basic idea behind variable-depth search is to allow unfavorable two-exchanges in a sequence to eventually obtain a favorable k-exchange without exhaustive search of the entire k-exchange neighborhood. For more information about the partitioning problem and its solution approach, the reader is referred to Aarts et al. [1] and De Kock et al. [13]. Related work on partitioning is presented by Lengauer [16].

The purpose of scheduling is to distribute the operations over the processing elements and the clock cycles and to distribute the operands over the silos such that overlapping operations are not executed on the same processing element and overlapping operands are not stored in the same silo. More precisely, one must find a processing element assignment, a silo assignment, and a time assignment that satisfy the phase constraints and the write constraints. The solution strategy is based on a combination of list scheduling, see French [9], and constraint satisfaction techniques, see Montanari [17]. In the list scheduling step one dynamically prioritizes the scheduling order of the operations based on time interval reductions that result from the precedence constraints and the overlap constraints. The precedence constraints are checked using the Bellman-Ford algorithm, see Lawler [15]. The overlap constraints are checked using graph coloring techniques based on sequential coloring, see Welsh & Powell [24], and kempe-chains, see Gibbons [10]. For more information about the scheduling problem and its solution approach, the reader is referred to Essink et al. [8]. Related work on periodic scheduling is presented by Korst [14] and Verhaegh [21].

7. Conclusion. We have presented a mathematical formulation for the mapping problem of signal flow graphs onto video signal processor systems. The mathematical formulation is based on well-defined signal flow graph transformations that extend the graphs with mapping information. Four decision variables covering processor binding, register binding, memory allocation, and timing complete the model. All constraints are formulated in terms of these decision variables.

Subsequently we have analyzed the computational complexity of the mapping problem which shows that the problem is NP-hard in strong sense. As a result we cannot expect to find an algorithm that solves the mapping problem in polynomial time.

Finally we have given an overview of a solution approach in which the mapping problem is decomposed into three subproblems called delay management, partitioning, and scheduling which are more commonly known from the literature. The literature describes good solution techniques to handle these subproblems, although they remain NP-hard in the strong sense.

The most important conclusion is that the presented mapping problem contains constraints that are typical for scheduling problems in embedded systems. We have demonstrated that they can be modeled in a mathematical way in order to analyze the computational complexity of the problem. This analysis often provides insight to the problem and the relation to other well-known problems in the literature. This usually opens the way towards a broad range of solution strategies.

REFERENCES

[1] Aarts, E.H.L., G. Essink, and E.A. de Kock, Recursive Bipartitioning of Signal Flow Graphs for Programmable Video Signal Processors, *Proc. ED&TC 96*, Paris, 1996, 460-466.

[2] Aarts, E.H.L. and J.K. Lenstra (Eds.), *Local search in combinatorial optimization*, Wiley, Chichester, 1997.

[3] Ahuja, R.K., T.L. Magnati, and J.B. Orlin, Network flows, M.J. Todd, G.L. Nemhauser, A.H.G. Rinnooy Kan (Eds.), *Handbooks in operations research and management science; Volume 1: Optimization*, North Holland, Amsterdam, 1989, 211-369.

[4] Bilsen G., M. Engels, R. Lauwereins, and J.A. Peperstraete, Cyclo-Static Dataflow, *IEEE Transactions on Signal Processing* 44 No. 2, 1996, 397-408.

[5] Bove, V.M., and J.A. Watlington, Cheops: A Reconfigurable Data-Flow System for Video Processing, *IEEE Transactions on Circuits and Systems for Video Technology* 5 no.2, 1995, 140-149.

[6] Coffman, E.G., Jr., M.R. Garey, and D.S. Johnson, Approximation algorithms for bin packing: An updated survey, G. Ausiello, M. Lucertini, and P. Serafini (Eds.), Algorithm Design and Computer System Design, *CISM Courses and Lectures* 284, Springer-Verlag, Vienna, 1984, 49-106.

[7] Dijkstra, H., H. Hollmann, K. Huizer, and R. Sluyter, New programmable delay element, *Electronic Letters* 25 no. 16, 1989, 1019-1021.

[8] Essink, G., E. Aarts, R. van Dongen, P. van Gerwen, J. Korst, and K. Vissers, Scheduling in programmable video signal processors, *Proc. IEEE International Conference on Computer Aided Design*, Santa Clara, 1991, 284-287.

[9] French, J., *Sequencing and Scheduling: An Introduction to the Mathematics of the Job-Shop*, Wiley, New York, 1982.

[10] Gibbons, A., *Algorithmic Graph Theory*, Cambridge University Press, Cambridge, 1989.

[11] Karp, R.M., Reducibility among Combinatorial Problems, *Complexity of Computer Computations*, Plenum Press, New-York, 1972, 86-103.

[12] Kernighan, B.W., and S. Lin, An efficient heuristic procedure for partitioning graphs, *Bell System Technical Journal* 49, 1970, 291-307.

[13] Kock, E.A. de, E.H.L. Aarts, G. Essink, R.E.J. Jansen, and J.H.M. Korst, A Variable--Depth Search Algorithm for the Recursive Bipartitioning of Signal Flow Graphs, *OR Spektrum* 17, 1995, 159-172.

[14] Korst, J.H.M., *Periodic Multiprocessor Scheduling*, Doctoral Thesis, Eindhoven University of Technology, 1992.

[15] Lawler, E.L., *Combinatorial Optimization: Networks and Matroids*, Holt, Rinehart and Winston, New York, 1976.

[16] Lengauer T., *Combinatorial Algorithms for Integrated Circuit Layout*, Wiley, Chichester, 1990.

[17] Montanari U., Networks of constraints: Fundamental properties and applications to picture processing, *Information Sciences* 7, 1974, 95-132.

[18] Niven, I., and H.S. Zuckerman, *An Introduction to the Theory of Numbers*, Wiley, Chichester, 1960.

[19] Roermund, A.H.M. van, P.J. Snijder, H. Dijkstra, C.G. Hemeryck, C.M. Huizer, J.M.P. Schmitz, R.J. Sluyter, A General-Purpose Programmable Video Processor, *IEEE Trans. on Consumer Electronics*, 1989, 249-257.

[20] Smeets, M.L.G., E.H.L. Aarts, G. Essink, and E.A. de Kock, Delay Management for Programmable Video Signal Processors, *Proc. ED&TC 97*, Paris, 1997, 126-133.

[21] Verhaegh, W.F.J., *Multidimensional Periodic Scheduling*, Doctoral Thesis, Eindhoven University of Technology, 1995.

[22] Veendrick, H.J.M., O. Popp, G. Postuma, and M. Lecoutere, A 1.5 GIPS video signal processor (VSP), *Proc. CICC 6.2.*, San Diego, 1994, 95-98.

[23] Vissers, K.A., G. Essink, P.H.J. van Gerwen, P.J.M. Janssen, O. Popp, E. Riddersma, W.J.M. Smits, and H.J.M. Veendrick, Architecture and programming of parallel video signal processors, M. Moonen and F. Catthoor (eds), *Algorithms and Parallel*

VLSI Architectures III, Elsevier, 1995, 373-390.

[24] Welsh, D.J.A., and M.B. Powell, An upper bound on the chromatic number of a graph and its application to timetabling problems, *The Computer Journal* **10**, 1967, 85-87.

[25] Yeung, A., and J. Rabaey, A Data-Driven Architecture of Rapid Prototyping of High Throughput DSP Algorithms, *Proc. VLSI Signal Processing*, Napa Valley, CA, October 1992, 225-234.

A REAL-TIME JAVA SERVER FOR REAL-TIME MACH*

AKIHIKO MIYOSHI [†], TAKURO KITAYAMA [‡], AND HIDEYUKI TOKUDA [§]

Abstract. We have developed a real-time Java[1] server on the Real-Time Mach micro-kernel which is suitable for embedded systems and distributed real-time systems. By implementing it as a user-level server on Real-Time Mach, applications such as WWW browsers and embedded applications can both execute Java byte codes. In this paper, we describe the real-time issues in Java and the architecture of our Java server. The real-time extension of the Java server and Java threads using kernel-level threads was also evaluated.

1. Introduction. Java[2] is an object oriented programming language very similar to C++ developed by Sun Microsystems. It was designed to be used in world-wide distributed computing environments, thus having security features and its code is compiled into architecture neutral byte codes. To execute Java code on a target machine or device, the virtual machine must interpret or dynamically translate Java byte code in to the target machine code. Java also supports a dynamic loading of classes across a network. Because of these unpredictable behavior during the code execution phase, it is often considered that Java is not appropriate for developing hard and soft real-time applications.

However, Java can provide portable multi-threaded programming interface and window system interface. Java can be used to develop object-oriented soft real-time systems with appropriate support. In this paper, we first discuss basic issues in the Java language for developing real-time applications. We then describe the Java server architecture and its extension based on the kernel level and user-level real-time threads and evaluate its performance.

2. Real-Time Issues in Java. Many issues in using Java for developing real-time applications can be classified into two categories: language specification and its execution environment. In this section we will discuss some of the problems which must be solved for real-time.

2.1. Language Specification. One of the missing real-time features of the Java language is the ability to specify explicit timing constraints. Since programmers cannot assume the performance of the target device which executes the application or the availability of system resources, specifying explicit timing constraints is important.

For instance, Java provides sleep(t) method where a running thread can suspend at least t milliseconds. This method alone is insufficient for many real-

---

*This research is conducted under the fund of Information-technology Promotion Agency, Japan (IPA).

†Keio Research Institute at SFC, Keio University, 5322 Endoh Fujisawa Kanagawa, Japan 240 (miyos@sfc.keio.ac.jp)

‡Keio Research Institute at SFC, Keio University, 5322 Endoh Fujisawa Kanagawa, Japan 240 (takuro@sfc.keio.ac.jp)

§Faculty of Environmental Information, Keio University, 5322 Endoh Fujisawa Kanagawa, Japan 240 (hxt@sfc.keio.ac.jp)

[1] Java is a trademark of Sun Microsystems, Inc

time programs.   Programmers would rather benefit from `sleep_until` (`time_of_day`) method, or `within` (`t`) `do s except q` construct[3]. Furthermore, explicit use of deadlines in thread attributes and the timing fault handler can be a better extension. By using the timing fault handler th programmer can get feedback whether it has missed the deadline or not, and determine if a recovery action is necessary.

Another missing feature of the language specification is the ability to provide resource abstraction. In current Java language it is difficult to express resources such as CPU time, memory, network and I/O bandwidth. Without the notion of resources, it is hard for programmers to maintain a certain level of quality of service (QoS) when a system is in a overload condition, or reserve resources needed for real-time activities.

2.2. Execution Environment. As for the execution environment, there are many unpredictable factors such as dynamic loading of classes, garbage collection, and effect of JIT (Just In Time) compilations. For a Java programmer, it is difficult to predict the time it will take to load a new class from a network or from local disks. When garbage collection occurs, an activity may be blocked for an arbitrary amount of time. If the virtual machine supports JIT, the execution time of a method may vary if that code is being JIT compiled. Although a previously JIT compiled code has predictable behavior in a controlled environment, it is extremely difficult to predict the time when JIT occurs. It may be caused by an external event. Or once JIT compiled code may be garbage collected and a JIT may occur again for the same code. Thus in current execution environment, it is extremely difficult to predict the behavior of Java programs.

Another source of unpredictability is the implementation of Java virtual machine itself. There are two models of implementation of Java virtual machine. One model is to implement it as an application or embed the virtual machine in applications such as WWW browsers. This model relys on the host OS it is on. Another model is to implement it without an host OS. Sun Microsystem's JavaOS[13] is an example of this model. Java programs running on different virtual machine architecture shows different characteristics even on the same hardware. This sometimes is caused by the effect of having a host OS and resulting in crossing of multiple layers of services. Often, there are unbounded priority inversions in the virtual machine and at the services of the host OS such as communication or window management. Thus for a Java program to be predictable, the virtual machine itself must be predictable. If it relys on the host OS, the services of the host OS must be also predictable.

3. Java Server Architecture. Considering the real-time issues in Java which we have discussed in the previous section, it is possible to provide soft real-time environments for Java. In this section, we first describe the structure of the user-level Java server and then discuss the two execution environment for Java server and its real-time features.

3.1. User-Level Java Server. We have implemented our Java environment as a user-level server on Real-Time Mach microkernel [18]. Real-Time

Mach is an extension of Mach 3.0 microkernel developed at Carnegie Mellon University, Keio University, and Japan Advanced institute of Science and Technology. Its objective is to provide a common real-time computing environment. Real-Time Mach provides distributed real-time computing environment for a wide range of target machines such as Pentium, SPARC, and MIPS architectures. It has real-time features such as real-time threads, real-time scheduler, real-time synchronization[17], high resolution clocks and timers, real-time IPC primitives[4], and processor capacity reservation[5].

By implementing the virtual machine as a user-level server on Real-Time Mach, it can be used as an engine for running basic operating software or application for embedded systems such as Network Computers. It can also be used from user application such as WWW browsers on another server such as the UNIX server. With this architecture, Java programmers can expect same characteristics from their programs whether it is executed in embedded system environment or from an application on a UNIX environment because Java server and UNIX server can coexist on the same machine.

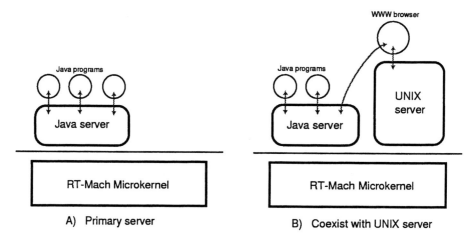

Figure 3.1 Two Execution Environment

Java server is based on RTS (Real-Time Server) [8] which is also a user-level server on Real-Time Mach. RTS is a simple object-based server which provides task management, file management, name service, and exception handling. Java server extends RTS and enables the server to interpret Java byte code as well as native binaries. It has an in-memory file system and different types of file system can be mounted from various media such as a floppy, hard disk or RAM disk. Files can be cached as continuous memory blocks. In our current implementation, Java server will mount Unix file system and copy necessary files (classes) from the local disks into its in-memory file system at initialization. This avoids blocking for disk I/O while executing Java methods, but devices with less

memory can choose to read from a mounted file system rather than to keep it
in memory or can request data from another server in the same machine or a
remote machine across a network. For the Java byte code interpreter, we used
a virtual machine called kaffe[19] which supports interpreting as well as JIT.

3.2. Configuration for Java Server. Java server can be booted on Real-
Time Mach as a primary server which is shown in Figure 3.1A. This configuration
will be small enough for devices with limited resources such as Network Computers, personal digital assistants, Internet-ready appliances. This configuration
is useful for embedded applications and embedded systems written in Java.

Another configuration that can be made is to coexist on Real-Time Mach
with other servers like the UNIX server [1]. It is shown in Figure 3.1B. Programmers can benefit from this environment because they can use developing
and testing tools while running Java applications. Or applications can communicate with the Java server and let it execute Java programs for them instead of
embedding the virtual machine in themselves like the WWW browser.

4. Real-Time Threads for Java.

4.1. Real-Time Threads. We have extended Java threads for real-time.
Real-time threads have been very effective in preserving timing constraints when
dealing with continuous media data and thus resulting in decrease of jitters and
noise in multimedia applications. Programmers can easily detect whether a
thread missed a deadline or not and change the QoS (quality of service) of continuous media dynamically[16]. For example, a movie player application can
adjust its performance by choosing to degrade the resolution of the picture or
reduce its frame rate when its working threads miss the deadlines specified because of reasons like low performance of the hardware or network, or because of
competing jobs in the same machine. The ability to adapt to the environment is
especially important for Java programs that cannot assume the platform which
it may run. 100 milliseconds of computation time in Java will have a totally different meaning for a program running on a highend workstation from a program
on a small PDA device.

Real-Time Mach has two implementation of real-time threads. One is kernel-
level threads called RT-Threads and the other implemented at the user-level,
called RTC-Thread [10, 11]. RT-Thread is scheduled by the kernel-level scheduler and timing management is done at the kernel using a clock device which
interrupts the kernel at short intervals. RTC-Thread separated timing management and thread management and put both functions at the user-level for
flexibility and efficiency. In both thread models, a thread becomes a real-time
thread by specifying its timing attributes.

As we shown in a C-like pseudo language in the following example, a real-
time thread, f( ) is created with its thread attributes f, Si, Ti, Di. f indicates its thread's function f( ), Si, Ti, and Di indicate thread f's start time,
period, and deadline respectively.

```
1.   root( )
2.   {
3.     thread_id f_id;
4.
5.     f_attr = {f, Si, Ti, Di};
6.            /* set thread attribute of f */
7.     rt_thread_create(&f_id, f_attr);
8.            /* creating f( ) as a thread */
9.   }
10.
11.    f(arg) {
12.      f's body
13.  }
```

Note that if thread f is periodic then it will automatically restart, or *reincarnate*, when it reaches the end of its function body.

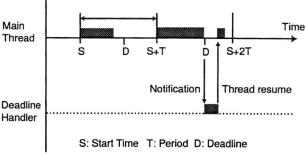

Figure 4.1 Real-Time Thread Model

We are implementing two models of real-time Java threads using RT-Threads and RTC-Thread as a base. We inherited the model of real-time threads in Real-Time Mach shown in Figure 4.1. Main thread will start at time S with a period of time T. If it misses its deadline D and a deadline handler is specified, main thread will be suspended and thread of control will be handed off to the deadline handler which is another thread. Deadline handler can specify a forward or backward recovery action as well as change the main threads attributes such as priorities, deadline time and period or some application specific attributes. For example, if a thread in a movie player application misses a deadline, the deadline handler can choose to reduce the frame rate or resolution of the movie.

4.2. Real-Time Java Threads. To use regular Java threads, a programmer would construct an object derived from **Thread** class and call **start()** as we show below. By invoking **start()** method, the thread starts execution by calling **run()** method of this **MyThread** object.

```
MyThread th = new MyThread( . . . );
```

```
th.start();
```

Real-time Java threads are created by instantiating a class extended from Thread class called RtThread as the following example. Si, Ti, and Di indicate the threads start time, period, and deadline respectively. By specifying a deadline hander, method meth will be invoked when it has missed its deadline. This can enable programmers to dynamically adjust attributes of its threads to provide better quality of service for continuous media applications.

```
RtThread rtth = new RtThread(Si, Ti, Di);
rtth.setDeadlineHandler(meth);
```

When constructing a real-time thread object, the virtual machine will actually create a RT-Thread or RTC-Thread. The thread will start interpreting from the run() method of this real-time thread object when the start() method is called in the Java program.

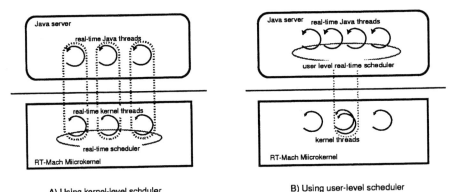

A) Using kernel-level schduler   B) Using user-level scheduler

Figure 4.2 Kernel-level and User-level Threads in Java Server

By mapping Java thread to RT-Thread, Java threads will be scheduled by the real-time scheduler in the kernel. As illustrated in Figure 4.2A, there is a one to one mapping of real-time Java threads and kernel threads. When RTC-Thread is used it will be scheduled by the user-level scheduler which is shown in Figure 4.2B and will not have a one to one mapping between Java threads and RTC-Threads.

In both cases, synchronization between threads is achieved by mutex locks and condition variables which avoids priority inversion problem[12].

4.3. RtThread.class. We provide a new class RtThread. This class extends the Thread class we usually use to create threads in Java. Thus programmers can use the same methods in the Thread class as well as new methods for real-time. RtThread class provides the following methods to support real-time.

- RtThread.setAttr(Time start, Time period, Time deadline)
  This method will set the timing attributes of the real-time thread.

- `Time RtThread.getStart()`
  This method will get the start time of the real-time thread.
- `Time RtThread.getPeriod()`
  This method will get the period of the real-time thread.
- `Time RtThread.getDeadline()`
  This method will get the Deadline of the real-time thread.
- `RtThread.setDeadlineHandler(method)`
  This method will set the deadline handler.

Using these methods programmers can express aperiodic threads and periodic threads. Aperiodic threads are expressed by specifying deadlines and starts when some external event occurs. Periodic threads can be expressed using start time, period and deadlines. A new instantiation of the periodic thread will be scheduled at the start time specified.

4.4. Programming Example. Here, we will show a simple self stabilizing programming example using real-time Java thread. By self stabilizing we mean that the thread itself can dynamically determine a runnable QoS level under current workload.

In lines 3-6, a periodic Java thread is created with start time set to 3 seconds after current time. (Current time is expressed using java.util.Date()) Period is set to 500 milliseconds and deadline to 400 milliseconds. Time is a class we introduced to express seconds and nanoseconds. In line 7, a deadline handler is set. If the main thread misses its deadline, deadline handler thread will start executing from `deadlineHandler` method. By calling the `start` method, the thread will start executing the `run` method.

In the `run` method of class `myRtThread` starting at line 17, the periodic thread we have just created will do some job, for example draw a video frame image for a movie application. There is a boolean flag called `missed` which indicates if the thread has missed its deadline previously. If it has not missed the deadline previously (flag is set to false), the period and deadline will be shortened as we show in line 26. The `adjustTiming` method starting from line 31 is the actual method that will change real-time threads timing attributes. If the main thread has previously missed its deadline, it will just change the value of `missed` flag from true to false.

If the main thread misses the deadline for such reasons as overload in the system, the deadline handler will be invoked. Deadline handler will increase the period and deadline of the main thread hoping that it will not miss its deadline next time and change the missed flag to true as we illustrate in lines 39-45. For the clarity of the code we have made the program very simple, but for a realistic program we can keep a counter and change the period when it has not missed its deadline for a certain amount of time to make it more stable.

By using real-time threads and deadline handlers, programs can dynamically adjust to the changing environment and stabilize to a feasible period and deadline by itself. This simple program illustrates that real-time Java threads and deadline handlers can be an effective tool for providing dynamic QoS control.

```
1. public myProgram{
2.    void main() {
3.       myRtThread rt =
4.          new myRtThread(Time(Date(), 3, 0),
5.                         Time(0, 500000000),
6.                         Time(0, 400000000));
7.       rt.setDeadlineHandler(deadlineHandler);
8.       rt.start();
9.    }
10. }
11.
12. class myRtThread extends RtThread {
13.    int count = 0;
14.    boolean missed = false;
15.    Time period, deadline;
16.
17.    public void run() {
18.       /*
19.        * do some job here
20.        * e.g. drawing a video frame image
21.        */
22.       synchronized (this) {
23.          if (missed) {
24.             missed = false;
25.          }else{
26.             adjustTiming(-10000000);
27.          }
28.       }
29.    }
30.
31.    public synchronized void adjustTiming(int d){
32.       private Time period, deadline;
33.       period = this.getAttrPeriod();
34.       deadline = this.getAttrDeadline();
35.       period.setNsec(period.getNsetc() + d);
36.       deadline.setNsec(deadline.getNsetc() + d);
37.    }
38.
39.    public deadlineHandler(RtThread rt){
40.       System.out.println("missed deadline");
41        rt.adjustTiming(10000000);
42.       synchronized (this) {
43.       missed = true;
44.       }
45.    }
46. }
```

5. Evaluation. We evaluated the performance of real-time Java threads on a Toshiba Dynabook Portege 610 Pentium 90MHz system with 16MB of memory. We have measured the time elapsed from the start time to the actual time where the Java method was interpreted using our real-time Java thread based on real-time kernel threads (RT-Thread) in Figure 5-1. We obtained the data from executing a periodic thread 1000 times and getting the average.

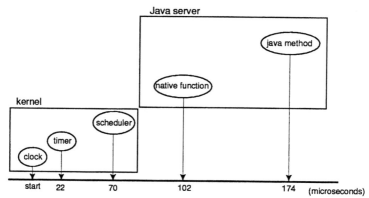

Figure 5-1 Time Elapsed From Actual Start Time

It takes 22 microseconds from the clock interrupt to the timer in the microkernel. If the timer decides that rescheduling is necessary (the clock interrupt is the start time for a thread), it will notify the scheduler which takes 48 microseconds. For the native function in the Java server to be executed, it takes 102 microseconds from the actual clock interrupt. For the Java method to be interpreted by the real-time thread it needs 72 microseconds inside the virtual machine to look for the methods that it is going to execute. The offset from the actual start time to the time Java method is executed totals to 174 microseconds. We are currently working to reduce this time for periodic threads, where a thread reincarnates every period and looks for the same method that it is going to execute, especially in the virtual machine using smart cache techniques.

Function	kernel-level thread	user-level thread
thread creation	$595.5\mu s$	$316.9\mu s$
get attribute	$49.8\mu s$	$0.9\mu s$
set attribute	$48.0\mu s$	$0.7\mu s$

Table 5 Basic Performance of User-Level and Kernel-Level Real-Time Threads

Another performance improvements we expect is from the support of real-time Java threads at the user-level using RTC-Threads. When many threads are running at the same time, user-level implementation is efficient and basic operations compared to kernel-level realt-time threads are better as we see in Table 5. But having a scheduler and managing the threads may cause the server to become too large for use in embedded systems. In a small system, using kernel provided thread may be practical. Thus we plan to provide an option for the user to select the type of thread implementation to use.

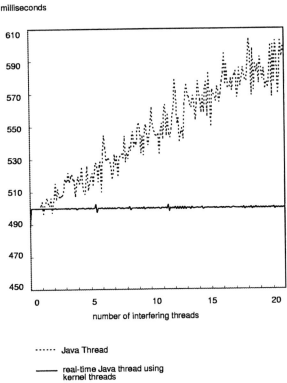

Figure 5-2 Timing Accuracy of Java Threads and Real-time Java Threads

In Figure 5-2 we compared regular Java threads and our real-time Java threads. For regular Java thread, to emulate periodic activity we have created a cyclic thread using `sleep()` method. Inside a `while` loop the thread will sleep for 500 milliseconds. We measured the interval time of the thread entering the head of the while loop.

For real-time Java threads, we created a periodic thread with a period of 500 milliseconds and measured its period. In both cases, cyclic thread or periodic thread will not do any work and we added a number of interfering thread which does random amount of work (with no I/O). All of these interfering threads have the same priority as the periodic or cyclic threads.

We can observe from Figure 5-2 that as interfering threads increases, regular

Java thread behaves more and more unpredictable. Scheduling delay occurs caused from competing threads, and when there are 20 other threads, the delay will increase up to more than 100 milliseconds. Our real-time Java thread will keep its period even when there are 20 other competing threads. This shows that predictability of real-time Java threads are high with overhead in the system.

6. Future Work. Although we have achieved several improvements to Java, there still remains work to be done. Our goal is to make all the component of the real-time Java environment predictable including services provided by the host OS such as window management and network support. Of course, components inside the virtual machine itself must be predictable. For example, garbage collecting algorithm used by many Java virtual machines, including our Java server, are mark and sweep algorithm. This is not suitable for real-time because a real-time activity may be blocked for an arbitrary amount of time while the garbage collector is running. We can think of this period the garbage collector is running, a critical section. Especially for multimedia interactive applications often seen in soft real-time application domains, long critical section reduces the responsiveness of the system and in a broad sense, cause priority inversion[6]. Thus we are currently investigating a garbage collection algorithm suited for real-time. Another feature we plan to add is the mechanism of reserving resources for the real-time activity to prevent non real-time activity from using up the resources.

Another source of unpredictability we must reduce is the invisible synchronization ovherhead in the standard Java library. We realized that there are many synchronization code in standard Java library provided in the file classes.zip (included in the JDK1.0.2). In Java, synchronization means locking of an object. Again, while the object is locked, other activity wishing to obtain the lock will be blocked. Thus the duration of the time an object is locked should be short, to prevent unresponsiveness and minimize priority inversion. But, often in Java programs which we have benchmarked, without the knowledge of the application programmer, there were many objects locked for a long time. For example, creation and running of an empty thread resulted in 9 locks all held for less than 10 microseconds, but for printing the word "HelloWorld" to the screen, there were 15 locks obtained. 13 of them locked under 2 microseconds but 2 of them were locked for approximately 2 milliseconds. These numbers do not include locking of objects inside the virtual machine to maintain shared data structure such as garbage collection information. These are very small examples, but we have experienced large number of locking with larger applications too, and some of them were locked for a long time. Our experience shows that, compared with C/C++ programs, there seems to be extremely more unvisible locking overhead involved leading to long unexpected critical sections. We are currently investigating the alternatives for implementing our own set of standard library tuned for real-time applications.

7. Related Work. There has been several efforts to use Java in embedded systems. For example, there are APIs such as EmbeddedJava[14], PersonalJava

[15] from Sun Microsystems and products such as JavaOS[13]. They target in making the footprint of the system small, but currently do not put emphasis on real-time requirements. Similar effort to make the system small can also be seen in [7]. In JavaOS most of the components such as device drivers and protocol stacks are implemented in Java language. [7] implements those functions in C. Our system is similar to [7] in that support for devices and protocol stack are not written in Java. We use the functionality of the microkernel to support these functions.

There will be many RTOS vendors which will provide real-time APIs and features for Java. One of them is work by Nilsen[9]. They propose different abstraction of real-time features and introduced statements such as `timed` and `atomic` statements. `timed` statements puts an upper bound on the execution time for a block of code, and `atomic` statements disable preemption for a block of code. To use their extension, a special compiler or a preprocessor is necessary. By using our real-time Java threads extensions, one can implement the statements proposed by their work.

8. Summary. We discussed the real-time issues in the Java language for developing real-time applications. We also described the architecture of the virtual machine which is implemented on Real-Time Mach microkernel. The merit of implementing it as a server on Real-Time Mach is that it can be used in various ways. It can be used from an application on another server or used as an engine for embedded systems. The server supports in memory file system to cache classes as continuous memory blocks to avoid blocking for disk I/O.

We have also added Java threads with real-time attributes. The ability to specify explicit timing constraints is important especially in the way Java is used in distributed environments since the programmer cannot assume the performance of the device which the program is running on. Currently there are two design of real-time Java threads. One based on kernel provided threads (RT-Threads), and the other based on user-level threads (RTC-Thread). Threads are synchronized using priority inheritance protocol to avoid priority inversion problem.

Experiment data shows the timing accuracy of real-time Java threads are high compared to regular Java threads even with overhead in the system. We are still improving the performance for periodic threads. Also, enhancements to our virtual machine such as garbage collectors are considered for a more predictable system.

Acknowledgements. We would like to thank all the members of MKng project for their valuable comments.

REFERENCES

[1] D. GOLUB, R. DEAN, A. FORIN, AND R.RASHID, *Unix as an application program*, in Proceedings of Summer USENIX Conference, June 1990.

[2] J. GOSLING, B. JOY, AND G. STEELE, *The Java Language Specification*, Addison Wesley, 1996.

[3] Y. ISHIKAWA, H. TOKUDA, AND C. MERCER, *An Object-Oriented Real-Time Programming Language*, IEEE Computer, 25 (1992).

[4] T. KITAYAMA, T. NAKAJIMA, AND H. TOKUDA, *RT-IPC: An IPC extension for Real-Time Mach*, in Proceedings of the USENIX Symposium on Microkernel and Other Kernel Architecture, Sept. 1993.

[5] C. MERCER, S. SAVAGE, AND H. TOKUDA, *Processor Capacity Reserves for Multimedia Operating Systems*, in Proceedings of the IEEE International Conference on Multimedia Computing and Systems, May 1994.

[6] C. MERCER AND H. TOKUDA, *Preemptibility in Real-Time Operating Systems*, in Proceedings of the 13th IEEE Real-Time Systems Symposium, May 1990.

[7] B. MONTAGUE, *The API of the UCSC Java Nanokernel(JN)*, Tech. Report UCSC-CRL-96-28, School of Engineering, University of California at Santa Cruz, Dec. 1996.

[8] T. NAKAJIMA, T. KITAYAMA, AND H. TOKUDA, *Experiments with Real-Time Servers in Real-Time Mach*, in Proceedings of USENIX 3rd Mach Symposium, 1993.

[9] K. NILSEN, *Java for Real-Time*, Real-Time Systems Journal, 11 (1996).

[10] S. OIKAWA AND H. TOKUDA, *User-Level Real-Time Threads*, in Proceedings of the 11th IEEE Workshop on Real-Time Operating Systems and Software, May 1994.

[11] S. OIKAWA AND H. TOKUDA, *Efficient Timing Management for User-Level Real-Time Threads*, in Proceedings of the 1995 IEEE Real-Time Technology and Applications Symposium, May 1995.

[12] L. SHA, R. RAJKUMAR, AND J. P.LEHOCZKY, *Priority inheritance protocols: An approach to real-time synchronization*, 1987.

[13] SUN MICROSYSTEMS, *JavaOS(tm): A Standalone Java Environment*, 1996. http://java.sun.com.

[14] SUN MICROSYSTEMS, *EmbeddedJava(TM)*, 1997. http://java.sun.com.

[15] SUN MICROSYSTEMS, *PersonalJava(TM)*, 1997. http://java.sun.com.

[16] H. TOKUDA AND T. KITAYAMA, *Dynamic QOS Control based on Real-Time Threads*, in Proceedings of the 4th Int. Workshop on Network and Operating Systems Support for Digital Audio and Video, 1993.

[17] H. TOKUDA AND T. NAKAJIMA, *Evaluation of Real-Time Synchronization in Real-Time Mach*, in Proceedings of USENIX 2nd Mach Symposium, Oct. 1991.

[18] H. TOKUDA, T. NAKAJIMA, AND P. RAO, *Real-Time Mach: Towards a Predictable Real-Time System*, in Proceedings of USENIX Mach Workshop, Oct. 1990.

[19] T. J. WILKINSON AND ASSOCIATES, *Kaffe A free virtual machine to run Java code*, 1997. http://www.kaffe.org.

INDEX